Voice, Silence and Gender in South Africa's Anti-Apartheid Struggle

New Historical
PERSPECTIVES

New Historical Perspectives is an open access book series for early career scholars, commissioned, edited and published by the Royal Historical Society and the University of London Press in association with the Institute of Historical Research. Submissions are encouraged relating to all historical periods and subjects. Books in the series are overseen by an expert editorial board to ensure the highest standards of peer-reviewed scholarship, and extensive support and feedback for authors is provided.

The series is supported by the Economic History Society.

ISSN 3049-5091 (print)
ISSN 3049-5105 (online)

INSTITUTE OF HISTORICAL RESEARCH | SCHOOL OF ADVANCED STUDY UNIVERSITY OF LONDON

ECONOMIC HISTORY SOCIETY

Voice, Silence and Gender in South Africa's Anti-Apartheid Struggle

The Shadow of a Young Woman

Rachel E. Johnson

UNIVERSITY OF LONDON PRESS

Available to purchase in print or download
for free at https://uolpress.co.uk

First published 2025 by University of London Press
Senate House, Malet St, London WC1E 7HU

A CIP catalogue record for this book is available from The British Library.

ISBN 978-1-915249-44-9 (hardback)
ISBN 978-1-915249-45-6 (paperback)
ISBN 978-1-915249-47-0 (.epub)
ISBN 978-1-915249-46-3 (.pdf)
ISBN 978-1-915249-99-9 (.html)

DOI https://doi.org/10.14296/rync2520

Cover image: On the streets of Soweto, Johannesburg everyone rejoiced at the news of Nelson Mandela's release. 11.02.1990. SueKramer / Africa Media Online.

Cover design for University of London Press by Nicky Borowiec.
Series design by Nicky Borowiec.
Book design by Nigel French.
Text set by Westchester Publishing Services UK in Meta Serif and Meta, designed by Erik Spiekermann.

Correction notice

In note 170 on p.138 and the Bibliography on p.156–7, the reference details for the book chapter by Annie E. Coombes were incorrect. The reference has now been corrected in both places to read Coombes, Annie E., 'The Gender of Memory in Postapartheid South Africa: The Women's Jail as Heritage Site'. In *Museum Transformations*, The International Handbooks of Museum Studies Volume 4, edited by Annie E. Coombes and Ruth B. Phillips, 207–226. Chichester: John Wiley and Sons, 2015. This correction has been made in all versions of the book.

For Myra and Sylvia – may your voices always be as loud and insistent as they are in our house.

Contents

Acknowledgements

This book has taken me a very long time to write and has therefore relied on the patience and continued support of many of my family, friends and colleagues. It had its beginnings in the research I conducted for my PhD thesis, undertaken at the University of Sheffield between 2006 and 2010. For inspiring me in that process, my first 'thank you' must go to Ian Phimister: I would not have thought to start out on this road without your encouragement. My thanks to Ian Phimister and Marion Wallace, who supervised that initial project and to Deborah Gaitskill and Henrietta Moore for examining it. It was during my viva that Henrietta Moore asked me if I knew anything more about Masabata Loate. At the time, I knew only of her first court appearance and her death. Thank you for that prompt to go looking for more.

For the writing of that thesis and this book I owe an unpayable debt to those women who spoke to me about their activism as young women in apartheid South Africa and, in equal measure, to those who refused to speak to me, or more accurately, spoke with me, but not about the past. As I describe in the introduction which follows, those encounters were so important in shaping the approach I take here. It took me a long time to work out what to do with those refusals. This is my considered response. My profound gratitude to Ntombi Mlakalaka for first introducing me to Soweto and to everyone in South Africa who has always made me feel so welcome there. I am acutely aware that I write about a painful past in this book and that this past belongs to real people. I have taken the responsibility of writing about shared life-stories very seriously and I have always tried to research, and write, with respect and sensitivity. My aim has been to restore a place for Masabata Loate, and other young women, within histories of South Africa's liberation struggle. In doing so I hope I have not misrepresented, or caused further pain to, anyone who was involved in the stories I retell.

Thanks must go to the staff at the archives in South Africa and the UK who made this research possible. In particular, I thank the National Archives in South Africa, the Historical Papers Research Archive at the University of the Witwatersrand, and the Women's Library at the London School of Economics. Special thanks go to the latter for enabling my access to the Women's Press material that had not yet been fully catalogued.

There was a long period, after the PhD, when I did not consider this book a possibility. Post-doctoral projects with Georgina Waylen and Shirin Rai took me in new research directions, even whilst they kept me focused on, and returning to, South Africa. Thank you, to you both. I am so grateful for those opportunities. I learnt so much from those projects and the people whom I was able to meet and work with, not least the ability to speak across disciplinary boundaries and to see, time and again, how much South Africa's history offered to theories of gender and politics. It is in this spirit that I have written the book – looking upwards and outwards – always conscious that I am not of South Africa and am distanced from the experiences I write about. I am hopeful the practice of history in other times and places is enriched by what South Africa has taught me.

It was the time and space of a job in a history department that gave me the opportunity to imagine this book. A job at Durham has included not just the stability of an open-ended contract and the proximity of my family but the chance to work with an amazing group of colleagues, particularly the members, both past and present, of the Durham University Centre for Contemporary African History (DUCCAH) including Justin Willis, Cherry Leonardi, Jacob Wiebel, Anne Heffernan, Bryan Kauma, Laura Channing, Nikki Kindersley, Ade Browne, Matt Benson, Gemma Barkhuizen, Neal Achary, Aida Abbashar and Chimwemwe Phiri. Teaching with you, talking with you, and learning from you since 2014 has been an enormous privilege. To my friends in the attic over the years – Helen Foxhall Forbes, Matthew Johnson, Jennifer Luff, Cathy McClive, Kevin Waite and Ana Diaz – thanks for all the corridor chats, lunches and friendship.

Some colleagues, both at Durham and beyond, have been instrumental in helping me formulate my ideas. Special thanks must go to Justin Willis for mentoring me through the book proposal and to Anne Heffernan and Julie-Marie Strange for invaluable input to that proposal. Two people in particular stand out for their unwavering support and interest in my work – Emily Bridger and Hilary Sapire. I am grateful that you read the thesis and found value in it. Thank you to Emily for reading an early draft of Chapter 2 and for always asking me when the book would be finished. I am extremely grateful to the newly formed 'History on Margins' cluster at Durham for letting me take over our first meeting and to Natalie Mears, Amanda Herbert, David Minto, Julie Marfany, Rebecca Clifford, Naomi Lloyd-Jones, Liam Liburd and Barabara Crosbie for reading the introduction for me in such a generous and thoughtful way. I want to thank Ruhan Fourie for translating from Afrikaans into English the extremely long, and long-winded, judgement from the case *State vs. Mary Masabate Loatse and others* – making sense of this without your skill would have been impossible for me.

I have been lucky enough to teach the material on which this book is based for the last two years, in a third-year undergraduate module called 'Voice and Silence in South Africa's Anti-Apartheid Liberation Struggle'. I am grateful to the students who joined me on the module in 2021–22 (Olivia Bothamley-Dakin, Dylan Cresswell, Lily Ellis, Minna Erith, Peter Firbank, Louisa Hanton, Ben Hovey, Grace Hutchinson, Philipp Jiang, Ned Kearton, Charlotte Styles, Max Taylor, Aoife Walter and Florence Ward) and 2022–23 (Scarlett Bedford, Lucy Chapple, Zarah Drummond, Dan Fitch, Joseph Furness, Cressida Harbottle, Cian Hutchinson, Issy Jackson, EJ Lord, Chloe Marsden, Molly Oglethorpe, Hannah Schultz, Oscar Scott and Alisha Tait). Your insights and enthusiasm pushed me to widen the scope of my thoughts and your ideas and research challenged and inspired me. I think many of you will be able to see the way our discussions influenced the book's final form.

I am enormously grateful to all those at the University of London Press and the Royal Historical Society's New Historical Perspectives book series who saw the potential in that original book proposal. Thank you to the three anonymous reviewers for their insight and feedback in the project's initial stages and to Annie Coombes for reading so generously a full draft of the manuscript. Throughout the process Elizabeth Hurren, co-editor of the series, has been extremely supportive and offered helpful and constructive advice and feedback at every stage. All of this has improved the book immeasurably – any remaining shortcomings are obviously entirely my own. I am grateful for the expert help, enthusiasm and patience of Emma Gallon at University of London Press. Thank you to Kate Dearlove at Africa Media Online for facilitating the use of Sue Kramer's beautiful photograph on the book's cover.

One of the reasons the book has taken so long to write is the birth of my two daughters in the midst of the process – Myra Jean, born 2017, and Sylvia Merle, born 2020. You two have taught me how to be in the world, in a whole new way, and so, you have also taught me how to be a historian anew. Without you, the book might have been finished sooner but I would not have valued the privilege of writing it in the same way. Mum and Dad – your emotional, practical and logistical support have made this possible. To the ever-widening Johnson and Saha families, thank you all for being there. And finally, to Jonathan Saha, always my first and last reader, in this, as in everything we do together, I cannot imagine how I could have done it without you. Thank you.

Durham, United Kingdom
June 2024

Abbreviations

ANC	African National Congress
ANCYL	African National Congress Youth League
APDUSA	African People's Democratic Union of Southern Africa
AZANYU	Azanian National Youth Unity
AZAPO	Azanian People's Organisation
BCP	Black Community Programmes
BPC	Black People's Convention
CASE	Community Agency for Social Enquiry
COSAS	Congress of South African Students
CRC	United Nations Convention on the Rights of the Child
DPSC	Detainee Parent's Support Committee
FEDSAW	Federation of South African Women
FEDTRAW	Federation of Transvaal Women
HRC	Human Rights Committee
IDAF	International Defence and Aid Fund
ISA	Internal Security Act 1982 (Amended 1986)
MDM	Mass Democratic Movement
MK	UmKhonto we Sizwe
MUFC	Mandela United Football Club
NPSL	National Professional Soccer League
NUSAS	National Union of South African Students
PAC	Pan African Congress
#RMF	#RhodesMustFall
SACOS	South African Council on Sport
SACP	South African Communist Party

SANSCO South African National Students' Congress

SASM South African Students' Movement

SASO South African Students' Organisation

SAYCO South African Youth Congress

SAYRCO South African Youth Revolutionary Council

SOYCO Soweto Youth Congress

SPRO-CAS Study Project on Christianity in Apartheid Society

SSRC Soweto Students' Representative Council

TRC Truth and Reconciliation Commission

UDF United Democratic Front

WRAB West Rand Administration Board

Introduction: the shadow of a young woman

It was 1978. After being held in detention without charge for over a year, a young South African woman who had just turned eighteen stepped into the witness box to testify for the prosecution, at Kempton Park Circuit Court, north-east of Johannesburg. She confirmed her name as Mary Masabata Loate. The prosecuting attorney-general of the Witwatersrand, Klaus Von Lieres, noted at the outset of her testimony that she was regarded as an accomplice to those on trial.[1] The trialists were the 'Soweto Eleven': ten young men and one young woman, aged between eighteen and twenty-three, and all members of the Soweto Students' Representative Council (SSRC). They were charged with sedition for their role in organising a march of Soweto schoolchildren on 16 June 1976, protesting against the Apartheid State's language policy in schools, which forced increasing numbers of them to learn in Afrikaans.[2] This language policy had become the focus of widespread frustrations for a newly militant and politically conscious urban youth culture by the early months of 1976.[3] When the school students' march was responded to violently by the South African police, the deaths of child protesters resulted in uprisings of anger and solidarity across South Africa. Organised protest actions continued into 1977 and reverberated around the world. The judge told Masabata Loate that, as an accomplice to those on trial, she could give evidence without the presence of the public. If her testimony was regarded as 'full and frank' she would be granted release. Justice H. Van Dyk commented: 'from her appearance she seems to be very nervous'. He went on, 'she need not be afraid, I only want to hear the truth in this case'.[4] Loate gave evidence as to her activities during 1976 and 1977. Under cross-examination by the defence advocate, Ernest Wentzel, she revealed something of the toll that being held in detention, for such a long period prior to the trial, had taken upon her. She told Wentzel she had lost 20lb in weight over that time. At the end of her testimony the judge turned to this young woman to instruct her that 'she may stand down. She is now going to be released'. He then added, 'She must watch her weight. I think she should not add another 20lbs again'.[5]

The shock of encountering this moment in the transcript of the trial has not dimmed for me. The violence of the judge's gaze and the licence he took in those circumstances to comment upon Masabata Loate's body is startling, even if it is not surprising. It lays bare in an instant the multiple vulnerabilities Loate was subjected to in that apartheid court room as a young, black woman.[6] Yet this moment of stark visibility, that wrenches Loate momentarily into full view, sits alongside a profound set of silences within the same archive about this young woman and others of her generation: silences surrounding what it was they did, what they thought and how they lived, amid the oppression of apartheid and the mobilisation of resistance to it. This was a silence made final in Masabata Loate's case by her death less than ten years after that moment in court. This book asks: What is it possible to learn about Masabata Loate from the multiple fragments of her life that can be found in the archives, written, oral and visual, that were generated during the struggle between the Apartheid State and its opponents at the end of the twentieth century in South Africa? How should we approach the silences that remain, in between those fragments and beyond them? At its heart, the book grapples with a fraught and complex relationship between speaking about politics and doing politics. I argue that any attempt to undo the historical silences surrounding Masabata Loate needs to pay careful attention to the ways in which speech, voice and silence were forged in the struggle itself. It is a 'problem' that needs 'twofold attention': attempting to re-read the archive for what it does tell us at the same time as noticing what remains 'absent, entangled and unavailable' and uncovering why that might be.[7]

I do not have the historical evidence to write a conventional biography of Masabata Loate.[8] What I attempt to do in these pages is something different: to give her a space in the historical narrative of the anti-apartheid liberation movement[9] – a space measured out, in part, by silence; to leave room to acknowledge that she breathed beyond the political struggles in which her life became enmeshed. Masabata Loate is a shadow we can see within the story of South Africa's liberation. She is neither silent nor absent in the archive(s), but she is easy to miss, and dismiss, as an insignificant, half-seen presence. This is not just because her age and gender made her a marginal figure within the liberation struggle; it is because our ways of knowing about that past are gendered. Whilst this is a project of reconstructing a life, it is necessarily a partial reconstruction. The ways in which it remains partial are important.

This much I do know: Masabata Loate was born on 20 October 1961 and lived in Orlando West, Soweto.[10] As a teenager she attended Orlando North High School. She became involved in anti-apartheid politics during the 1976 Soweto Uprisings, and she was arrested and detained in June 1977, outside John Vorster Square police station, after visiting those students already being held there. The *Rand Daily Mail* reported on 22 June 1977 that over a thousand of her fellow students stayed away from school in 'sympathy' with her and the two other students arrested at the same time (Christopher More and one other unnamed student).[11] She was held in detention, without charge, for a year before she appeared as a state witness during the trial of the Soweto Eleven that took place between September 1978 and April 1979. That winter, after her release from detention she entered several beauty contests and was crowned 'Miss Mainstay' in August 1979. She worked as the face of Mainstay, makers of a South African sugar cane spirit, pictured in newspapers, complete with crown and sash.[12] At the same time, Loate's earlier testimony as a state witness resulted in threats to her safety and she was shot in the leg. She next reappears in the archive as the Soweto branch organiser for the Azanian National Youth Unity (AZANYU) when it was established in 1981. AZANYU was, according to one of its founding members, 'operating like a cultural movement but pushing the politics of the [banned and exiled] Pan African Congress (PAC)'.[13] Loate was also involved, both romantically and politically (the balance or distinction between the two is blurred), with former SSRC leader Khotso Seatlholo in establishing a presence within South Africa for another organisation, the South African Youth Revolutionary Council (SAYRCO), which had been formed in exile in 1979.[14] For this she was arrested and tried alongside Seatlholo in 1982, on charges of terrorism and recruiting others to violently overthrow the State.[15] Both were found guilty. Loate was sentenced to ten years in prison; Seatlholo to fifteen. Loate was released part-way through her sentence in 1986 and returned to Soweto. That same year, she was murdered, or 'necklaced' (reports differ) just before her twenty-sixth birthday, by a large gang of men on the streets of Soweto. According to her mother she was killed for speaking out against the kind of violent tactics being used within the liberation struggle, to which she then fell victim herself.[16] To be necklaced was to be killed as a traitor to the struggle, following accusations of being a state informer or of some other form of collaboration with the State or a rival organisation.[17] For a young woman, a necklacing might also be the result of refusing the sexual advances of a comrade, fraternising with an alleged informer or simply being an available proxy for a man.[18] Stories of Masabata Loate's death have been told, and re-told, in post-apartheid South Africa. There are confusions and contradictions in the various accounts that leave us without a clear sense of why she was killed and what her death might mean, both for her life, and for the national liberation struggle.

This introduction situates Masabata Loate within South African history. Chapter 1 then provides a theoretical and methodological introduction to using voice, speech and silence, for the writing of shadow histories. In the chapters which follow, I retell Masabata Loate's life and death as it is contained within various archival fragments: principally the two trials in which she was involved, as well as the glimpses of her that can be found in newspapers, the Truth and Reconciliation Commission (TRC), oral remembrances and written autobiography. Each of these chapters poses a question about Masabata Loate. Can we know what she thought? Was she a beauty queen *and* an activist? What did her death mean? In answering these questions, I tell a wider story, of the gendered shape of our knowledge about South Africa's anti-apartheid liberation struggle and I offer a methodology for historians of the marginalised, who can, intermittently, hear the voices they are listening for, and see the shadows they are chasing.

Young women in the liberation struggle

In the ten years between 1976 and 1986 Loate's life followed the arc of youth politics in South Africa as it evolved in the aftermath of the Soweto Uprisings. The fragments of her life that we do have are the result of the State's concerted attempts to contain the challenge to its authority that had emerged from within the Bantu Education system in the 1970s.[19] Whilst young South Africans were certainly not apolitical before 1976 and university students had been organising explicitly anti-apartheid actions in the early 1970s, the events of 16 June mobilised those as young as ten, and to an extent never before seen, across the country.[20] It was after 1976 that 'the youth' as a defined constituency within the liberation struggle became visible politically, the subject of popular discussion, and of academic studies.[21] Those who had acted in June 1976 were widely perceived to belong to a new political generation. Their politics were something new – combining the repertoires and ideas of the national liberation movements that preceded them with the 'philosophy of African self-reliance' that had emerged on black university campuses, known as Black Consciousness.[22] The inspiration that many of the school students drew from Black Consciousness was read variously as a marker of their political distinctiveness and/or a certain political immaturity by some.[23] The South African Students' Movement (SASM) that had been involved in planning the 16 June march, and the Soweto Students' Representative Council (SSRC) that led the ensuing uprising, were banned in October 1977. At the same time, so were the Black Consciousness organisations that had come before them (the South African Students' Organisation, the Black People's Convention, Black Community Programmes), and *The World*, the newspaper that had documented the movement and its rise.[24] As the trial of the Soweto Eleven drew to a close, the question of what would happen *after* Soweto loomed large.[25]

Many young people involved in the Uprisings left the country. Some 6,000 to 10,000 students went into exile and whilst many joined the structures of the older liberation movements – the African National Congress (ANC) and Pan African Congress (PAC) – there were those, Khotso Seatlholo and Masabata Loate amongst them, who persisted with attempts to organise young people separately from those political traditions.[26] By the time of Loate's death those attempts had largely ceased. New organisations were founded, notably the Congress of South African Students (COSAS) in 1979. COSAS was open to all students (secondary and night-school students) irrespective of political affiliation and was initially, Anne Heffernan has argued, 'a relatively permissive space for diverse ideological engagement'.[27] Within a few years that space had narrowed. Support for the ANC through the adoption of the 1955 Freedom Charter as the blueprint for a future South Africa, described as 'Charterism'; 'Africanism', which signalled dissent from some key aspects of the Charter; and 'Black Consciousness', became 'sharply delineated points of self-identification' during the 1980s, within what has been characterised as 'a politics of enmity' (rather than clear-cut ideological differences).[28] COSAS declared its support for the Freedom Charter in 1980.

If the politics of the 1980s saw a widespread realignment away from the ideas of Black Consciousness that had suffused the 1970s, towards the non-racialism of the Freedom Charter, then it seems Loate may too have followed the direction of these currents. One account of Loate's death suggests that on her return to Soweto in 1986 she had become involved in the street committees that were taking control of urban areas, as the official local governance structures collapsed in the face of sustained insurrection.[29] These street committees underpinned the work of the ANC-aligned United Democratic Front (UDF). Yet she is also listed online by the organisation founded in 1978 as the custodian of Black Consciousness, the Azanian People's Organisation (AZAPO), as a Black Consciousness Movement heroine. The historical record is unclear on her political affiliation – and yet this was a time when affiliation to one or other strand within the liberation struggle – the Congress tradition, Africanist or Black Consciousness – could be a matter of life or death. Soweto in the mid-1980s saw open conflict between rival organisations over recruiting members and areas of influence. According to the TRC's final report, tensions between AZAPO and UDF-aligned activists erupted in Soweto in 1985 and the resulting conflict 'involved abductions, kidnappings, killings, bombings and attacks on homes'.[30] Violence was inculcated and encouraged by state security forces and their network of informers and askaris.[31]

Young people were central to the sustained urban opposition to apartheid in the 1980s. Alongside worker and community or civic organisations, 'youth' groups played a central role in many localities, with young people operating in a loose (and at times fraught) affiliation with the new nationwide organisations like the UDF and the Mass Democratic Movement (MDM).[32] Beginning in the late 1970s, over the course of the 1980s and into the 1990s, 'youth' accreted very particular meanings in South African politics.[33] It was always a racialised term: writing in the early 1990s, David Everatt of the Community Agency for Social Enquiry (CASE) project introduced a sociological study, *Black Youth in Crisis*, by commenting that 'South Africa has white teenagers but black youth'.[34] 'Youth' is a relational term, referring to a space in between childhood and adulthood. In late twentieth-century South Africa, youth was an identity sometimes imposed and rejected, at other times embraced or aspired to, by people, not all of whom were necessarily young.[35] As Chapter 1 explores, the 'youth' of 1976 were also implicitly male, a phenomenon which became explicitly noted as young black men were increasingly visible, and visibly violent, within the township uprisings of the 1980s.[36] The form of violence that was used to kill Loate in 1986, perpetrated by a large group of young men, has been explained by some as a result of a 'fusion' of youth political culture with that of urban gangs – in which young women's bodies were viewed as an extension of territory, to be controlled and fought over.[37]

Masabata Loate was not typical or representative of young activists who joined the liberation struggle in 1976 – indeed, as I will argue, she was in many ways very unusual in combining her political activism with a career as a beauty queen and in her apparent willingness to speak in contexts that others, and particularly young black women, did not. Yet I suggest that the ways in which the speech, voice and silence of Masabata Loate have been recorded and recalled is emblematic – emblematic of the processes by which gendered narratives of the liberation struggle have been made. The fragments of her life caught in the archive can help us to reappraise our understandings of political participation in late twentieth-century South Africa. If Loate was a member of the 1976 generation, hers is not a story which aligns comfortably or closely with the powerful public histories of this watershed moment in South African history.[38] She is a liminal figure, in the sense that she exists – we can hear her voice and see her body – at the edges of identities and categories in formation. Masabata Loate emerges as a shadow within the narratives of the masculinised politicisation and mobilisation of the youth – a shadow that throws these processes into sharp relief. Hers is a shadow that appears more than once, and in multiple archives. From Loate's appearances and disappearances we can learn what has rendered so many of her contemporaries more fully invisible and silent.

Loate's voice and silence do not stand in for others but can show us how the 'ensemble of relations' that was South Africa's liberation struggle created certain patterns of knowledge about the past.[39] Over the course of the liberation struggle young women could be, and were, mobilised as women, as workers, as youth and as community-based activists – they had no specific organisational home. As a result, amongst the many voices of the liberation struggle, a collective voice for young women is rarely found. The existing historiography points to the liminality of young women within both youth organisations *and* women's organisations. If youth groups were dominated by young men and women's groups by older women, young black women were, in the words of one activist, 'in limbo'.[40] In 1991 Suzi Nkomo wrote as a member of the South African National Students' Congress (SANSCO), active on the University of Witwatersrand campus in the mid-1980s:

> So we, as black women activists, remained in limbo. On the one hand we could not claim a space for ourselves politically in the way that men had on campus. On the other our association with the Federation of Transvaal Women (Fedtraw) defined for us the 'legitimate' women's concerns. The problem was that a programme geared for older community women, did not cater for a constituency of young women, who were arguably not triply oppressed, or in fact mothers of youth, but youth themselves. We could not even rely on constant debate within the non-racial alliance with the National Union of South African Students (Nusas) women to develop a critical analysis of the role of young women in the struggle. In a sense we were a disempowered grouping.[41]

Nkomo's experiences, recounted here, point to the ways in which the making of collective voices of 'youth' and 'women' left no space for young black women to 'debate'. Her race, gender, age and identity as a student all jostled and ultimately acted to exclude her from one space after another. The desire for 'constant debate' is significant – it was space to speak that Ncomo felt she, and others, lacked. That the archive captured Masabata Loate's speech between 1976 and 1986 – as filtered, mediated and coerced as it was – is relatively rare.

Jon Soske has argued that the anti-apartheid struggle was 'a family affair', in the sense that many of those involved 'saw family and gender (either through their radical transformation or their restoration to a Christian or precolonial ideal) as central to national liberation'.[42] Shireen Hassim notes that the 'familial' structure of the ANC as well as the codes of address in the movement – 'father' or 'uncle' for older men, 'mother' for older women and 'buti' (brother) and 'sisi' (sister) for cohorts – simultaneously created a positive 'sense of nurture and belonging' and a 'conservative acceptance of gerontocracy' that reinforced patriarchal masculinities.[43] Young women had a particular place within these imaginaries.[44] According to Elleke Boehmer, within narratives of post-colonial nationalism the figure of the daughter is a 'non-subject' who is 'if not subordinate, peripheral and quiet, then virtually invisible'.[45] If this was the case, it has not always remained so.

What place South African nationalism has offered to young women post-1994 has arguably never been a more urgent question. I first began researching the material that underpins this book during 2006, when the rape trial of then former deputy president, later to be president, Jacob Zuma, hit the headlines. For many, the trial, in which Zuma was acquitted, became not only a test of this one man's guilt, but of South Africa's commitment to the gender equality enshrined in its post-apartheid Constitution. Amongst the issues that it brought to the fore was that 'sexual violence was the dark shadow of political conflict in South Africa'.[46] During the trial, the personal history of Zuma's accuser 'Khwezi' was used as evidence to discredit her, including three incidents where she had been raped as a child when living in exile during the 1980s. Her story prompted discussion of young women as silenced victims of the liberation struggle. One woman wrote to the *Sunday Times* telling them that she too had been raped in exile as a young woman but that 'she was afraid that if she spoke out, her trauma would have derailed the process of attaining freedom for South Africa'.[47] The opprobrium directed at 'Khwezi', who regarded Zuma as an uncle due to his close relationship with her father, a fellow ANC comrade, revealed that her public accusation of Zuma broke with established hierarchies of gender and age.[48] As one female supporter of Zuma put it: 'this young girl is crazy and does not respect older people'.[49]

Since then, rates of gender-based violence have continued to rise and, whilst young women are not the only victims, the dynamics of what Pumla Dineo Gqola has memorably called the 'fear factory' has profound impacts upon girlhood and young womanhood.[50] This has been visibly and vocally challenged by South African women.[51] Most recently, within the Fallist movements that emerged on South Africa's university campuses in 2015, young Black womxn argued for the importance of intersectionality *within*

Black liberation as part of their critique of South Africa's 'transformation' as incomplete.[52] Black womxn were integral to organising the Fallist movements and theorised their own position within it. The #RhodesMustFall (#RMF) Mission Statement of 2015 seemingly addressed the very problem Suzi Nkomo had earlier expressed:

> We all have certain oppressions and certain privileges and this must inform our organising so that we do not silence groups among us, and so that *no one should have to choose between their struggles*. Our movement endeavours to make this a reality in our struggle for decolonisation [emphasis added].[53]

In one spectacular instance of using the power of gender to disrupt, at the University of the Witwatersrand in 2016, three Black womxn activists bravely used their 'nude' bodies to halt the violence being enacted on protesting students.[54] As Hlengiwe Ndlovu, one of these womxn recalled, 'we took off our tops and charged towards the policemen who were our target . . . They stopped shooting at that moment'.[55] However, these womxn's experiences have also shown that the repertories of political action available (still) did not adequately address their oppression. As Mbalenhle Matandela puts it: 'although womxn are visible, recognised and have voice in the context of the #RMF movement, they *still* experience physical, spiritual, sexual, linguistic and psychological violence from both the opposition and the culture of Black liberation politics' [emphasis added].[56] 'Still' is central to these understandings, which are based upon a (re) appraisal of the gendered politics of Black Consciousness thought that Fallism draws upon, as well as an analysis of present-day lived realities. 'Still' names this as a problem *of* the past. What I want to do with this book is unsettle the picture of the past we have, by focusing on how it has been made.

Picturing the struggle

In tracing the appearance and disappearance of Masabata Loate's voice in the archives of struggle this book shows how the making of collective voices – of masculine youth and public motherhood – did in fact involve young women and indeed at times, relied on their presence and participation. They are hiding in plain sight in these archives. Quite literally when it comes to the photographic record. To take one example, the combination of visibility and silence that we noted as marking Masabata Loate's first court appearance can be found writ large in the story of young black women's participation on 16 June 1976. Photographs of the march that day are full of large numbers of young women and men alike. However, as Helena Pohlandt-McCormick notes, the accounts of many young men participants, on 16 June and in the subsequent uprisings, 'would have us believe' that young women were merely 'in the background'.[57] This contradiction is noted in one of the volumes of the South African Democracy Education Trust's huge project to (re)write the history of South Africa's liberation struggle, *The Road to Democracy*, which focuses on reinterpretations of June 1976. At the very end of a chapter on the 'Anatomy of the Crowd', Sifiso Mxolisi Ndlovu includes a photograph that shows the body of a young woman lying face down on the ground next to a police vehicle, whilst a number of white, armed police officers stand close by, nonchalantly ignoring her presence, and her dying or recent death.[58] It is a chilling image of white indifference for a black life. It is included by Ndlovu as symbolic of the silence of young female participants in the march. At several points in the chapter he notes the significant presence of young women in the photographic record of that day, alongside what he calls the 'failure' of historians to 'record, narrate and publish the liberating stories of these extra-ordinary unsung heroines'.[59] In concluding the chapter he notes the numbers of young women detained in the aftermath of the march and that they were amongst the dead before noting 'we cannot recover the voices of those who were silenced by death'.[60] In Ndlovu's account of 16 June 1976, this image of one young woman killed that day speaks for the silence of many others on their participation.

There is, however, another way of depicting the relationship of young women with 16 June. Consider the image on the front cover of this book. The photograph was taken in 1990 in Soweto, following the release of Nelson Mandela from prison. I do not know the name of the young woman who is central to the image but the joy on her face is palpable. Her raised fist is accompanied by a wide smile. She is wearing a T-shirt. It is a little hard to make out, but I think the image on the T-shirt is the famous Sam Nzima photograph, taken on 16 June 1976. The words above the image, 'Soweto Massacre' are clearly visible. Ruth Kerkham Simbao has written about this iconic photograph that shows the dying Hector Pieterson being carried by Mbuyisa Makhubu, with Hector's sister, Antoinette Sithole, running alongside, as an image that contains shadows and silences.[61] She argues that during the 1980s, at the height of anti-apartheid mobilisation, the photograph became ubiquitous and was reproduced in countless contexts as an image of resistance, on T-shirts, posters and placards. This young woman's T-shirt is one such reproduction. In these processes Kerkham Simbao argues that the image was flattened, and the trio's shadow was removed, thereby simplifying the picture in more than one respect. For Simbao, the shadow in the Nzima photograph represents the ongoing silences that exist within narratives of 16 June and the contested and multiple views of the past that can, and should, be allowed to emerge in the ongoing post-apartheid moment.[62] But what might it mean for this young woman to wear this photograph in 1990?

In her hand the young woman holds a sign that says 'Viva the Spear of the Nation' written on cardboard – a reference to the fact that Mandela's release was unconditional, and that amongst his first acts he reiterated that he did not renounce the armed struggle.[63] There was no straight line linking June 16 to the release of Mandela, but this young woman carries the one historical moment into the other – on her body. For me, this photograph captures the way in which the Soweto Uprisings framed youth political action in the years which followed, and it shows us a young woman inhabiting that history. It shows us her, clothed in that history. This is what I seek to focus upon: the way young women move through gendered narratives of the liberation struggle, some of which even deny their presence. It looks as though she has paused, to pose in front of the photographer. I do not think it is a coincidence that the photographer was a woman, Sue Kramer. This too, is part of what I hope to capture in the book, the processes by which we come to know about women in the struggle, and how often this is the result of the work of other women.

The extent to which the youth politics that followed on from the Soweto Uprisings offered a space for young women's voices has been disputed. The 1980s were shaped by the National Party's simultaneous attempts to provide limited openings for political participation within the apartheid system, such as the Tri-Cameral Parliament that offered 'representation' within the national legislature for Asian and Coloured communities, or the 'independence' offered to the Bantustans, alongside the increased securitisation and militarisation of the white State.[64] New alliances and co-ordination between sites of struggle – trade unions, civic organisations, human rights campaign groups, and women's and youth organisations – emerged under the UDF, initially founded to oppose the Tri-Cameral Parliament. The township uprisings of the mid-1980s, triggered by the material realities of urban life for black South Africans, were crucibles for the political language of 'People's Power' and millenarian beliefs in the end of apartheid.[65]

For many years the most widely cited interpretation of the gender politics of township youth groups of the 1980s was Jeremy Seekings' study of the Tumahole Youth Congress, which was conducted in early 1986. Seekings noted that when he spoke with them, 'young male comrades dismissed the idea that women could be involved in any political activity despite the extensive involvement of women in rent protests, student organisations and even the youth congress one or two years before!'[66] Thus, Seekings argued that the mid-1980s saw the marginalisation of young women from such youth organisations through an increasing use of violence that was rooted in a 'crisis of masculinity'.[67] However, this picture has been challenged by studies based on more recent interviews that evidence young women's active participation in violent political activity.[68] Organisations like COSAS could, as Emily Bridger has shown, offer young women possibilities for participation throughout the 1980s. One former COSAS member, Florence, told Bridger in a 2014 interview: 'with COSAS I felt I had a voice; as a human being, as a South African, and as a woman'.[69] Post-apartheid interviews offered these former COSAS activists a chance to assert that experience of finding voice again. The importance of oral evidence in establishing both pictures of youth politics, points to an important reconfiguration of women's voices within the liberation struggle that unfolded in the years after Loate's death.

Women were leaders in the development of political opposition to apartheid and formed an important constituency within the struggle. Yet they often had to fight for inclusion within the liberation struggle and for recognition of the ways in which their gender identities shaped that inclusion. As Natasha Erlank has noted, early African nationalism was 'saturated' with language 'calling for the reassertion of a denied manhood'.[70] African women were not allowed to apply for formal full membership of the ANC until 1943. Organisational inclusion, when it came, was often predicated on a particular framing of women as mothers. For many years historians have been divided over whether 'motherhood' was an inherently socially conservative basis for political mobilisation or if, especially in the second half of the twentieth century, it became 'militant' in ways that offered women chances to challenge prevailing gender ideologies.[71] Neatly sidestepping this issue, Meghan Healy-Clancy has recently argued that we instead notice the 'multivalent' possibilities of 'public motherhood'.[72] According to Healy-Clancy, for activists of the multi-racial Federation of South African Women (FEDSAW), founded in 1954, and operating most actively until 1960 when its major affiliate the ANC Women's League was banned, public motherhood was a 'strategic discourse'. She argues women could invoke public motherhood 'in order to make themselves legible as social actors, both to agents of the white-controlled state and to allies in South Africa and across transnational networks'.[73]

This is a compelling argument. Even as a strategy however, it places young women in a particular relationship with women's movements. Writing about the militancy of some women within UDF structures in Natal under the 1985 State of Emergency, Beall et al. noted that 'while mothers are creating space for themselves', through the articulation of radical motherist demands, 'they may be limiting it for their daughters'.[74] The ways in which age shaped the relationships within women's organisations has rarely been the focus of study, but what can be gleaned from the details in existing scholarship is that younger women often found themselves in tension with older women activists with socially conservative views about what it was appropriate for women to wear, say and do in public.[75]

The space for women's voices to be heard was transformed by two developments: women and queer activists, organising within and outside the liberation movement that highlighted the heteronormative masculinity of the struggle; and the wider centrality of 'voice' within South Africa's transition to democratic governance. The emergence of new women's organisations in the 1980s was interlinked with the creation of some explicitly feminist spaces – for example, *Agenda*, a feminist journal founded in 1987.[76] This process has sometimes been mapped onto generational struggle within the women's movement – with younger women seen as leading these developments.[77] The importance of these ambivalent and contested spaces as sites for the articulation of women's voices is explored in Chapter 4. Most women's organising was not overtly feminist. Sheila Meintjes has recalled, 'feminism was what we *did*, but not what we *spoke*'.[78] However, women's voices were accorded a new status in the transition years. In May 1990, the ANC issued a 'Statement on the Emancipation of Women', over thirty years after the Freedom Charter, in which it called for a new Charter of Women's Rights, 'so that in their *own* voice women define the issues' [emphasis added].[79] Such a charter would be according to the ANC 'a major agency for stimulating women to break the silence imposed on them'.[80] The ANC's National Executive did not delineate exactly who had imposed silence upon women but this framing of women's speech as 'breaking silence' was ubiquitous in the early 1990s. That women would take a prominent place within South Africa's post-apartheid political settlement was seen as one of the most important breaks with the apartheid past. As Shireen Hassim puts it, 'women came to occupy a peculiar status as the proving ground for the extent to which the new order would be inclusive, participatory, and permeable to socially excluded groupings'.[81]

Meg Samuelson has questioned the claim that in the early 1990s, the end of apartheid and the transition moment 'provided an opening in which previously silenced female voices [could] be heard'.[82] Similarly Fiona Ross has pushed back against the rhetoric which surrounded the TRC, that what preceded the Commission was 'voiceless-ness and silence about the apartheid past'.[83] The TRC was a quasi-judicial body established by the Government of National Unity in 1994, tasked with helping the new South Africa come to terms with the apartheid past through collecting testimony of human rights abuses suffered, some of which were given in public hearings, applications for amnesty for abuses committed and the writing of a report. Ross points out that much 'was already known about apartheid', 'told in diverse genres' and that the TRC was just a new formalised structure for voices to be heard in.[84] However, the dominance of voice and speech as *the* way in which the past can be known in the post-apartheid moment has important and ongoing consequences for the writing of histories. It is to voice, speech and silence as ways of knowing the past, that we will now turn in Chapter 1.

Notes

1. Supreme Court of South Africa (Transvaal Provincial Division), *State vs. W.W.C. Twala and Ten Others*, case K/P 282/78; WHP: AD1450: Box 5: Record of Proceedings, 1084.

2. The historiography on 16 June 1976 is voluminous. For accounts that stress the importance of Afrikaans as a medium of instruction in schools as the issue motivating student protests see, in particular: Helena Pohlandt-McCormick, *'I Saw a Nightmare . . .': Doing Violence to Memory, The Soweto Uprising, June 16, 1976* (New York: Columbia University Press, 2008), http://www.gutenberg-e.org/pohlandt-mccormick/index.html; *The Road to Democracy in South Africa: Volume 7: Soweto Uprisings: New Perspective, Commemorations and Memorialisation* (Cape Town: Unisa Press, 2017).

3. Jonathan Hyslop, *The Classroom Struggle; Policy and Resistance in South Africa, 1940–1990* (Pietermaritzburg: University of Natal Press, 1999), 150–65.

4. *State vs. W.W.C. Twala*, Record of Proceedings, 1085.

5. *State vs. W.W.C. Twala*, Record of Proceedings, 1096.

6. I have used the lower-case black in this instance, whereas at other points in the book I have used the upper-case Black. This is a position based on the accepted practice in South Africa and the arguments that whilst Black gives appropriate status and recognition to an identity claimed by Americans of African descent it may obscure more plural ways of being black outside of North America and the global north. In 1970s South Africa, Black Consciousness thinkers argued that 'Black' was an identity that belonged to all those oppressed by apartheid, dissolving distinctions made by the Population Registration Act (no. 30 of 1950) between 'African', 'Asian' and 'Coloured'. Where a capital has been used by an individual, I have retained its usage, but I have not imposed it upon anyone. Here using lower case is a way of signifying that in this instance black is how Loate was seen by others, not necessarily a claim she was making for herself. Masabata Loate did appear to lay claim to an identity as Black during her testimony in her trial in 1982, when she stated, 'I am aware that a black man in this country is oppressed'. The ambiguities of this statement are discussed in Chapter 3. For more on using upper and lower case for black see: 'To cap? Or not cap "Black"?', Who We Are, posted 8 August 2021, https://www.who-are-we.online/article2.html.

7. Lisa Lowe, 'The Intimacies of Four Continents', in *Haunted by Empire: Geographies of Intimacy in North American History*, ed. Ann Laura Stoler, American Encounters/Global Interactions (Durham: Duke University Press, 2006), 208; Jean Allman describes such an approach as 'agnotology', the study of what we do not know and why we do not know it. Jean Allman, 'The Disappearing of Hannah

Kudjoe: Nationalism, Feminism, and the Tyrannies of History', *Journal of Women's History* 21, no. 3 (11 September 2009): 13–35, https://doi.org/10.1353/jowh.0.0096.

8. Biography is by far and away the most popular genre of non-fiction in post-apartheid South Africa. For a discussion of this phenomenon see: Nancy J. Jacobs and Andrew Bank, 'Biography in Post-Apartheid South Africa: A Call for Awkwardness', *African Studies* 78, no. 2 (3 April 2019): 165–82, https://doi.org/10.1080/00020184.2019.1569428; As Ciraj Rasool has argued, auto/biographical practices held an enduring place within the liberation struggle, and in particular international solidarity campaigns, beginning with the biographies of the defendants at the 1956 Treason Trial produced by the Treason Trial Defence Fund. Ciraj Rassool, 'Rethinking Documentary History and South African Political Biography', *South African Review of Sociology* 41, no. 1 (April 2010): 28–55, https://doi.org/10.1080/21528581003676028.

9. As Elaine Unterhalter has noted, when reading the autobiographies of struggle participants, it is impossible to disentangle the 'personal political narrative' from the 'material and discursive forms of the anti-apartheid struggle'. In Loate's case the fragmented narratives of her life that we have are embedded in the material and discursive forms of the anti-apartheid struggle. Elaine Unterhalter, 'The Work of the Nation: Heroic Masculinity in South African Autobiographical Writing of the Anti-Apartheid Struggle', *European Journal of Development Research* 12, no. 2 (December 2000): 160, https://doi.org/10.1080/09578810008426770.

10. Orlando West is one of the oldest parts of Soweto. It was established in the 1930s, intended as a 'garden city' to house Johannesburg's African population then largely residing in inner-city areas that authorities regarded as properly 'white areas'. Noor Nieftagodien and Sally Gaule, *Orlando West, Soweto: An Illustrated History* (Johannesburg: Wits University Press, 2012), https://www.cambridge.org/core/books/orlando-west-soweto/3C379146F2C62F49B9EC6EF41C0DCE4C.

11. 'Orlando stayaway goes on', *Rand Daily Mail* (Township Edition), 22 June 1977, 1.

12. For two examples see: *Rand Daily Mail* (Township Edition), 3 August 1979, 16, and 28 August 1979, 26.

13. Tshepo Moloi, 'Youth Politics: The Political Role of AZANYU in the Struggle for Liberation: The Case of AZANYU Tembisa Branch, 1980s to 1996'. (Research Report, Johannesburg, University of the Witwatersrand, 2005), 106, https://core.ac.uk/download/pdf/39664456.pdf.

14. What is known about SAYRCO is, as Toivo Asheeke has put it, 'scant at best'. It was an organisation formed, primarily by former members of the SSRC, to fight an armed struggle against the Apartheid State. Asheeke's work gives us the fullest account of the organisation yet available. Khotso Seatlholo was central to the organisation, serving as its first President and persuading Nosipho Matshoba to return to Botswana from the United States to help establish the organisation. According to Matshoba, SAYRCO was fiercely independent: 'people did not want to go through the ANC . . . they did not want to go through the PAC . . . so the only way to do this was to form a different political movement'. See: Toivo Tukongeni Paul Wilson Asheeke, *Arming Black Consciousness: The Azanian Black Nationalist Tradition and South Africa's Armed Struggle*, African Studies Series (Cambridge: Cambridge University Press, 2023), 3 and also 146–50, and 158–9. Khotso Seatlholo, despite his leading role in the SSRC (he was the second President in 1977–78) has not received much historiographical attention. He was released from prison in 1990 but did not regain political prominence. When he died in 2004 his wife reportedly refused to allow his funeral to be 'glamorised' by politicians claiming his legacy, stating 'why should he be treated like that after his death when he was neglected while he was alive?' See, Thami Nkwanyane, 'No lavish funeral for Seatlholo, icon of '76', City Press, 21 February 2004, https://www.news24.com/citypress/southafrica/news/no-lavish-funeral-for-seathlolo-icon-of-76-20100614; For more

on Tsietsi Mashinini, the first President of the SSRC, see: Kealeboga J. Maphunye, 'Legacy Underplayed or Ignored? Tsietsi Mashinini: The Forgotten Warrior of South Africa's Liberation Struggle', *African Historical Review* 49, no. 2 (3 July 2017): 22–47, https://doi.org/10.1080/17532523.2017.1414675. Schuster's account of Tsietsi Mashinini is based in part on interviews with Seatlholo. Lynda Schuster, *A Burning Hunger: One Family's Struggle Against Apartheid* (Athens, OH: Ohio University Press, 2006).

15. *State vs. Mary Masabate Loatse and others*, case: 41/4115/81 Magistrates Court, District of Johannesburg; WHP: AD2021: SAIRR Security Trials 1958–82. Boxes 19–20. Digitised trial proceedings, accessed July 2023, http://www.historicalpapers.wits.ac.za/?inventory/U/collections&c=AD2021/R/.

16. Maria Loate gave an interview to the *Sunday Star*. For a summary drawing on the stories published in various South African newspapers see: Laurinda Keys, 'Woman Activist Slashed to Death', *AP News*, 19 October 1986; as of 24 July 2019, https://apnews.com/0c77c01ccad449910d3a2fa2a4fa97a1. [Site inactive on 30 September 2024. Screenshot available from author.]

17. On the controversies and contestations of necklacing as a form of political action within the liberation struggle see: Riedwaan Moosage, 'A Prose of Ambivalence: Liberation Struggle Discourse on Necklacing', *Kronos* 36, no. 1 (2010): 136–56.

18. For the gendered nature of necklacing see: Nyasha Karimakwenda, 'Safe to Violate: The Role of Gender in the Necklacing of Women During the South African People's War (1985–1990)', *Journal of Southern African Studies* 45, no. 3 (4 May 2019): 559–74, https://doi.org/10.1080/03057070.2019.1642646.

19. The Bantu Education Act was introduced in 1953. It replaced a system in which the majority of African children attended state-aided mission schools, with one in which all schools had to be registered with the State and were run by a central Department of Education. A separate curriculum was introduced, designed to ensure that Africans were educated to be 'hewers of wood, and drawers of water'. There was widespread opposition to Bantu Education when it was first introduced but teachers and schools had few choices but to comply and outright opposition had dissipated by 1960. See: Hyslop, *The Classroom Struggle*; for more on the nature of Bantu Education in Soweto see: Clive Glaser, 'Soweto's Islands of Learning: Morris Isaacson and Orlando High Schools Under Bantu Education, 1958–1975', *Journal of Southern African Studies* 41, no. 1 (2 January 2015): 159–71, https://doi.org/10.1080/03057070.2015.991573.

20. Julian Brown, 'An Experiment in Confrontation: The Pro-Frelimo Rallies of 1974', *Journal of Southern African Studies* 38, no. 1 (1 March 2012): 55–71, https://doi.org/10.1080/03057070.2012.644978.

21. The events of 1976 became the lens through which the subsequent involvement of young people in the 1980s was interpreted. For example, analysing the role of young people during the township uprisings of the mid-1980s, Colin Bundy argued for a theory of 'generational units' as actors within history in 1976 and the 1980s. Colin Bundy, 'Street Sociology and Pavement Politics: Aspects of Youth and Student Resistance in Cape Town, 1985', *Journal of Southern African Studies* 13, no. 3 (April 1987): 303–30, https://doi.org/10.1080/03057078708708148; For Shaun Johnson, the classroom boycotts of 1980 were almost 'an action replay of Soweto', Shaun Johnson, ed., *South Africa: No Turning Back* (Basingstoke: Macmillan, 1988), 108.

22. Anne Heffernan, 'Blurred Lines and Ideological Divisions in South African Youth Politics', *African Affairs* 115, no. 461 (1 October 2016): 667, https://doi.org/10.1093/afraf/adw052.

23. For three early responses to the Uprisings that attempted to analyse the students' motivations see: John Stuart Kane-Berman, *Soweto: Black Revolt, White*

Reaction (Johannesburg: Ravan Press, 1978); Baruch Hirson, *Year of Fire, Year of Ash: The Soweto Revolt: Roots of a Revolution?* (London: Zed Press, 1979), 195. Hirson was critical of the revolutionary potential of the SSRC, commenting 'a student council, fighting for student rights is inevitably something different from a council that is directing the population in revolt'. Alan Brooks and Jeremy Brickhill, *Whirlwind Before the Storm: The Origins and Development of the Uprising in Soweto and the Rest of South Africa from June to December 1976* (London: International Defence and Aid Fund for Southern Africa, 1980).

24. Daniel R. Magaziner, *The Law and the Prophets: Black Consciousness in South Africa, 1968–1977* (Athens, OH: Ohio University Press, 2010), 183.

25. The academic and activist Frank Molteno put it like this in a 1979 article: 'During 1976 it was popularly believed that things would never be the same again – nor are they. And yet, what precisely has changed?' Frank Molteno, 'The Uprising of 16th June: A Review of the Literature on Events in South Africa 1976', *Social Dynamics* 5, no. 1 (June 1979): 55, https://doi.org/10.1080/0253395790 8458236.

26. Such numbers are estimates. These particular numbers are drawn from Hyslop, *The Classroom Struggle*, 168.

27. Heffernan, 'Blurred Lines and Ideological Divisions', 671.

28. Heffernan, 'Blurred Lines and Ideological Divisions', 675.

29. Nomavenda Mathiane, *Beyond the Headlines: Truths of Soweto Life* (Johannesburg: Southern Book Publishers, 1990), 132.

30. Truth and Reconciliation Commission of South Africa, *Truth and Reconciliation Commission of South Africa Report*, vol. 3 (Cape Town: Truth and Reconciliation Commission, 1998), 669.

31. 'Askaris' in the South African context were former members of the liberation struggle armies who changed sides to work with apartheid security forces. As the Truth and Reconciliation Commission noted, in South Africa contra-mobilisation of security forces by the State involved 'the fostering of conflicts' between organisations within the liberation struggle, along ethnic and ideological fault-lines. See: Truth and Reconciliation Commission of South Africa, *Truth and Reconciliation Commission of South Africa Report*, vol. 2, 299; volume 3 of the TRC's final report details the few cases from this conflict that came before the Commission. Two mothers of sons killed in the conflict between AZAPO and the UDF in Soweto testified before the Human Rights Violation Committee: one whose son was allegedly killed by AZAPO activists, the other by UDF activists. Truth and Reconciliation Commission of South Africa, *Truth and Reconciliation Commission of South Africa Report*, 1998, vol. 3, 669; For a first-hand account of this period see: Sibongile Mkhabela, *Open Earth and Black Roses: Remembering 16 June 1976* (Braamfontein, South Africa: Skotaville Press, 2001); See also: Monique Marks, *Young Warriors: Youth Politics, Identity and Violence in South Africa* (Johannesburg: Witwatersrand University Press, 2001).

32. Jeremy Seekings, *The UDF: A History of the United Democratic Front in South Africa, 1983–1991* (Oxford: James Currey, 2000); Ineke Van Kessel, *Beyond Our Wildest Dreams: The United Democratic Front and the Transformation of South Africa* (Charlottesville: University Press of Virginia, 2000); Franziska Rueedi, *The Vaal Uprising of 1984 and the Struggle for Freedom in South Africa* (Woodbridge, Suffolk: James Currey, 2021).

33. Jeremy Seekings, *Heroes or Villains? Youth Politics in the 1980s* (Johannesburg: Ravan Press, 1993).

34. David Everatt and Elinor Sisulu, eds., *Black Youth in Crisis: Facing the Future* (Braamfontein: Ravan Press, 1992).

35. Rachel E. Johnson, 'Making History, Gendering Youth: Young Women and South Africa's Liberation Struggles after 1976', PhD Thesis, University of Sheffield, 2010: 19.

36. The principle study of the gender politics of youth politics was for many years that of Jeremy Seekings, 'Gender Ideology and Township Politics in the 1980s', *Agenda* 10 (1991): 77–85, https://doi.org/10.2307/4065458; The picture Seekings drew has been challenged in recent years, most thoroughly by Emily Bridger, see: Emily Bridger, 'Soweto's Female Comrades: Gender, Youth and Violence in South Africa's Township Uprisings, 1984–1990', *Journal of Southern African Studies* 44, no. 4 (4 July 2018): 559–74, https://doi.org/10.1080/03057070.2018.1462591; Emily Bridger, *Young Women against Apartheid: Gender, Youth and South Africa's Liberation Struggle* (Woodbridge, Suffolk; Rochester, NY: James Currey, 2021).

37. Clive Glaser, *Bo Tsotsi: The Youth Gangs of Soweto, 1935–1976* (Oxford: James Currey, 2000), 189. See also: Peter Delius and Clive Glaser, 'Sexual Socialisation in South Africa: A Historical Perspective', *African Studies* 61, no. 1 (2002): 27–54, https://doi.org/10.1080/00020180220140064.

38. For some important publications see: Khangela Ali Hlongwane, Sifiso Mxolisi Ndlovu and Mothobi Mutloatse, eds., *Soweto '76* (Houghton: Mutloatse Arts Heritage Trust, 2006); Pohlandt-McCormick, *'I Saw a Nightmare'*; *The Road to Democracy in South Africa*; for work that situates 1976 within a wider context of student politics in South Africa see: Anne Heffernan et al., *Students Must Rise: Youth Struggle in South Africa before and beyond Soweto '76* (Johannesburg: Wits University Press, 2006).

39. The phrase is Luisa Passerini's. She uses it in relation to the idea of an Italian working class not 'fixed in a still image' but an 'ensemble of relations': Luisa Passerini, *Fascism in Popular Memory: The Cultural Experience of the Turin Working Class*, Studies in Modern Capitalism (Cambridge: Cambridge University Press, 2010), 11.

40. Suzi Nkomo, 'Organising Women in SANSCO: Reflections on the Experience of Women in Organisation', *Agenda* 10 (1991): 10–15, https://doi.org/10.2307/4065449.

41. Nkomo, 'Organising Women in SANSCO', 12.

42. Jon Soske, 'The Family Romance of the South African Revolution', in *Love and Revolution in the Twentieth-Century Colonial and Postcolonial World: Perspectives from South Asia and Southern Africa*, ed. G. Arunima, Patricia Hayes and Premesh Lalu, Palgrave Studies in the History of Social Movements (Cham: Springer International Publishing, 2021), 178, https://doi.org/10.1007/978-3-030-79580-1_7; in developing this argument, Soske draws upon the work of Lynn Hunt, in Lynn Hunt, *Family Romance of the French Revolution* (London: Routledge, 1992), https://doi.org/10.4324/9781315003306.

43. Shireen Hassim, 'Democracy's Shadows: Sexual Rights and Gender Politics in the Rape Trial of Jacob Zuma', *African Studies* 68, no. 1 (1 April 2009): 63, https://doi.org/10.1080/00020180902827431.

44. For one example, see a profile of Lindiwe Sisulu in the ANC's journal in exile, *Sechaba*, subtitled 'daughter of the struggle', in which she is described as 'a slim wisp of determined womanhood, eyes bright with the courage of the freedom fighter, though shadowed with the pain of the ordeals she has undergone'. 'The Torture of Lindiwe Sisulu', *Sechaba*, 1978.

45. Elleke Boehmer, *Stories of Women: Gender and Narrative in the Postcolonial Nation*, Knowledge Unlatched (Manchester: Manchester University Press, 2009), 106, https://doi.org/10.2307/j.ctt155j4ws.

46. Hassim, 'Democracy's Shadows', 65.

47. Letters Page, *Sunday Times*, 26 March 2006.

48. For discussion of Jacob Zuma's rape trial and what it meant for post-apartheid South Africa's gender politics see: Mmatshilo Motsei, *The Kanga and the Kangaroo*

Court: Reflections on the Rape Trial of Jacob Zuma (Sunnyside: Jacana, 2007); Vasu Reddy and Cheryl Potgieter, '"Real Men Stand up for the Truth": Discursive Meanings in the Jacob Zuma Rape Trial', *Southern African Linguistics and Applied Language Studies* 24, no. 4 (2006): 511–21, https://doi.org/10.2989/16073610609486438.

49. M. Tolsi, K.Sosibo, T.Makgetla and M. Dibetle, 'This mama is speaking lies', *Mail and Guardian*, 24–30 March 2006.

50. Pumla Dineo Gqola, *Rape: A South African Nightmare* (Auckland Park, South Africa: MF Books Joburg, 2015), 78–79; see also Bridger's discussion of sexual violence and its impact on girlhood in South Africa in Bridger, *Young Women against Apartheid*, 38–42.

51. For a rare discussion of the history of rape within South Africa see: Emily Bridger, 'Apartheid's "Rape Crisis": Understanding and Addressing Sexual Violence in South Africa, 1970s–1990s', *Women's History Review* 33, no. 2 (23 February 2024): 265–84, https://doi.org/10.1080/09612025.2023.2219535. Bridger sets out the responses of South African women, including the founding of feminist anti-rape organisations in the 1970s, women organisers within trade unions and the township anti-rape marches of the 1990s, alongside the responses of police and vigilante groups.

52. I have used 'womxn' within my discussion of the Fallist movements since this is the term preferred by participants. Matandela explains the term thus: 'womxn refers to a definition of womanhood that aligns itself with decolonial theory, which is inclusive of the LGBTI community and challenges the dichotomy of "man" and "woman" . . . [it is] therefore a revolutionary term for understanding how gender has been challenged in the times of Fallism'. See: Mbalenhle Matandela, 'Redefining Black Consciousness and Resistance: The Intersection of Black Consciousness and Black Feminist Thought', *Agenda* 31, no. 3–4 (2 October 2017): 11–12, https://doi.org/10.1080/10130950.2017.1402410.

53. As quoted and discussed in: Matandela, 'Redefining Black Consciousness and Resistance', 15.

54. I used 'nude' in quotation marks, as one of the participants herself does in her theorising of the moment, as a way of signalling its controversial status as an act of protest. See: Hlengiwe Ndlovu, 'Womxn's Bodies Reclaiming the Picket Line: The "Nude" Protest during #FeesMustFall', *Agenda* 31, no. 3–4 (2 October 2017): 68–77, https://doi.org/10.1080/10130950.2017.1391613.

55. Ndlovu, 'Womxn's Bodies Reclaiming the Picket Line', 74–5.

56. Matandela, 'Redefining Black Consciousness and Resistance', 27.

57. Pohlandt-McCormick, *'I Saw a Nightmare'*, chapter 4, 10.

58. Sifiso Mxolisi Ndlovu, 'The Anatomy of the Crowd', in *The Road to Democracy in South Africa: Volume 7: Soweto Uprisings: New Perspective, Commemorations and Memorialisation* (Cape Town: Unisa Press, 2017), 77.

59. Ndlovu, 'The Anatomy of the Crowd', 49.

60. Ndlovu, 'The Anatomy of the Crowd', 77.

61. Ruth Kerkham Simbao, 'The Thirtieth Anniversary of the Soweto Uprisings: Reading the Shadow in Sam Nzima's Iconic Photograph of Hector Pieterson', *African Arts* 40, no. 2 (1 July 2007): 52–69.

62. Prominent amongst those ongoing silences is the unknown fate of Mbuyisa Makhubu after June 1976, when he left South Africa. Simbao, 'The Thirtieth Anniversary of the Soweto Uprisings', 65.

63. As he put it: 'The factors which necessitated the armed struggle still exist today. We have no option but to continue. We express the hope that a climate conducive to

a negotiated settlement would be created soon so that there may no longer be the need for the armed struggle'. See Nelson Mandela's address to rally in Cape Town on his release from Prison, 11 February 1990. Verbatim transcript, accessed June 2024, https://atom.nelsonmandela.org/index.php/za-com-mr-s-16.

64. At the centre of the apartheid project was the idea that races and ethnic groups should be physically separate from one another. In apartheid theory only whites belonged in South Africa, Asians and Coloureds should be contained within their townships in urban areas and Africans should only be in white areas to support the white population – otherwise they belonged to ethnically defined homelands or Bantustans, made up of the land allocated to 'Natives' by the 1913 and 1936 Land Acts. By the 1980s the National Party attempted to channel black political aspirations by offering these Bantustans 'independence' and providing representation to Asians and Coloureds in a reconstituted parliamentary system. In both cases ultimate power remained within white hands. The white chamber of Parliament outweighed the other two chambers combined. All of the 'independent' Bantustans were economically dependent on South Africa.

65. For two examples of studies that take seriously the beliefs of participants in township uprisings see: Belinda Bozzoli, *Theatres of Struggle and the End of Apartheid* (Edinburgh: Edinburgh University Press, 2004); Rueedi, *The Vaal Uprising of 1984*.

66. Seekings, 'Gender Ideology and Township Politics', 82.

67. Seekings, *Heroes or Villains?*, 84.

68. Bridger, 'Soweto's Female Comrades'; Bridger, *Young Women against Apartheid*; Marks, *Young Warriors*; Janet Cherry, '"We Were Not Afraid": The Role of Women in the 1980s Township Uprising in the Eastern Cape', in *Women in South African History: They Remove Boulders and Cross Rivers*, ed. Nomboniso Gasa (Cape Town: HSRC Press, 2007), 281–314.

69. Bridger, *Young Women against Apartheid*, 48.

70. Natasha Erlank, 'Gender and Masculinity in South African Nationalist Discourse, 1912–1950', *Feminist Studies* 29, no. 3 (2003): 653–72, https://www.jstor.org/stable/3178733.

71. For a summary of this debate see: Cherryl Walker, 'Conceptualising Motherhood in Twentieth Century South Africa', *Journal of Southern African Studies* 21, no. 3 (September 1995): 417–37, https://doi.org/10.1080/03057079508708455.

72. Meghan Healy-Clancy, 'The Family Politics of the Federation of South African Women: A History of Public Motherhood in Women's Antiracist Activism.', *Signs* 42, no. 4 (2017): 851, https://doi.org/10.1086/690916.

73. Healy-Clancy, 'The Family Politics of the Federation of South African Women', 844.

74. Jo Beall et al., 'African Women in the Durban Struggle, 1985–6: Towards a Transformation of Roles', ed. G. Moss and I. Obery, *South African Review* 4 (1987): 102.

75. For work on an earlier period that tackles the relationship between generations of women, see: Deborah Gaitskell, '"Wailing for Purity": Prayer Unions, African Mothers and Adolescent Daughters 1912–1940', in *Industrialisation and Social Change in South Africa: African Class Formation, Culture, and Consciousness, 1870–1930*, ed. Shula Marks and R.J.A.R. Rathbone (Harlow: Longman, 1982), 383; The following include details of tensions between older/younger women activists. For example, Cherry, '"We Were Not Afraid": The Role of Women in the 1980s Township Uprising in the Eastern Cape'; Shireen Hassim, *Women's Organizations and Democracy in South Africa: Contesting Authority* (Madison: University of Wisconsin Press, 2006), 66, especially her profile of the Natal Women's Organisation (NOW) in which she notes, 'older women were wary of the younger women who belonged to NOW, often considering them to be disrespectful and "too

westernised"'. See also the suggestion that in the Western Cape, 'although it was never openly discussed, younger women (below 35) were encouraged to join the youth groups . . . often younger women felt they were not taken seriously' in the United Women's Organisation and its successor the United Women's Congress: Gertrude M.N. Fester, 'Women and Citizenship Struggles: A Case of the Western Cape, South Africa 1980–2004' (PhD, Gender Institute LSE, 2007), 272.

76. For an overview of women's mobilisation both within and outside the mainstream liberation organisations see: Hassim, *Women's Organizations and Democracy in South Africa.*

77. This is suggested in Hassim, *Women's Organizations and Democracy in South Africa.*

78. As quoted in Hassim, *Women's Organizations and Democracy in South Africa*, 77.

79. 'Statement of the National Executive Committee of the African National Congress on the Emancipation of Women in South Africa', *Agenda* 6, no. 8 (1 January 1990): 23, https://doi.org/10.2307/4065629.

80. 'Statement of the National Executive Committee of the African National Congress on the Emancipation of Women in South Africa', 23.

81. Hassim, *Women's Organizations and Democracy in South Africa*, 161–2.

82. Meg Samuelson, *Remembering the Nation, Dismembering Women? Stories of the South African Transition* (Scottsville, South Africa: University of KwaZulu-Natal Press, 2007), 120.

83. Fiona Ross, 'On Having Voice and Being Heard: Some After-Effects of Testifying before the South African Truth and Reconciliation Commission', *Anthropological Theory* 3 (2003): 327, https://doi.org/10.1177/14634996030033005.

84. Ross, 'On Having Voice and Being Heard'.

Chapter 1

A methodology for fragments: voice, speech and silence

Introduction

If Masabata Loate and young women have been made liminal within narratives of the liberation struggle, in another sense, Loate's story is central. The spaces and records through which we can know Masabata Loate (and the impossibility of knowing her) are those through which we know the liberation struggle: photographs; trials – their processes, proceedings and the evidence they created; political speeches; newspapers; human rights reportage; creative fiction, drama, poetry and song; autobiography and memoir; the Truth and Reconciliation Commission (TRC) and oral histories. In approaching these various archives of struggle this book traces cycles of voicing and silencing within them. This is an approach that treats all archives as 'storied' spaces, where lives are made and remade in the unfolding tangle of political mobilisation, state oppression and individual self-fashioning.[1] Looking for 'cycles of voicing and silencing' is a conscious attempt to move away from a linear understanding of subjecthood, in which once silent/silenced subjects have their voices found or given, and thereby enter into 'History'.[2] The politics and practices of voice, speech and silence are much richer and more complex than this. It is the argument of this book that, if we acknowledge that voice and silence are not opposites of one another, but rather always entangled in any act of speech, we can position ourselves to learn much from the shadows. Below, I introduce my approach to voice, speech and silence, situating each within the historiography of South Africa's liberation struggle and a wider methodological discussion. These are the tools I have used when drawing Masabata Loate's shadow; they might be used for navigating the interplay of light and dark in the archives of many other times and places.

Voice

To possess and to be able to use your voice is something we can distinguish from the straightforward ability to speak. As Sean Field puts it, having voice is perhaps more accurately about having 'sufficiently enabled' access to public spaces to speak and be heard.[3] To have a voice is to achieve recognition. It is both a political demand and a deeply personal experience. It is also about the connection between speech and a sense of self. Having voice is to be able to achieve a recognition and expression of selfhood through speech. In the chapters which follow I listen for the expressions of individuals and collectives. There are many voices, nested inside one another: South Africans, Africans, Black, white, women, men, the youth, nationalists, feminists, to name but a few. Exactly who has a voice and when, or what claims are made for and by individuals, is a history of the many threads contained within South Africa's anti-apartheid liberation struggle. Sometimes individuals are contained and constrained by the collective claims made through and by them; sometimes competing voices drown each other out or silence those within; and sometimes they can amplify one another.

The emergence and evolution of African nationalism in Southern Africa can be understood in a very simple way as a fight to claim a political voice for all within the nation of South Africa, the borders of which were drawn in 1910. South Africa was a nation created out of the violent encounter between the British Empire, white settlers of Dutch origin and the indigenous communities of Southern Africa. As soon as that nation was constituted, those who had already been working for political recognition within the early colonies and settler states in the region, developed claims for their right to a voice within the Union of South Africa.[4] An organisational history of African nationalism begins with the founding of the South African National Native Congress, later renamed the African National Congress (ANC), in 1912. The ANC was not always the driver of political action or demands over the course of the twentieth century – the liberation struggle was wider and deeper than any single organisation – but it maintained a constant presence and ultimately led the process that negotiated a non-racial democracy in the 1990s. Demands for a political voice always existed alongside those for access to land, especially following the 1913

Land Act that dispossessed 'Natives' of the right to buy or hire all but 7 per cent (later 13 per cent) of South Africa's territory and controlled access to that remnant through a reconstituted tradition of Chieftaincy.[5] For others, the driver was economic opportunities, and, for some, the struggle was guided by a vision of economic and political revolution.[6]

The fight for political voice in South Africa acquired a new dimension when the white segregationist State was reconfigured as the Apartheid State after 1948. Apartheid legislation conceived of South Africa as a white nation and sought to control all aspects of life based on a person's racial classification as either White, African, Asian or Coloured.[7] After 1948 African nationalist demands were bound up with a fight for racial justice against institutionalised white supremacy. This had a global dimension in the anti-apartheid solidarity movement, interconnected with the rise of human rights discourses. In the late 1960s and early 1970s the ideas that came to be collectively named 'Black Consciousness' sought nothing less than to 'transform identity' and 'instil dignity and confidence' in those who were oppressed – ideas which, Dan Magaziner has argued, by the 1980s gave way to 'the far more limited, if laudable goal of ending apartheid'.[8] Achieving a political voice for all South Africans through electoral democracy was thus not necessarily always the principal demand of those who participated in the liberation struggle. Yet, to have a voice was a continuous demand and a desire running through these various currents, even if the articulation and meaning of this demand changed over time and location, and in response to the State's attempts to suppress opposition.

Natasha Erlank has suggested that there are two different ways of thinking about nationalism. The first is to conceptualise African nationalism as a response to the white State. 'It speaks to a desire for equal rights for black and white South Africans' and is a project aimed at producing a political community that takes place in the public sphere.[9] The second is to consider what is contained within this process of producing a political community and look for the ways nationalism is shaped – the imaginative repertoires it calls upon and creates.[10] Using voice as a lens brings both into focus: asking who speaks, when and where; what claims they make; how; and with what consequences? If we approach nationalism in this way, it becomes a space rich with struggles over speech, drawing upon and in dialogue with other ideologies and currents of thought – Christianity, socialism, communism, Black Consciousness, feminism, queer activism – through which individual and collective voices were forged.

We should note that there were specific conditions under which voices, public voices striving for recognition, were articulated in South Africa after 1976, shaped by the struggles which had preceded 16 June, and the shocks that the Uprisings themselves unleashed. Those who opposed apartheid were targeted by an array of security legislation which evolved over the forty years of National Party rule, through measures such as censorship, banning orders, banishments, detention and torture – many of which targeted the right (and in the case of torture the ability) to speak or write. Whilst legislation like the Suppression of Communism Act was laid down in the 1950s, the systematic and concerted suppression of political opposition to the Apartheid State deepened after 1960. The State of Emergency declared to quash the response to the Sharpeville Massacre on 21 March, when sixty-nine unarmed anti-pass protesters were shot (in the back) by police, saw the mass detention of political activists. In April 1960 the ANC and the PAC, the latter the organisation which had organised the Sharpeville protest, were banned. By the mid-1960s most of the leadership of these organisations, and their armed wings (both launched in 1961), as well as that of the South African Communist Party (SACP), and other organisations of the Congress Alliance, were detained, imprisoned or in exile. This has resulted in a common characterisation of the 1960s as the 'silent decade' within the history of the liberation struggle.[11] The idea that political organising ceased in the face of state repression has been shown by Julian Brown and others to be inaccurate.[12] However, we might instead see the 1960s as the point at which silence became an ever more necessary tactic within the struggle. From the 1960s onwards secrecy and silence were central to political lives.[13] Voices had to be ever more carefully composed, shaping the forms of speech available and limiting what was sayable. We can include within this the stifling silences operating within white society – what Helena Pohlandt-McCormick has recalled as 'the potent mixture – for whites – of silence, secrets, complicity, indifference, guilt, habit and decree' that upheld apartheid laws and the means used to do so.[14]

The legal space to voice opposition to the State shrank again in the wake of 16 June 1976. The Internal Security Amendment Act that was passed during the Uprisings allowed for the indefinite preventative detention of those suspected of endangering the security of the State, or law and order.[15] It also enabled the detention of, and prohibition of bail for, potential witnesses to violations of internal security. This was the form of detention without trial that many young people involved in the Soweto Uprisings, including Masabata Loate, were subjected to.[16] Into the 1980s detention became the principal weapon utilised by security forces to curtail the activities of youth groups, trade unions and women's, church and civic organisations that were mobilising in opposition to the State's attempts to retain apartheid through reform.[17] Another Internal Security Act (ISA) was passed in 1982 and amended in 1986. The powers of the ISA were, in the words of the Human Rights Committee of South Africa (HRC), 'truly awesome'.[18] Writing in 1990, the HRC noted that, 'there is hardly a form of political expression, which is not blocked, controlled or threatened by one or other provision of the ISA'.[19] The Act allowed for three forms of detention: detention for interrogation (Section 29), preventative detention (Section 28, 50 and 50A) and witness detention (Section 31). The power to detain was widened still further by the States of Emergency declared in 1985 (partial) and 1986 (national) that lasted until 1990. Under the Emergency any member of the security forces was empowered to detain and interrogate. Those detainees had no automatic right of access to lawyers, family or friends and could be held for the duration of the Emergency. Even the naming of those held in detention under the Emergency was prohibited. In the context of 1970s and 1980s South Africa then, speech and silence had meaning and importance beyond the content of such acts – simply to speak and to be silent could have extraordinary resonance and meaning in and of itself.

As many have noted, including the TRC, the violence of the Apartheid State in these years and the effects of this violence on memory and speech have been profound. Helena Pohlandt-McCormick identifies a 'collusion between violence and silence' that can, and has, 'obstructed the ability of individuals to place themselves in history'.[20] Veena Das who thinks deeply about the experience of world-annihilating violence suggests that such violence can have the effect of rendering someone 'voiceless' but 'not in the sense that one does not have words but that these words become frozen, numb, without life'.[21] Similarly, Elaine Scarry argues that: 'world, self, and voice are lost, or nearly lost, through the intense pain of torture'.[22] If violence has profound effects on voice, then the gendered patterns of state violence, and that which took place within the liberation struggle, shape both speech and the record it leaves us.

Voices were the stuff of the liberation struggle; they are also very often how we know about that liberation struggle. Given the restrictions on the public articulation of political voices under apartheid, oral history has been for historians one of the most important ways of accessing the liberation struggle both at the time and in the post-apartheid present. As Jeremy Seekings has noted, South Africa's liberation struggle is perhaps unusual in the extent to which it was documented by academics as it was unfolding.[23] Voices were central methodologically to the social historians of the second half of the twentieth century. The aim of 'giving voice to the voiceless' can be found within social history, oral history and feminist research at this time.[24] It was certainly not always put as bluntly and simplistically as this. However, a sense of the authenticity of voices, that are 'out there' to be found and restored to history by the historian and can thereby redress the gaps in the written archives, still lingers within South African historiography.[25] Yet there are also important critiques of such an approach that have emerged from all three intellectual traditions, social, oral and feminist histories, which equip us with the tools to explore voices as I have suggested above,[26] to hear them as constructed claims, speech striving for recognition, crafted by speakers in dialogue with others, and under conditions that shape what was sayable and by whom in specific circumstances.

The centrality of voices within South African historiography means that struggles over voice criss-cross apartheid and post-apartheid spaces. Those who were conducting research during the 1990s noticed the profound affect that the ending of the Apartheid State had upon talk about the liberation struggle. Helena Pohlandt-McCormick has recounted how researching the Soweto Uprisings before the 1994 election she found people 'cautious, reluctant and unwilling to talk' but that after the election 'much of the tension had been replaced by relief and a new willingness to think about the past', and 'interviews were now tinged with humour and the heady feeling of victory'.[27] The 1990s may have seen the creation of new openings for speech and changing attitudes from former participants in the liberation struggle 'as a range of inhibitions and security concerns dissipated', but these openings were not universally accessible and many individuals have maintained significant silences.[28] Thus, the cycles of voicing and silencing that this book traces continue beyond the end(ings) of apartheid.

The ongoing creation of oral histories of political participation is a part of a longer history of speaking about the struggle.[29] This means recognising sites of speech that were heavily coerced, such as the statements of young people in court and their possible relationship with subsequent acts of speech and silence.[30] Those who speak now about their pasts of political participation do so after having traversed the terrain of speech and silence within the liberation struggle for many years. The interconnectedness of different sites of speech can sometimes be uncomfortable. For example, during an interview I conducted back in 2008 with a woman named Rebecca Musi, who became politically active as a university student at the University of the North, this interconnectedness became audible in a moment that initially passed me by in the flow of conversation.[31] It was only later when I was transcribing the interview that her words pulled me up short. We were talking about her time in detention in 1977:

> In all my interrogations etc, you'd have, you always had the good guy, the bad guy, the mediocre guy (laughs). And the good guy would always come to you and thinking well, *speak like we are speaking*, and

> you give them all the information, and the other guy, if the other two guys realised he's not winning then they come and the aggressive guy comes and those are the guys who actually beat you up and you know all sorts of things. [emphasis added][32]

Speak like we are speaking. This was, of course, perhaps just a simple way of explaining the differences in tactics between security police. It was a reminder too of the ways my whiteness shaped our interactions. However, it also brought home to me the way in which moments of speech about the struggle are layered upon one another. Talking to me then, Rebecca Musi was recalling the way she spoke to police during her interrogations, and how she tried to maintain her silence, in the face of 'all sorts of things'. This euphemistic reference to torture points to the ongoing effect of the experience. That earlier moment of speech and silence was part of our conversation. There was, I hope, a huge difference between those moments but Rebecca Musi's words suggest that even if just for a second, the two collapsed into one another. This layering of speech is something the chronological structure of the book emphasises – the palimpsest effect of speech in the struggle, across multiple sites, and over time, is important. However, the ways in which speech and silence recollect and revisit earlier moments should also disturb any straightforward notion of chronology. The potency of speaking about the struggle as an act breaks down divisions between the past, present and future.

Speech

There are many forms of speech – and it should be noted, languages – through which voices emerge from within the liberation struggle and in its aftermath.[33] There are spectacular and highly choreographed moments, for example, Nelson Mandela's speech from the dock at the Rivonia Trial. When the publication of his words and image were banned, Mandela took the opportunity to make a statement to the court instead of testifying, and spoke, uninterrupted for over four hours. The speech detailed a personal history of his involvement in the struggle, that of the ANC and the decision to launch the armed struggle.[34] Alongside this, are more everyday kinds of political discussion or debate, such as the *umrabulo* of the COSAS activists on Soweto streets, which Emily Bridger's interviewees discussed with her. Bridger's research suggests that at the centre of young men and young women's differential participation in youth politics in the late 1980s was speech. Florence told Bridger that from young men's easy access to the street flowed the ease of their participation:

> It's easy for them to communicate. We used to say *umrabulo* [a political discussion or debate] . . . it was easy for them to *umrabulo*-ise, to make understand or make one politically aware. So, it was easy because one guy would go chat, they'd start smoking, passing it, and chatting about whatever.[35]

As both of the above examples attest, all forms of speech had gendered dynamics. Certain modes of speech, and spaces, were more and less accessible to men and women. Speech – who talks, when and where – takes us to the heart of the ways in which participation in the liberation struggle was navigated through inter-personal relations. The vast majority of speech does not leave behind any archival traces. The spectacular is more likely to leave a trace than the everyday. In a striking example of the ways in which the repressive machinery of the State shaped speech in the struggle, Murphy Morobe, a member of the SSRC and one of the Soweto Eleven, has recalled clandestine meetings with underground ANC activists during the 1970s. Testifying at the TRC, Morobe recalled meeting with ANC operative Joe Gqabi, who was a banned individual at the time: 'Each time we came to his house, we did not speak, you know, everything will be written on paper and we will just exchange paper because the houses will be bugged and after all, those papers, he would take those papers and burn them'.[36] Yet, as I argued above, speech and silence do leave traces in subsequent acts of talking and not talking. These unspoken meetings resurfaced in Morobe's TRC testimony.[37]

Most of the material that I work with in the book is speech rendered as text. Captured in this way we lose much about the act of speaking – body language, tone, demeanour, fluency. Yet recorded speech is still different from written prose. Walter J. Ong has argued that: 'by keeping knowledge embedded in the human life world, orality situates knowledge, within a context of struggle'.[38] This quality of speech, as a form of struggle, can certainly still be found within speech rendered as text, such as the trial transcripts that underpin Chapters 2 and 3 in this book. The oral historian Luisa Passerini has described how working with written archives can be a work of oral history too 'in so far as it seeks to uncover a culture of the spoken word'.[39] I argue that in the archives of South Africa's liberation struggle we can uncover cultures of the spoken word that shaped what was sayable and by whom. These cultures I call 'struggle speech'.

Struggle speech has three dimensions: speech *about* the struggle, speech *as* the struggle and the struggle *to* speak. In an individual's efforts to speak about their own actions within the anti-apartheid struggle, as a way of critiquing and publicising the injustices of apartheid, one can see all three dimensions of struggle speech: a struggle to talk about liberation and to use speech as a means of winning it. In each of the chapters which follow I question one aspect of the life of Masabata Loate by focusing on one dimension of struggle speech. I argue that each of the three dimensions of struggle speech had gendered dynamics and was, and is, part of the ongoing reiteration and negotiation of gender as a lived experience. Whilst in individual chapters I think repeatedly about moments of speech and silence, the whole book is also an attempt to think instead about what is sayable. The term is borrowed from Judith Butler and is an attempt to capture something more than the straightforward question of what people can say in a given context because of social or political norms or personal interests. As Butler puts it, 'the question is not what it is that I will be able to say but what will constitute the domain of the sayable within which I begin to speak at all?'[40]

What is sayable is what underlies having a voice – staying within the bounds of the sayable helps speech to be recognised as a voice. Struggle speech is a particular 'domain of the sayable', the boundaries of which shifted over time through cumulative acts of speech and silence. The violence used to constitute that domain, state violence and liberation violence, was productive of gendered narratives and experiences of struggle. Who can talk, where and when, and what they might say, are not, as Butler argues, the kinds of 'rules' that are written down or even necessarily conscious.[41] It is very often through moments of rupture or transgression that we can glimpse the domain of the sayable: acts of silence or silencing, of speech which is spoken but unheard, or that which is deemed unspeakable, can show us just what was and is sayable. It is through struggle speech and the ways in which she both conformed and did not conform to its conventions, that we come to know, and cannot know, Masabata Loate.

In this endeavour, maintaining the distinction between speech and voice, or having a voice, helps us to think more precisely about when, and how, speech becomes a moment of voicing. As Chapter 4 demonstrates, written prose plays an important role in the making of voices – both collective and individual. Veena Das puts it this way: 'voice is not identical to speech, nor does it stand in opposition to writing'.[42] Written prose, particularly in the form of memoir and autobiography, also contains traces of earlier moments of speech and silence. For example, in composing her autobiography, trade unionist and anti-apartheid activist Emma Mashinini began with the transcripts of recorded conversations she had with the film-maker Betty Wolpert.[43] She explains the process in a preface to her book:

> During the shooting of the film, [*Mama I'm Crying*] Betty interviewed me and recorded my story on every possible occasion, even on aeroplane journeys. She would then post the tapes to Ruth Vaughan, her collaborator in London, who would rapidly transcribe them so that I could immediately work on the rough draft. With time I gained confidence and got into the groove of writing chapters myself. It was Betty who took my manuscript to The Women's Press, and it was at her house in London that I completed the final draft and worked with my editor, Alison Mansbridge.[44]

However, what Walter Ong's recognition of the special character of orality, that we noted earlier, does usefully draw attention to, is that speech and writing often occur in (and require) different kinds of spaces and moments. This is evident in Mashinini's account above.

In the chapters which follow I explore the gendered dynamics of 'talking', 'speaking up' and 'speaking out' as certain kinds of speech within the struggle which were archived. Each of these forms of speech played a role in capturing Masabata Loate's story, drawing fragments of her life into the archive. These forms of speech were recorded particularly through the legal system and the human rights activism which emerged to monitor, publicise and campaign against the Apartheid State's use of legal and extra-legal methods of supressing political dissent. I consider 'talking' as a form of speech that resulted from the unbearable weight of state oppression on individuals. Talking is speech that was the result of detention and often torture. It is the kind of speech recorded as the testimony of state witnesses. Talking can involve claims to voice (seeking a recognition of a self) but often involve a high degree of dissembling. We might think of dissembling as speech that seeks to protect a self through misinformation, half-truth and silence. Trial transcripts are full of talk, to such an extent that many researchers have cautioned against their use for writing struggle histories. For example, as Belinda Bozzoli and Franziska Rueedi have shown, the trial scenario silences particular actors and amplifies others.[45] It thus cannot be read as representing an accurate picture of struggle politics – particularly its gender and generational dynamics. The life stories that might emerge from these encounters between the State and its subjects or opponents are, as Gready has noted, a 'violently collaborative' effort.[46] The pressures of speech in such a context may well produce utterances which are 'precisely not testimony' and those who talk may 'no longer coincide' with themselves.[47] Whilst fully acknowledging this, I argue that trial versions of events mattered, and perhaps even more so, who spoke and from what position during trials had consequences beyond the courtroom. The life and death of Masabata Loate demonstrates this rather starkly. In addition, whilst 'talk' may not always give us access to an accurate picture of 'who did what' it does often and in surprising ways reveal the emotions of activists amidst oppression and points to what was sayable in this context.

At times, talk morphs into an act of 'speaking out' against the injustices of the Apartheid State. This was much more commonly the case in the high-profile political show trials of the late 1950s and early 1960s. The Treason Trial (1956–61), the Incitement Trial (1962) and the Rivonia Trial (1963–64) all included moments where defendants were able to articulate openly and, at times at great length, their political ideology, the actions they had taken in opposition to apartheid, and justify their beliefs.[48] The State removed these possibilities for subsequent political defendants, and it should be remembered that the majority of political trials took place far from the glare of the international or even national media, with large portions closed to the public.[49] For those young people detained in the 1980s, in particular under the Emergencies, there was often no trial at which to speak or stay silent. In this context acts of 'speaking out' were recorded by human rights groups like the Detainee Parent's Support Committee (DPSC) through their advice offices, daybooks and public campaigns.

In September 1981, just a few months before Seatlholo and Loate's trial began, a large number of activists were detained in a countrywide swoop. By January 1982, over a hundred people were detained.[50] The State at this time targeted some of the newly resurgent ANC-aligned activists as well as trade unionists, such as Emma Mashinini, and a number of white students, including Keith Coleman. Keith Coleman's parents, Dr Max and Audrey Coleman, and Emma Mashinini's husband, Tom, were among the founding members of the first DPSC.[51] In 1983 the DPSC affiliated to the newly formed United Democratic Front. Two weeks before a partial State of Emergency was declared in 1985 the DPSC opened an advice office in Johannesburg at Khotso House, where the South African Council of Churches was also based. By 1987 the DPSC operated advice offices in 'all major centres and several small towns'.[52] It was named a banned organisation by the State in February 1988 but continued to operate until 1990 when the office in Khotso House was finally closed.[53] The DPSC actually had two organisational components: the Detainee Parent's Support Committees which were made up of parents, friends and relatives of detainees and thus had an ever changing membership; and the Descoms which had a much wider membership and carried out the organisation's education campaigns, provided support to DPSC branches and undertook 'information gathering' and 'crisis and emergency work'.[54] Underpinning this information gathering were the advice offices and their 'daybooks'.

The daybooks recorded testimony from newly released detainees, family members of the recently detained, those affected by the violence of the State and, as the 1980s unfolded, inter-organisational conflict. The DPSC was deeply enmeshed in the politics of struggle speech since it had to work closely with other organisations whose membership was being targeted for detentions if they wanted to provide support to detainees and 'gather information' from them about the repressive tactics of security forces. As Audrey Coleman explained in 2007, 'the different organisations within the townships seconded people to our office because of the sensitivity of the information we were receiving. So, they wanted to know that reliable people were getting the information as we debriefed detainees'.[55] The DPSC's position, and, with that, its ability to assist detainees and access information, depended upon it being trusted. In the increasingly fraught political landscape of the late 1980s trust gained through, for example the organisation's affiliation with the UDF, would have had far from a universal purchase. Even amongst UDF affiliates there could be considerable tensions.[56] Coupled with this, under the Emergencies of the late 1980s, as the DPSC itself became a target for state repression, members of other organisations were often needed to step in and help run the advice offices. Audrey Coleman remembers relying upon friends from the Black Sash to help her keep Khotso House running in 1985 when the first State of Emergency sent other activists underground.[57]

The DPSC daybooks contain glimpses of people's lives at moments of crisis. In each case the testimony recorded was prompted by an intrusion into a friend's, a relative's or the testifier's own life. The archived daybooks are not systematic or comprehensive. They cannot provide an overview of human rights abuses during the Emergency. That they exist, that they were created, is what interests me. This was the emergent context for Loate's second trial and the circumstances in which she found herself on her release in 1986. There is a terrible immediacy to the testimonies even read at a physical and temporal distance. However, each testimony was mediated by a statement-taker working in the DPSC advice offices. Judging from the surviving daybooks, different statement-takers, and witnesses, had differing approaches. The DPSC's guidelines make clear the organisation's interest in dates, times, places and names which would make up a factual statement of what had happened to each person. Nevertheless, this did not constrain some individuals from making fuller and more personal statements. Occasionally it appears that individuals wrote their own testimony directly into the daybooks. One such example can be found in a testimony written by a young man from Klipspruit West,

Gerald Lewis Williamson. The entry is written in a mixture of upper and lower-case letters; he describes his detention and treatment angrily as dehumanising and barbaric. His testimony ends: 'an injury to one is an injury to all! KILL THE BOER, THE FARMER! I hate WHITES!'[58] The writing of these slogans and the final statement, 'I hate WHITES!' take up most of a single page; the form of the writing itself seems to convey the emotions of this act of speaking out and to suggest that this has been written directly by Williamson. In most cases the role of the statement-taker is obscured by the use of the first person.[59] In this way, the daybooks are more than composite and mediated accounts of the Emergency – they are sites of struggle themselves, of speech as struggle. They are evidence of an important set of processes by which experiences of detention and abuse were (re)framed for individuals so that speaking out about such experiences became itself an act of confrontation with the State, a responsibility of resistance. They are records of decisions to speak out made by many activists and non-activists alike: the counter to the testimonies delivered and silences maintained within the courtroom.

Finally, 'speaking up' is a form of speech that has not so often been archived. We can think of this as the internal discussions that took place within liberation organisations – debates over strategy or practice. As Chapter 4 demonstrates, more of this kind of speech within the struggle began to emerge publicly in the late 1980s and during the relative freedom of the 1990s. It often accompanied the (re)making of collective voices for women and queer activists within the liberation struggle. All of these forms of speech within the struggle had gendered dynamics which is important, because of the centrality of voices to our understanding of political participation, especially since these archived forms of speech do not stand in opposition to oral histories of the struggle. There are important ways in which genres and forms overlap and shape one another across time and space: trial testimonies, human rights reportage, activist interviews and oral histories echo, and recall, one another in ways of speaking in the struggle.

Speech might also be seen to have a particular relationship with emotion and thereby help us to understand the 'projects of desire' within anti-apartheid political activism.[60] The idea of a special connection between speech and emotion has been put forward in an influential set of arguments by William Reddy. According to Reddy there are particular speech acts which can be defined as 'emotives', whereby sensory, biological and bodily experiences are translated into expressions of emotion.[61] He argues that 'when we speak of our emotions, they come into a peculiar, dynamic relationship with what we say about them'.[62] Emotives 'are influenced directly by, and alter, what they refer to'.[63] Speech thus offers historians glimpses of the normative regimes of emotional management which individuals navigate in specific contexts. An individual's ability to navigate their feelings is at the core of emotional liberty which, for Reddy, must underpin any definition of political freedom.[64] Reddy's insistence that 'emotions are of the highest political significance' converges with the second-wave feminist mantra, 'the personal is political'.[65] Put another way: claims to self and voice are inherently political, and politics is enacted through embodied subjectivities.

Many have recognised that histories of the liberation struggle are necessarily intimate and emotional.[66] Jon Soske has drawn attention to the ways in which, in researching and writing histories of the liberation struggle, historians are often working with 'intimate knowledge'. In his definition, 'intimate knowledge' is derived from 'lived experience', from 'direct personal involvement; it is embodied in individual relationships (and therefore possesses an affective dimension) and it incorporates the knower within that which is known'.[67] However, Soske argues that the 'intimacies of black anti-apartheid politics' have often been obscured in academic accounts. In his own work Soske restores the emotional depth of the past by noticing not just what former participants have told him, but *how* those stories are told. He reflects on the way one interviewee chooses to tell a story 'off the record', in the form of a secret, despite the information actually imparted being well-known.[68] When confronted with the emotional intensity of speech about the struggle it is not long before the question of silences appears.

Silence

In thinking about silence, I want to return to a moment of failure, as I experienced it. In 2008 I was in Johannesburg, conducting oral history interviews with women who had been activists when they were young. I encountered both refusals and acceptances, but one set of refusals left me with a profound sense of unease, which has informed my approach to the past ever since. This set of refusals from a group of women was courteous but firm. They did not want to speak with me about their activist pasts. It might help me, but it certainly would not help them. They did not need recognition from me as historical subjects and they did not need my intervention. Initially, the meaning I took from these refusals was that I was not the historian who should be writing their histories – after all, my foreignness, race and age (for I was a very young researcher then) undoubtedly informed our interaction.[69] Over time, I have come to see another meaning there, too, that those refusals to speak were important archival acts. In a place like South Africa, where oral history is so obviously necessary for vast swathes of the past to be remembered and understood, how can we honour some people's decisions not to speak? Should it be that a decision to stay silent results in being written out?

Jacob Dlamini has considered the issue of silence and refusal within the public discourse on the liberation struggle in his work on police collaborators, the so-called askaris, former liberation soldiers and activists who were 'turned' to work for the South African security forces. In beginning to write the histories of informing and collaboration Dlamini touches on one of the loudest silences within public narratives of the liberation struggle. He makes this plea:

> There are stories that continue to refuse to be told. How might we go beyond that refusal? One way, it seems to me, is to engage honestly with the fatal intimacy at the heart of human relations in South Africa. It is in our persons that the secrets of the past have found a home. We must open up these archives and tell these stories.[70]

Yet Dlamini reveals just how difficult this 'opening up' can be by telling his readers a story he asks us to 'treat as fictional', in which a young man 'keen on history' decides against following his suspicions and finding out whether one of his uncles had been an informer for the apartheid police.[71] Dlamini describes this young man as coming 'face to face with the notion of a legitimate secret'.[72] What Dlamini makes clear is the way in which certain silences can be woven into the warp of social worlds and that the costs of unravelling them may be too high a price to pay. In this context there is a moral and ethical urgency to Nthabiseng Motsemme's call for historians to 'learn to read silences just as we would speech and action',[73] since to 'break' some silences might have very real social consequences for those involved in carrying controversial pasts.

When thinking about the silences of individuals, Obioma Nnaemeka makes an important distinction between 'to be silenced' and 'to be silent'.[74] Whilst the first fits quite obviously with an understanding of oppression, the second is more complicated. As Nnaemeka puts it, 'one exercises agency when one chooses not to speak; the refusal to speak is also an act of resistance that signals the unwillingness to participate'. By choosing to remain silent an individual may in fact 'gain attention that initiates talk'.[75] Or, as Motsemme has noted, silence may offer a form of emotional protection amidst conditions of oppression.[76] I argue that to read a silence held by an individual as what Reddy would term an 'emotive' is possible and indeed, necessary, to understand the gendered navigation of feeling in the liberation struggle.[77] On an individual level speech and silence are not opposites of one another. As social acts, and archival traces, silence and speech contain the possibility of each other within one another. This has long been recognised by oral historians who argue that the silences, errors or 'even the lies' within oral accounts of the past are what make them truthful; they reveal the creative processes by which lives lived become memories and stories to be told and retold in the present.[78] This is the 'unique and precious element' of oral sources: they tell us 'not just what people did, but what they wanted to do, what they believed they were doing, and what they now think they did'.[79] They do so through acts of silence, just as they do through speech.

'Talk' as a form of speech heavily shaped by coercive power is particularly full of silences. Dissembling – saying one thing but meaning another, or speech that misleads and misdirects – was central to daily life under apartheid. The need for black South Africans to speak in particular ways to (often white) authority in order to survive is captured particularly within poetry of the Black Consciousness era. For example, in 'Gumba Gumba Gumba',[80] a poem that catalogues the sights, sounds and feelings of life in a South African township, Mafika Gwala describes:

> Struggle is when
> You have to lower your eyes
> And steer time
> With your voice bent
> [. . .]
>
> Jerk your talk
> Frown in your laughs
> Smile when you ain't happy
> That's struggle.[81]

Jeremy Cronin has called this a 'paradoxical voicing of voicelessness', which explores the rich (and painful) emotional depths of the silences imposed and maintained under apartheid.[82] The terrain of speech in the liberation struggle was significantly reshaped in the late 1960s and through the 1970s by the emergence of Black Consciousness, which placed a renewed emphasis on voice. Dan Magaziner has argued that the ability 'to speak with the self-conscious assurance of an adult' was of central importance to Black Consciousness thought.[83] In another set of reflections on silence from the early 1970s, in his poem, 'And Yet . . .', Don Mattera points to a complex relationship between silence and emotional expression which underlay his own ideas about his place in the world. Mattera, who had been working as journalist for the newspaper *The Star* and an activist within the Black People's Convention (BPC), was banned by the State in 1973.

> I have known deep silences
> when thoughts like angry waves
> beat against the shores of my mind[84]

Within this silence Mattera remembers painful experiences and in particular recalls the wounding of his sense of masculinity.[85] The recent flowering of scholarship on Black Consciousness has shown that the movement's ideas and practices were marked by gendered formulations such as this.[86] Magaziner emphasises the 'conscious silences and stressed syllables' of the famous mantra 'Black man you are on your own'.[87] According to Magaziner, Black Consciousness 'was both a marker and a process; to call oneself 'Black' was to 'assert one's consciousness of oneself as such'. He suggests that despite an initial interest in exploring women's consciousness of themselves as women, over time the movement became more ascriptive of distinct gendered roles and soon the 'options open' to women within Black Consciousness organisations were to be 'one of the boys' or a mother.[88] As 'one of the boys' it was possible for women to speak with 'defiant adult voices' but they were not always heard in this way. By way of example, Magaziner cites press coverage of the Black Renaissance Conference in 1974 that denigrated the young women delegates from the South African Students' Organisation (SASO) as 'hysterical girls'.[89] All of this points us to the importance of the contexts in which speech and silence are heard, which can shape the meaning of both. These 'deep silences' show us that a historical silence is not simply an absence or lack of speech or noise. It is something more akin to a limitation on knowledge about the past. Silence is a limit in the sense that it marks the boundary between one kind of knowledge and another. Silence can be one of the ways in which we come to know about the past.

In his influential work on the Haitian Revolution, Michel-Rolph Trouillot talks of four crucial moments at which 'silence enters the process of historical production': 'the moment of fact creation (the making of sources); the moment of fact assembly (the making of archives); the moment of fact retrieval (the making of narratives); and the moment of retrospective significance (the making of history in the final instance)'.[90] Paying attention to when and where silences are made, Trouillot suggests, is vital for understanding that 'not all silences are equal' and therefore 'they cannot be addressed – or redressed – in the same manner'.[91] Archives, written and oral, can be silent about things which we know happened. That they are partial is axiomatic. Asking how and why we do not know, about marginalised people in any given context, can be extremely revealing. As Ann Laura Stoler has argued, we can read 'along the archival grain'; to see the workings of governmental mind-sets within the making of state archives with logics, desires and anxieties shaping what was recorded and how.[92]

Colonialism, genocide and slavery are all processes of annihilation, of people and of worlds, and enact foundational silences at the moment of source creation. Historians who have sought to write about societies and peoples subjected to such annihilation have faced many questions about what it is possible to know in these contexts. These historians often conceive of themselves as telling stories of the unspoken, the unspeakable or the impossible. In her iconic essay 'Can the Subaltern Speak?', Gayatri Spivak argued that 'if in the context of colonial production, the subaltern has no history and cannot speak, the subaltern as female is even more deeply in shadow'.[93] For Spivak, subaltern women are 'doubly in shadow' or 'in the shadow of shadows',[94] and the possibility of learning to 'speak to the subaltern woman' lies in 'unlearning' the postcolonial intellectual's privilege by 'measuring silences, if necessary into the object of investigation'.[95] I take this to mean we must unlearn the privilege *to know*.

Conclusions

Writing about the silence of enslaved women in the Americas, Saidiya Hartman observes that: 'the loss of stories sharpens the hunger for them. So, it is tempting to fill in the gaps and provide closure where there is none'.[96] Hartman resists this temptation in her work and argues for a refusal to fill in gaps and an imperative to 'respect black noise' as that which was not sayable.[97] Following Hartman and other feminist historians and theorists who have drawn attention to *how* stories are told I have aimed to keep Loate's story contained within the fragments that hold her.[98] Working with fragments and keeping them as such – noticing their sharp jagged edges and holding the incomplete pieces alongside one another – helps us to see moments of voicing and silencing and what makes them possible, necessary or likely.

The silences and silencing of Masabata Loate occur at every stage that Trouillot identifies. Her voice emerges only through the apartheid legal system and its regimes of torture; her face is captured by the beauty-seeking camera; her death is subsumed under wider patterns of violence within mid-1980s Soweto. Within the archives, in her trial alongside Khotso Seatlholo, the records misspell name her as 'Masabate Loatse'. In the transcripts of the TRC's public hearings she is 'Masabata Luate'. *The Financial Mail* when reporting her death described her as 'one of the best known activists during the Soweto 1976 upheavals' – yet her name is rarely to be found within wave upon wave of scholarship on 16 June and its aftermaths.[99] She is mentioned in Helena Pohlandt-McCormick's, *I Saw A Nightmare*, only because of the large number of documents archived as having been found in her possession when she was arrested in 1977.[100] In this last instance it is the record itself that almost obscures her. Chapter 2 begins with this – the archive which bears Loate's name – and asks what it can tell us, if anything, about her. After this, Chapter 3 explores Loate's seemingly different appearances as beauty queen and terrorism suspect. Chapter 4 examines the multiple stories of her death. These fragments are kept as such, glimpses of a life and a person, a shadow moving through the archive. Throughout the book I do not attempt to recover whole voices but rather work with fragmented speech and silence to reveal both what we know and how we know it.

Notes

1. Ciraj Rassool has pioneered this approach in a South African context with his focus on processes of biographical production, or the creation of 'storied lives'. See: Ciraj Rassool, 'The Individual, Auto/Biography and History in South Africa' (University of the Western Cape, 2004), 9.

2. Wendy Woodward, Patricia Hayes and Gary Minkley, eds., *Deep Histories: Gender and Colonialism in Southern Africa* (Amsterdam: Rodopi, 2002), xxiv.

3. Sean Field, 'Turning up the Volume: Dialogues about Memory Create Oral Histories', *South African Historical Journal* 60, no. 2 (1 June 2008): 187, https://doi.org/10.1080/02582470802416393.

4. Bernard Magubane, *The Making of a Racist State: British Imperialism and the Union of South Africa, 1875–1910* (Trenton, NJ: Africa World Press, 1996); André Odendaal, *The Founders: The Origins of the ANC and the Struggle for Democracy in South Africa* (Johannesburg: Jacana Media, 2012); Peter Limb, *The ANC's Early Years: Nation, Class and Place in South Africa before 1940* (Pretoria: University of South Africa, 2010), https://doi.org/10.25159/882-5; Thula Simpson, *History of South Africa: 1902 to the Present* (London: C. Hurst & Co Publishers Ltd, 2022).

5. For one argument about the importance of land for early ANC leaders see: Philip Bonner, 'Fragmentation and Cohesion in the ANC: The First 70 Years', in *One Hundred Years of the ANC: Debating Liberation Histories Today*, ed. Arianna Lissoni et al. (Johannesburg: Wits University Press, 2012), 1–12.

6. For histories of the place of communism and socialism within the liberation struggle see: Tom Lodge, *Red Road to Freedom: A History of the South African Communist Party 1921–2021* (Woodbridge, Suffolk; Rochester, NY: James Currey, 2022); Allison Drew, *Discordant Comrades: Identities and Loyalties on the South African Left* (London: Routledge, 2019).

7. For a concise overview of the apartheid state see: Saul Dubow, *Apartheid, 1948–1994* (Oxford: Oxford University Press, 2014).

8. Daniel R. Magaziner, *The Law and the Prophets: Black Consciousness in South Africa, 1968–1977* (Athens, OH: Ohio University Press, 2010), 12.

9. Natasha Erlank, 'Christianity and African Nationalism in South Africa in the First Half of the Twentieth Century', in *One Hundred Years of the ANC: Debating Liberation Histories Today*, ed. Arianna Lissoni et al. (Johannesburg: Wits University Press, 2012), 83.

10. Erlank, 'Christianity and African Nationalism in South Africa', 84–5.

11. This shorthand is widespread – for a recent example see the chapter title 'The Silent Sixties' in Simpson, *History of South Africa*.

12. Julian Brown, *The Road to Soweto: Resistance and the Uprising of 16 June 1976* (Woodbridge, Suffolk: James Currey, 2016); Steven Friedman, 'The Sounds of Silence: Structural Change and Collective Action in the Fight against Apartheid', *South African Historical Journal* 69, no. 2 (3 April 2017): 236–50, https://doi.org/10.1080/02582473.2017.1293719.

13. As Gillian Slovo, daughter of Ruth First and Joe Slovo recalls. In the aftermath of Sharpeville, her father was detained under the Emergency and her mother went into hiding. Slovo remembered, 'Secrecy which had been part of our lives for as long as we could remember, now ran riot'. Gillian Slovo, *Every Secret Thing / Gillian Slovo* (London: Little, Brown, 1997), 53.

14. Helena Pohlandt-McCormick, *'I Saw a Nightmare' . . . : Doing Violence to Memory: The Soweto Uprising, June 16, 1976* (New York: Columbia University Press, 2008), chapter 1, 30, http://www.gutenberg-e.org/pohlandt-mccormick/.

15. The Internal Security Amendment Act 79 of 1976, accessed May 2024, https://www.gov.za/documents/internal-security-amendment-act-16-jun-1976-0000.

16. For more on the changes to the legal landscape after 1976 see: Michael Lobban, *White Man's Justice: South African Political Trials in the Black Consciousness Era* (Oxford: Clarendon Press, 1996), 144–51.

17. See 'The Detention Weapon' in Max Coleman, *A Crime Against Humanity* (Cape Town: David Philip, 1998).

18. See 'Internal Security Act' (July 1990), reprinted in Coleman, *A Crime Against Humanity*.

19. Coleman, *A Crime Against Humanity*.

20. Pohlandt-McCormick, *'I Saw a Nightmare': Doing Violence to Memory*, chapter 6, 5.

21. Veena Das, *Life and Words: Violence and the Descent into the Ordinary* (Berkeley: University of California Press, 2006), 8.

22. Elaine Scarry, *The Body in Pain: The Making and Unmaking of the World* (New York: Oxford University Press, 1985), 35.

23. Jeremy Seekings, 'Whose Voices? Politics and Methodology in the Study of Political Organisation and Protest in the Final Phase of the "Struggle" in South Africa', *South African Historical Journal* 62, no. 1 (2010): 7–28, http://dx.doi.org/10.1080/02582471003778300.

24. Luise White, Stephan Miescher and David William Cohen, *African Words, African Voices: Critical Practices in Oral History*, African Systems of Thought (Bloomington: Indiana University Press, 2001).

25. This is a critique put forward in Field, 'Turning up the Volume'.

26. For some examples, drawn from each of these overlapping and loosely defined fields see: Jenny Robinson, '(Dis)Locating Historical Narrative: Writing, Space and Gender in South African Social History', *South African Historical Journal* 30 (May 1994): 144–57, https://doi.org/10.1080/02582479408671788; Luisa Passerini, *Fascism in Popular Memory: The Cultural Experience of the Turin Working Class*,

Studies in Modern Capitalism (Cambridge: Cambridge University Press, 2010); Woodward, Hayes and Minkley, *Deep Histories: Gender and Colonialism in Southern Africa*.

27. Pohlandt-McCormick, *'I Saw a Nightmare': Doing Violence to Memory*, chapter 1, 40.

28. Arianna Lissoni et al., eds., *One Hundred Years of the ANC: Debating Liberation Histories Today* (Johannesburg: Wits University Press, 2012), 35.

29. Field, 'Turning up the Volume', 176.

30. Helena Pohlandt-McCormick has argued for something similar when it comes to the statements of student activists before the government inquiry into the Soweto Uprisings, the Cillie Commission. She suggests, 'they cannot be discounted, because to discount them would be to discount the struggle of participants to assert, in the face of severe and threatening repercussions, and even in the smallest of ways, their own voices'. Pohlandt-McCormick, *'I Saw a Nightmare': Doing Violence to Memory.*

31. The world of student politics which Rebecca Musi was part of at the University of the North and its importance for the development of national student movements is explored in Anne Heffernan, *Limpopo's Legacy: Student Politics and Democracy in South Africa* (Woodbridge, Suffolk: Boydell & Brewer, 2019), https://doi.org/10.2307/j.ctvc16j21.

32. Rebecca Musi, interview with author, Johannesburg, September 2008.

33. Liz Gunner makes this point – even if the 'official' language of the ANC was English, that organisation's history was 'acted out, experienced and recorded through a variety of languages': Liz Gunner, 'The Politics of Language and Chief Albert Luthuli's Funeral, 30 July 1967', in *One Hundred Years of the ANC: Debating Liberation Histories Today*, ed. Arianna Lissoni et al. (Johannesburg: Wits University Press, 2012), 192, https://www.cambridge.org/core/books/one-hundred-years-of-the-anc/politics-of-language-and-chief-albert-luthulis-funeral-30-july-1967/E613C1E81B5CD1EFE8F8052C8EA2AC04.

34. Awol Allo, *The Courtroom as a Space of Resistance: Reflections on the Legacy of the Rivonia Trial* (London: Routledge, 2016), https://doi.org/10.4324/9781315615073.

35. Emily Bridger, *Young Women against Apartheid: Gender, Youth and South Africa's Liberation Struggle* (Woodbridge, Suffolk; Rochester, NY: James Currey, 2021), 45.

36. Murphy Morobe, Truth and Reconciliation Commission, Human Rights Violations Committee Public Hearings, Soweto – June 16 Hearings, Day 1, 22 July 1996, accessed February 2024, http://www.doj.gov.trc.hrvtrans/soweto/morobe.htm.

37. For a discussion of the significance of these links see: Simpson, *History of South Africa*, 239.

38. As quoted in Alessandro Portelli, 'Oral Testimony, the Law and the Making of History: The "April 7" Murder Trial', *History Workshop*, no. 20 (1985): 5–35, https://www.jstor.org/stable/4288647.

39. Passerini, *Fascism in Popular Memory*, 9.

40. Judith Butler, *Excitable Speech: A Politics of the Performative* (New York: Routledge, 1997), 133.

41. As Butler puts it: 'one speaks according to a tacit set of norms that are not always explicitly coded as rules'. Butler, *Excitable Speech*, 134.

42. Das, *Life and Words*, 8.

43. Mashinini discusses this process in the preface to her autobiography. I discuss this book and its origin story more fully in Chapter 4. Emma Mashinini, *Strikes Have*

Followed Me All My Life: A South African Autobiography (London: Women's Press, 1989).

44. Mashinini, *Strikes Have Followed Me All My Life*, xvi.

45. Belinda Bozzoli, *Theatres of Struggle and the End of Apartheid* (Edinburgh: Edinburgh University Press, 2004). Franziska Rueedi, 'Narratives on Trial: Ideology, Violence and the Struggle over Political Legitimacy in the Case of the Delmas Treason Trial, 1985–1989', *South African Historical Journal* 67, no. 3 (3 July 2015): 335–55, https://doi.org/10.1080/02582473.2015.1092573.

46. Paul Gready, *Writing as Resistance: Life Stories of Imprisonment, Exile, and Homecoming from Apartheid South Africa* (Lanham, MD: Lexington Books, 2003), 10.

47. These are Louise Bethlehem's evocative descriptions of the speech of a 'boy prisoner' character, Jerry, in Mary Benson's novel, that used verbatim excerpts from political trials. Louise Bethlehem, 'Stenographic Fictions: Mary Benson's At the Still Point and the South African Political Trial', *Safundi* 20, no. 2 (3 April 2019): 198–9, https://doi.org/10.1080/17533171.2019.1576963.

48. Referring to the trial of Nelson Mandela for incitement in 1962, for which he was sentenced to five years, as the Incitement Trial, is a shorthand suggested by Catherine Cole, 'Justice in Transition: South African Political Trials, 1956–1964', in *The Courtroom As a Space of Resistance: Reflections on the Legacy of the Rivonia Trial*, ed. Awol Allo, Emilios Christodoulidis and Sharon Cowan (London: Taylor & Francis Group, 2015), 81–122.

49. See for example the Post-Rivonia trials of activists in the Eastern Cape attended by Mary Benson as a journalist for the British newspaper the *Observer*. Benson describes the 'terrible pall of anonymity' which fell over these trials, held in camera and often without counsel or press in attendance. As discussed in: Bethlehem, 'Stenographic Fictions'.

50. Seekings, *The UDF: A History of the United Democratic Front in South Africa, 1983–1991* (Oxford: James Currey, 2000), 38.

51. 'History of the DPSC', (1987), WHP, AG2523, Box A1.

52. 'History of the DPSC', (1987), WHP, AG2523, Box A1.

53. Max and Audrey Coleman, interview by Craig Matthews, John Vorster Square Police Station, Johannesburg, April 10, 2007. *Between Life and Death: Stories from John Vorster Square* (Doxa Productions, 2007), DVD

54. 'Detainee Support Committees', WHP, AG2523, Box A1.

55. Interview with Max and Audrey Coleman in *Between Life and Death.*

56. For example, Seekings suggests a very strained relationship between COSAS and the UDF. Seekings, *The UDF*, 134.

57. Interview with Max and Audrey Coleman in *Between Life and Death.*

58. Gerald Lewis Williamson, Kliptown/Klipspruit Daybook, 1985–86, WHP, AG2523, Box G21.4.1.1.

59. The DPSC did not have a policy on this except that statement-takers should be consistent. In a March 1987 document it was suggested that 'when taking down the statement we should try to be consistent. Either we should use "I" all the time, or "He/She". That way it will not be confusing to read'. 'Detainee Interview Checklist of Statement Taking', (March 1987), WHP, AG2523, Box M1.12.1.6.

60. This evocative phrase is Rachel Sandwell's, see: Rachel Sandwell, 'Fantasy States: Nationalism, Intimacy, and Transgression in South African Women's Political Memoirs', *Signs: Journal of Women in Culture and Society* 47, no. 3 (March 2022): 765–87, https://doi.org/10.1086/717734.

61. William M. Reddy, *The Navigation of Feeling: A Framework for the History of Emotions* (Cambridge: University Press, 2001), 96–104, https://doi.org/10.1017/CBO9780511512001.

62. Reddy, *The Navigation of Feeling*, 64.

63. Reddy, *The Navigation of Feeling*, 104.

64. Reddy, *The Navigation of Feeling*, 113.

65. Reddy, *The Navigation of Feeling*, 124; The phrase 'the personal is political' was coined by Carol Hanisch in a 1970 essay, reprinted in Carol Hanisch, 'The Personal Is Political', in *Radical Feminism: A Documentary Reader*, ed. Barbara A. Crow (New York: New York University Press, 2000), 113–16.

66. Shireen Hassim has also explored what she terms 'the sphere of the intimate-political' in her work on Winnie Madikizela-Mandela and her marriage to Nelson Mandela. In this work she also cautions us not to 'reduce the personal to the political'. See: Shireen Hassim, 'Not Just Nelson's Wife: Winnie Madikizela-Mandela, Violence and Radicalism in South Africa', *Journal of Southern African Studies* 44, no. 5 (3 September 2018): 901, https://doi.org/10.1080/03057070.2018.1514566; Shireen Hassim, 'The Impossible Contract: The Political and Private Marriage of Nelson and Winnie Mandela', *Journal of Southern African Studies* 45, no. 6 (2 November 2019): 1152, https://doi.org/10.1080/03057070.2019.1697137.

67. Jon Soske, 'Open Secrets, Off the Record: Audience, Intimate Knowledge, and the Crisis of the Post-Apartheid State', *Historical Reflections / Réflexions Historiques* 38, no. 2 (2012): 58, http://www.jstor.org/stable/23267796.

68. Soske, 'Open Secrets, Off the Record'.

69. As Gerald Sider and Gavin Smith have put it, in urging historians to consider the positionality of their potential subjects, 'the silenced, may be particularly silent precisely to us': Gerald Sider and Gavin Smith, 'Introduction', in *Between History and Histories: The Making of Silences and Commemorations*, ed. Gerald Sider and Gavin Smith (Toronto: University of Toronto Press, 1997), 14.

70. Jacob Dlamini, *Askari: A Story of Collaboration and Betrayal in the Anti-Apartheid Struggle* (Johannesburg: Jacana Media, 2014), 255.

71. Dlamini, *Askari*, 256.

72. Dlamini, *Askari*, 257.

73. Nthabiseng Motsemme, 'The Mute Always Speak: On Women's Silences at the Truth and Reconciliation Commission', *Current Sociology* 52, no. 5 (2004): 910, https://doi.org/10.1177/0011392104045377.

74. Obioma Nnaemeka, 'Imag(in)Ing Knowledge, Power and Subversion in the Margins', in *The Politics of (M)Othering: Womanhood, Identity and Resistance in African Literature*, ed. Obioma Nnaemeka (London: Routledge, 2005), 4.

75. Nnaemeka, 'Imag(in)Ing Knowledge, Power and Subversion in the Margins', 4.

76. Motsemme, 'The Mute Always Speak'.

77. Reddy, *The Navigation of Feeling*.

78. Alessandro Portelli, *The Voice and the Text – Writing, Speaking and Democracy in American Literature: Writing, Speaking, Democracy, and American Literature* (New York: Columbia University Press, 1994), 53.

79. Alessandro Portelli, *The Death of Luigi Trastulli, and Other Stories: Form and Meaning in Oral History* (Albany, NY: State University of New York Press, 1991), 50.

80. Gumba Gumba was a slang term used in township English that referred to hi-fis used to play music loudly, particularly at drinking sessions.

81. Robert Royston, ed., *Black Poets in South Africa*, African Writers Series (London: Heinemann, 1974), 24.

82. Jeremy Cronin, '"The Law That Says/Constricts the Breath-Line (. . .)" South African English Language Poetry Written by Africans in the 1970s', *English Academy Review* 3, no. 1 (January 1985): 27, https://doi.org/10.1080/10131758585310031.

83. Daniel R. Magaziner, 'Pieces of a (Wo)Man: Feminism, Gender and Adulthood in Black Consciousness, 1968–1977', *Journal of Southern African Studies* 37, no. 1 (1 March 2011): 53.

84. Don Mattera, 'Six Poems', *Index on Censorship* 3, no. 4 (1974): 24, https://doi.org/10.1080/03064227408532368.

85. Mattera, 'Six Poems', 24.

86. Magaziner, 'Pieces of a (Wo)Man'; Magaziner, *The Law and the Prophets*; Leslie Anne Hadfield, 'Challenging the Status Quo: Young Women and Men in Black Consciousness Community Work, 1970s South Africa', *Journal of African History* 54 (2013): 247–67, https://doi.org/doi:10.1017/S0021853713000261; Leslie Anne Hadfield, *Liberation and Development: Black Consciousness Community Programs in South Africa* (East Lansing, MI: Michigan State University Press, 2016); Ian M. Macqueen, *Black Consciousness and Progressive Movements under Apartheid* (Scottsville, South Africa: University of KwaZulu-Natal Press, 2018), 138–64.

87. Magaziner, 'Pieces of a (Wo)Man', 48.

88. Magaziner, 'Pieces of a (Wo)Man', 49.

89. The coverage was in *Drum* and *The World*, as cited in Magaziner, 'Pieces of a (Wo)Man', 56.

90. Michel-Rolph Trouillot, *Silencing the Past: Power and the Production of History, 20th Anniversary Edition*, 2nd Revised edition (Boston, MA: Beacon Press, 2015), 26.

91. Trouillot, *Silencing the Past*, 27.

92. Ann Laura Stoler, *Along the Archival Grain Epistemic Anxieties and Colonial Common Sense* (Princeton, NJ: Princeton University Press, 2009).

93. Gayatri Chakravorty Spivak, 'Can the Subaltern Speak?', in *Marxism and the Interpretation of Culture*, ed. Lawrence Grossberg and Carry Nelson (Urbana, IL: University of Illinois Press; Basingstoke: Macmillan, 1988), 288.

94. Spivak, 'Can the Subaltern Speak?', 289; Gayatri Chakravorty Spivak, 'The Rani of Sirmur: An Essay in Reading the Archives', *History and Theory* 24, no. 3 (1985): 265, https://doi.org/10.2307/2505169.

95. Spivak, 'Can the Subaltern Speak?'

96. Saidiya Hartman, 'Venus in Two Acts', *Small Axe* 12, no. 2 (2008): 8, https://doi.org/10.1215/-12-2-1.

97. Refusal and respect are both central to what Hartman calls a method of 'critical fabulation' for 'telling impossible stories' about enslaved women 'to amplify the impossibility of [their] telling'. Critical fabulation disrupts chronological 'tellings' of events and introduces multiple perspectives as a way of making visible the production of historical silences. Hartman, 'Venus in Two Acts', 12.

98. See for example: Clare Hemmings, *Why Stories Matter: The Political Grammar of Feminist Theory* (Durham, NC: Duke University Press, 2011).

99. *Financial Mail*, 24 October 1986, 57.

100. Pohlandt-McCormick, *'I Saw a Nightmare': Doing Violence to Memory.*

Chapter 2

The Soweto Eleven and the sayable: speaking about the struggle

Introduction

On 17 June 1977 Masabata Loate was arrested outside John Vorster Square police station in Johannesburg.[1] She was taken to the ninth floor and searched. She had in her pocket a press statement that she was supposed to give to *The World* newspaper. Earlier that day she had been discussing its contents with student detainees already being held at the station. After her arrest, she was taken by Detective Warrant Officer Trollip to two addresses in Orlando West, Soweto – 7798 and 7804. A stash of papers and books were taken from 7798.[2] These remain in the archives of the South African State. As a part of the State's response to the Soweto Uprisings, eleven young South Africans were tried for sedition, between 25 September 1978 and 30 April 1979. Ten of the eleven were young men. One was a young woman. Shadowing those on trial, another eleven young people testified as state witnesses for the prosecution's case. Of these witnesses, six were young women, and five were young men. Masabata Loate was one of them. She would live with the fall-out from her appearance at the trial for the rest of her short life.

In 1978 she told the court about the two houses she had been taken to after her arrest: 'I live in both houses, and sleep at different days in both houses'.[3] In amongst the papers the police seized from 7798 was a handwritten document titled 'My Thoughts'. This is what it said:

> We have been living through an unforgettable period. Here is history in the making, with all its terrific drama and all its tragic interest. For

> our age is transitional. Its very uniqueness prepares the way for a unique renaissance. We must learn to meet bad times with better thoughts. We must struggle for a new era characterised by heartfelt universality. It is for us to spell the riddle of the future with letters drawn from the alphabet of the present. It is for us to evaluate the movements disclosed by history and follow its own logic. It is for us to draw wise lessons out of the vanished centuries for our own ethical guidance and material profit.
>
> When intelligence is only partial, immature and incomplete, it leaves man cunning, selfishness and materialism [*sic*]. When full, mature and perfect, it teaches him wisdom, selflessness and truth.
> Struggle there must be, for all life is a struggle of some kind.
>
> For what man will not learn by reason he must learn by pain. He who will not think, must suffer.
>
> Hatred is a sharp boomerang which not only hurts the hated but also the hater, they will hesitate twice and thrice before yielding to this worst of all sins.[4]

No author is attributed. Most of the other papers do have authors given to them in the labels of the police, or historians have matched the handwriting of other unattributed documents with those that do have names.[5] This document was not referred to during the trial of the Soweto Eleven. 'My Thoughts' were archived as part of another court case that took place in the aftermath of 1976. In the civil courts the West Rand Administration Board (WRAB) that administered Soweto brought a case against Santam, the insurance company that covered WRAB against riot damage. In amongst the evidence submitted during this process were many papers produced by students, particularly South African Students' Movement (SASM) documents seized during a raid on their headquarters in October 1977 and those confiscated from Masabata Loate at 7798 Orlando West. Helena Pohlandt-McCormick, who first uncovered this archive, suggests we read 'My Thoughts' as a 'prose poem', reflective of the 'eloquence of an empowered thinking student consciousness'.[6] Here, it seems, is a thoughtful and poetic mind, a young person aware of themselves within history and thinking deeply about their experiences.

However, this sense of authorship and voice is disrupted by a simple online search for the text. The lines labelled 'My Thoughts' by a writer in 1970s Soweto are taken, mostly without editing, from a book first published in 1941, *The Hidden Teaching Beyond Yoga*, by Paul Brunton.[7] Paul Brunton was itself a pen name for Raphael Hurst, a British man who travelled to India in 1930 and thereafter embarked on a life as a travelling spiritual 'researcher' and teacher.[8] He wrote a number of books of spiritualism, drawing upon Hinduism and Buddhism. The question of who these thoughts belong to, is a complex one. Brunton was himself performing an act of translation, in bringing 'Eastern' philosophies and religious thought to a Western audience. 'Struggle there must be, for all life is a struggle of some kind', is a quote Brunton attributes to Buddha.[9] In his intellectual history of Black Consciousness, Dan Magaziner has noted that the activists of SASO, SASM's forerunner, 'did not exactly respect copyright'. Their writings often included 'an endless succession of purloined phrases'.[10] Yet, as Magaziner argues, 'activists copied, but they also translated; they read words from one context and wrote them into their own'.[11] There is no doubt these words, written by Brunton during the Second World War in India, with some minor edits and a process of careful selection, seem to speak as if directly out of Soweto in 1976. Two edits were made to the first long paragraph. Firstly the line, 'the ravages of the war will need to be repaired' was omitted, which clearly altered the context of the ideas.[12] Secondly, 'it is for us to evaluate the movements disclosed by history and follow its own logic' originally referred to history's 'iron logic'.[13] Too deterministic a sentiment perhaps? By writing down these lines, taken from different passages in the book, and compiling them into 'My Thoughts', a new voice is made. We can still hear this as 'an empowered student consciousness', albeit with a more nuanced grasp of the processes of making such a voice. Who exactly was involved in articulating this 'student consciousness' is unclear. Is it just as plausible that these thoughts were written down by a young woman, as it is that they were written by a young man? Did these ideas belong to Masabata Loate?

In 1978 Loate told the court that the papers had been given to her 'for safe keeping'.[14] So, even if she did not write these thoughts down, she possessed them in another sense. At the very least we can say that Loate (literally) held these thoughts on behalf of others. She shared the responsibility of holding them. The sense of being part of a collective 'we' is strong within 'My Thoughts'. The writer takes on responsibilities with the repeated phrases, 'we must' and 'it is for us'. In her evidence in 1978 Loate talked about a 'we' who was planning an event that the press release in her pocket pertained to. Asked who she meant by 'we' she clarified: the Soweto Students' Representative Council.[15] The SSRC was formed in August of 1976 and was made up of two representatives from each high school and secondary school in Soweto and comprised about a hundred individuals.[16] Its formation came two months after the initial march and the ensuing violence, and followed the reopening of Soweto's schools in July. It was an organisation forged out of the events of 16 June. It included activists who had been involved in earlier student political formations and the planning of the original march, but also drew in a wider group. Micheal Lobban has described the SSRC as 'an ambiguous organisation'.[17] It was perceived during the Uprisings as articulating genuine grievances, possessing moral authority and even seen as a 'moderating voice' that repeatedly espoused non-violence.[18] Yet, the State sought to brand it as led by dangerous agitators – a characterisation which was based on the intimidation used to enforce the stayaways the SSRC called for, as well as violence directed at members of the Urban Bantu Council, acts of sabotage and the destruction of government property carried out by members and some leaders.[19]

There were different levels of involvement and politicisation within the SSRC. For example, one former President of the organisation and one of the Soweto Eleven, Dan Montisisi, spoke years later of a 'Shadow Committee' within the SSRC that sought military training and had links with the ANC underground that were not known about by other students.[20] Whilst we do not know the depth of her involvement, Loate, it seems, saw herself as part of the SSRC, and students saw her as one of them. It was reported in the *Rand Daily Mail* that a few days after her arrest, over a thousand pupils at Orlando High School stayed away from classes 'in sympathy' with Loate and the two others arrested at the same time as her.[21] Yet the trial of the Soweto Eleven positioned, and heard her, as a liminal figure, on the edges of the events of 1976 and 1977 at best. Her testimony as a state witness meant that once the trial was over, that marginality was confirmed. Back on the streets of Soweto, she was no longer trusted.[22] This chapter looks closely at the framing of young women during the trial of the Soweto Eleven and the wider public discourses surrounding it, which fed into the making of the '1976 generation' as a collective voice within South African history. This was a trial that was focused on what had happened on 16 June and in the year and half afterwards; its battleground was the recent history of the Uprisings and how they should be explained and understood. The narratives that it produced were gendered in ways that shaped the speech and silence of young women.

On reading the transcript of the Soweto Eleven trial, it was not what Loate said, but what was said to her, that first caught my attention. The judge's parting comment on the weight she had lost during detention – 'She must watch her weight. I think she should not add another 20-lbs again' – is a moment that exemplifies how young women have so often been seen, but not heard within the unfolding of youth political activism in South Africa.[23] It was only later that I would return to Loate's testimony and pore over every word, looking for clues as to what lay beyond the simple and mostly unrevealing statements she made in court. There is nothing there to suggest that Loate could have been the compiler of 'My

Thoughts'. That document feels a little like the first draft of a speech – certainly there is strong rhetorical energy in the first paragraph with the repeated phrases and the sense of audience. There were several papers identified as 'notes for a speech' in the same file, listed as confiscated from Loate, as well as drafts for press releases, pamphlets and books, some of which were banned. The trial heard evidence that both young men and young women of the SSRC made speeches, at schools and during organised protests. Yet the unresolved question of who wrote 'My Thoughts' points us to the ongoing silences of many who participated in the 1976–7 Uprisings and the boundaries of what was sayable, and for whom, as events were unfolding and later as they were retold in court.[24] It is a reminder of the ways individual thoughts, drawn from many sources, became collective statements during this 'unforgettable period' of 'history in the making'. The tantalising possibility remains that if Loate did write 'My Thoughts', there is very little chance the historical record would credit her with them.

There are two inventories of the papers and books taken from Masabata Loate.[25] In one the following books are listed:

Religious Beliefs and White Prejudice, by Robert Buts
Notes of a Native Son by James Baldwin
Black Viewpoint by The Study Project on Christianity in Apartheid Society (SPRO-CAS)
Black Theology and Black Power by James H. Cone
Nobody Knows My Name by James Baldwin
Naught for Your Comfort by Father Trevor Huddleston (Two Copies)
Détente in Southern Africa by South African Institute of Race Relations
Some Implications of Inequality by SPRO-CAS
Uncle Tom's Cabin by Harriet Beecher Stowe
The Eastern Philosophers by E W F Tomlin
Assault on Private Enterprise: The Freeway to Communism by A. D. Wassenaar
Not Yet Uhuru: Autobiography by Odinga Oginga
Inside the KGB by Aleksei Myagkov[26]

The inventory points to the range of thought the young participants in the Soweto Uprisings drew upon. Kasonde T. Mukonde has recently made the case for the existence of a 'vibrant reading community amongst high school students in Soweto in the 1960s and 1970s'.[27] This is evident in the list above which includes African nationalist texts (Odinga Oginga) alongside African American thought (the two James Baldwin books); a good dose of liberation theology (James H. Cone) and theologically influenced critiques of apartheid (the volumes produced by SPRO-CAS); as well as texts introducing Marxist theory (Wassenaar) and Hinduism, Buddhism and Islam (Tomlin). The two copies of Huddleston's account of the destruction of Sophiatown (*Naught for Your Comfort*) point to the knowledge of historical episodes in the liberation struggle.[28] Texts like *Détente in Southern Africa*, which analysed the policies of then South African Prime Minster John Vorster towards Rhodesia and the surrounding region, alongside the insider account of working in the KGB by Aleksei Myagkov, reveal a potentially wide-ranging political sphere of interest.

The list contains many that Dan Magaziner has highlighted as influential in shaping Black Consciousness thought in its early years. For example, of the Sophiatown forced removals which *Naught for your Comfort* chronicles, Magaziner argues 'the failure to save Sophiatown . . . and the helplessness that defeat engendered' was the 'critical intellectual context' for what Black Consciousness sought to address.[29] Oginga Odinga was Steve Biko's African nationalist of choice, who by the time of the publication of *Not Yet Uhuru* had emerged as a critical voice within the project of the independent African postcolonial nation (specifically Kenya).[30] Magaziner considers the intellectual contribution of James H. Cone at length – highlighting in particular his ideas of Christ as a political actor.[31] However, as well as the content of these books, the sociality of reading underlines what having this list of books may have meant about Loate.

Mukonde argues that within the reading culture of Soweto High school students banned books circulated much less widely. Even so, many books which were not, in fact, banned, were perceived as such, and treated as illicit by students. Indeed, even books with no political content at all, like the thriller novels of James Hadley Chase, circulated and were read in subversive ways. Reading Chase became a marker of generational identity that challenged the conservatism of South African society and created a network of readers which might then later be used in the exchange of radical literature.[32] With these books in her possession, we can assume that Masabata Loate was one of these readers. In her 1982 testimony as a defendant on trial on charges of terrorism, she stated quite plainly: 'I did not deny that I am a person who is politically minded, I am in possession of banned literature'.[33] If Loate was a radical reader, who through their practices 'created a new social order', then surely there is every possibility she was a radical thinker too?[34]

The existence of the papers, titled intimately (albeit deceptively) 'My Thoughts' stand in stark contrast to the speech of Loate and her contemporaries during the trial. Loate spoke, but she and the other young witnesses did so under the severe and pressing constraints of ongoing detention. This was the kind of speech we can think of as 'talk' – deeply shaped by the coercive circumstances that produced it. Helena

Pohlandt-McCormick has urged us to consider those students who spoke during the trials that followed the Uprisings and in front of the government-instituted Cillié Commission of Inquiry as voices struggling to be heard.[35] Acts such as the refusal to confirm or to deviate from statements extracted through torture were ways of reclaiming voice, through silence.[36] Speaking about the struggle in this context was a deeply gendered act. Loate and the other young women witnesses who testified during the trial, as well as the only young woman defendant, Sibongile Mkhabela née Mthembu, were framed by the prosecution and defence alike in such a way that their speech was marginalised before it was uttered. Yet these processes of silencing required the presence and speech of those same young women and girls, pointing to a more complex picture of political participation than their words alone suggest.

Speaking about the struggle

As we noted in the introduction to this book, there are powerful and abiding narratives of youth political action in the liberation struggle. In academic, popular and official histories alike, it has been held that over time youth organisations became more aggressively masculine and that an increase in violence and confrontation marginalised young women from the activities of the 'comrades' or the 'youth', by the 1980s.[37] The explanations as to why this process took place are at times circular: violence causes masculinisation causes violence; and sometimes they rely problematically on normative constructions of masculinity in suggesting that apartheid emasculated black men and thus provoked hyper-masculine responses.[38] Such narratives suggest, as Leslie Hadfield has noted, that men alone possessed the agency or ability to alter gender relations: young women were simply, 'victims or unwitting contributors to the construction of masculinities'.[39] Hadfield argues that we need to rethink how we define political participation, in order to properly locate and understand young women's place within the Black Consciousness movement. Her argument applies across the various organisational currents of the liberation struggle. If political activity became more violent this is not quite the same thing as violence constituting politics.[40] We need to re-examine the ways in which connections between violence, political participation and masculinity were made and reinforced over time. This means looking closely at the production of gendered narratives of struggle. When and where did ideas about youth politics, violence and masculinity appear? This takes us towards an approach which focuses upon an analysis of 'struggle speech'.

'Struggle speech' is a way of trying to capture the inseparability of speaking about political activity from that activity itself, and the simultaneous distinctiveness of speech as a social act. To speak about taking part in a march or a demonstration is different from going along or organising one. Such speech is a part of participating but, depending on context, it is also a reflection on political practice and a way of (re)making its meaning. In the trial of the Soweto Eleven the meaning and nature of youth political actions on 16 June and its aftermath were discussed at great length. This trial came at a time when masculinisation was supposedly not so aggressive or dominant within school-based political groups. Clive Glaser and Peter Delius have described the student leadership of the 1970s as 'less physically aggressive and more respectful of women's sexual choices' than was the case subsequently in the 'fusion' of student and gang culture that pervaded the youth groups of the 1980s.[41] The work of constructing stories of youth that are traceable in the Soweto Eleven trial reveals the interest both the state prosecutors, and those defending young activists, had in producing narratives of masculine youth political action – gendered narratives which had very real repercussions for Masabata Loate. The presence and speech of young women in constructing these narratives of youth politics show us that they were not straightforward reflections of exclusively male activity. Speaking about the struggle had gendered dynamics of its own. In interpreting the speech and silence that are the focus of this chapter I borrow the idea of the 'sayable' from Judith Butler to try to draw into focus a broader sense of the context for speech about youth politics. As I outlined in the introduction, Butler asks us to consider 'what constitutes the domain of the sayable within which I speak at all?'[42] As well as thinking about young witnesses' fear and the consequences of their speech during the trial itself, this means asking what could be said by whom, how, and what was heard when it was uttered.

Youth on trial

According to the prosecution, the eleven accused were members of SASM and the 'Action Committee' which had organised the march of school children on 16 June 1976. This march, an expression of SASM's policy of rejecting the system of education in South Africa and, specifically, the use of Afrikaans as a medium of instruction, was deemed a 'seditious gathering',[43] an argument that was ultimately accepted by the judge. The State also alleged that the Action Committee had changed its name to the SSRC sometime in July or August, and the SSRC was responsible for a series of further gatherings which stretched from June 1976 to October of 1977 that were also seditious.[44] These included four stayaways in 1976; marches such as those that aimed to call for the release of detainees in August 1976 and June 1977, and the anti-Kissinger demonstrations of September 1976; the 'Black Christmas' campaign in December of 1976 that called for the closure of shebeens, the suspension of football games and other leisure activities, the boycott of white-owned shops, and the observance of a period of mourning; protests targeting the Urban Bantu Council (which eventually resulted in the mass resignation of the Councillors); and a series of events commemorating the first anniversary of 16 June. The charges brought by the State alleged that the eleven accused had committed sedition as well as conspiracy to sedition, incitement to sedition, and a secondary charge of 'participation in terroristic activities'.[45]

In his study of the political trials of the 1970s, Michael Lobban argues that the trial of the Soweto Eleven marked a change in the South African State's legal assault on Black Consciousness organisations. According to Lobban, the decision to regard the eleven as seditionists and not revolutionaries was an 'attempt to dilute the political mixture' that the trial represented both domestically and abroad.[46] Observers in the 1980s noted this move to the use of common law crimes such as sedition and treason as a response to criticisms of state security laws.[47] The Soweto Eleven trial was, as the *Rand Daily Mail* reported at the time, South Africa's first sedition trial in thirty years.[48] In a number of earlier political trials the State had failed to link the SSRC as an organisation to specific acts of violence or to a conspiracy with the ANC, as it had hoped to and, perhaps, believed was the case.[49] By 1978 the Cillié Commission of Inquiry into the 'riots' had been running for two years and the events of 16 June and its aftermath had been publicly discussed at length inside and outside South Africa. The trial of the Soweto Eleven began whilst the Cillié Commission was ongoing. It was enmeshed in both the State's attempts to rationalise and justify its response to 16 June and the ongoing efforts of parents, the liberation movements in exile, and other observers, to make sense of the events. Alongside the shock of the young age of participants and the perception that there were legitimate grievances behind student protests, the State was up against widespread scepticism, even within white South African society, that agitators might explain the size and scale of the unrest.[50] According to Lobban, 'the trial was an exercise in retrospective self-justification by the State'; one that sought to 'establish plainly the boundaries of illegitimate protest'.[51] The prosecution thus moved away from attempting to prove grand conspiracy theories of a unified liberation struggle directed from exile by the ANC and instead argued that by challenging Bantu Education the SSRC was actually assailing the authority of the State.

Since Bantu Education was administered by the Department of Bantu Education, a branch of the State, to attack the former was construed as an attack on the latter. As Lobban points out, the logic of this was to make almost any black protest against the government seditious but the prosecution selectively emphasised the 'ensuing violence' as the mark of seditious intent.[52] Playing upon public perceptions about legitimate grievances the prosecution argued that the Action Committee was 'irresponsible in calling the march' on 16 June, considering the background of anger and tension that existed in Soweto.[53] It was alleged that since the Action Committee knew the march would bring about conflict with the police they were aiming to assail the authority of the State. The result of this choice of arguments and battleground was that both prosecution and defence spent a lot of time debating the nature of youth political action and the position of the 16 June march and uprisings in wider understandings of liberation politics to that date. It was the prosecution which put forward what might be recognised now as the more orthodox nationalist version: that the students acted with political intent but were limited by their youth. The defence found itself in an awkward position, trying to play down the students' political ambitions and emphasising the social aspects of youth political action, evoking a more innocent and naive youthfulness. Both prosecution and defence had constructions of youth, often overlapping, which they wished to emphasise to condemn or absolve the eleven accused. These constructions were sometimes explicit and were drawn out of evidence given by witnesses but were also implicit in certain arguments and courtroom practices.

The accused were named in court as: Wilson Welile 'Chief' Twala aged 18 in 1978; Daniel Sechaba Sediane Montsisi aged 23; Seth Sandile Mazibuko aged 19; Murphy Mafison Morobe aged 22; Jeferson Khotso Wansi Lenganu aged 21; Susan Sibongile Mthembu aged 22; Ernest Edwin Thabo Ndabena aged 21; Kennedy Kgotsietsile Mogama aged 19; Reginald Tejobo Mngomezulu aged 21; Michael Sello Khiba aged 20; and George Nkosinati Yami Twala aged 23. Throughout the proceedings defence advocate Ernest Wentzel tried to emphasise the young age of his clients, drawing upon a discourse of youth as innocent and vulnerable in the face of determined efforts by the prosecution to suggest the opposite. In South Africa at this time the age of criminal responsibility was seven.[54] In the case of defendants aged between seven and fourteen, the onus was on the prosecution to prove that the accused were aware that whatever act they committed, contravened the law. Defendants older than fourteen were treated as adults. At the outset of the trial in 1978 the prosecution asked that the witnesses they regarded as accomplices, the second Soweto eleven, be allowed to give evidence *in camera*. Defence advocate Wentzel reacted with indignation at the suggestion that those witnesses were potentially in danger from his clients: 'M'Lord, I am representing school boys and school girls. This is not the African National Congress, or some body which is in hostile antagonism with the Republic of South Africa. These are school children'.[55] However, the court accepted the prosecution's arguments. In other instances too, Wentzel's emphasis on the innocent youth of his clients did not prove all that successful within the courtroom. Once, the judge himself intervened to disagree with Wentzel's use of 'child' when describing a defendant. Wentzel was cross-examining Walter McPherson of the South African Police, who was in charge of detainees at John Vorster Square, and was asking him how long Sibongile Mthembu had been in solitary confinement for:

> **Adv. W:** What about this child here, accused No.6, how long was she there in those conditions?
>
> **BY THE COURT:** I don't know whether accused No.6 can still be described as a child, she is well over twenty.[56]

Justice Cillié sounded a similar complaint in his report, published in 1980: 'witnesses referred in a misleading manner to young people as children . . . with the object of arousing sympathy for them, because they were supposed to be children and not blameworthy'.[57] The meaning of the age of the accused was thus highly contested. Indeed, this was in part because, during the 1970s in South Africa, 'childhood, youth and adulthood' became blurred in the context of social changes that were particularly acute in urban areas.[58] Schooling was not compulsory for Africans and many school-going children had to work alongside their studies. In addition, as Ndlovu has argued, through their actions and their shouldering of political responsibility, of which the writer of 'My Thoughts' was so aware, the young participants of 16 June and the SSRC 'brought forth' a 'new age category of their own making, between adolescence and maturity'.[59]

The sayable

The trial was lengthy. The Soweto Eleven first appeared in court for a remand hearing in July 1978 after having already been held in custody for up to a year. The trial then began in September of 1978 with the prosecution's case heard for three months. The defence case began again in February of 1979 and the Eleven were sentenced in May. The three-month gap between prosecution and defence cases in particular prompted media reflections on the nature of the trial experience and its effects on the young accused. This manifested itself in the sympathetic English-language press as a focus upon their appearance. In February 1979 when the accused reappeared to the public, Zwelakhe Sisulu reported for the *Rand Daily Mail* that: 'nine of the 10 young men either had or seemed to be in the process of cultivating Afro hairstyles. The sole exception was accused number four Mr Mafison Morobe. He had the Yul Brynner look'.[60] The young accused's Afro hairstyles were thus read as a way of signalling a radical Black Consciousness politics.

Also in February 1979, another portrait of the accused was published in *Sash* magazine circulated to the members and supporters of the Black Sash – a women's anti-apartheid campaign group. The author Janet Sahil sought to reassure the Black Sash membership of predominantly white middle-class women about the potential association between youth and violence, or at the very least unruly behaviour, in the case of the Soweto Eleven. This resulted in an emphasis on the absence of 'Afro clothes' as opposed to the *Rand Daily Mail*'s focus on the presence of 'Afro hairstyles':

> Just before 10.00 the 11, whose ages range from 19 to 23, came into the dock. They looked fit, slim, shiningly clean, almost unreally like the sort of advertisement in 'Post' which projects a sophisticated, affluent image of black youth. Some wore tracksuits with stripes of white, enhancing the basic maroon or navy. Bongie [Sibongile], the only girl, wore a mohair jersey over a pleated skirt, made even more elegant by an ivory pendant. Some of them had wanted to wear Afro clothes, but their parents had forbidden it. Such is the cohesion of their family life that they had simply obeyed.
>
> They exuded, collectively and individually, a feeling of youth, but a curiously mature, highly disciplined youth . . . The combination of high intelligence, drive, sensitivity and toughness impressed itself on me again and again as I watched their successive changes of expression during the proceedings: scepticism, potential dislike, humour and impassivity.[61]

Janet Sahil presented the Soweto Eleven as full of youthful promise. Their very appearance was a contradiction to their position as defendants in a criminal trial. The reference to the accused as appearing like an 'advertisement in the Post' together with the movie star reference to Yul Brynner in the *Rand Daily Mail* suggests a certain glamour was attached to the Soweto Eleven. The presence of a young woman amongst the accused was often mentioned by the press. For Sahil, Sibongile Makhabela's presence was a marker of the respectability of the group, as was their obedience to their parents' wishes. Sahil had been invited to attend the trial by Jill

Wentzel, the wife of Ernest Wentzel, the Eleven's defence advocate. Sahil's account was part of a broader defence of the young accused and the battle over the meaning of youth political action. All of this tied in with the defence portrayal of the Soweto Eleven as teenagers.

The accused did not testify during the trial. Lobban suggests this was the result of an awareness of the strength of the case against them.[62] Their comparative silence is something that Sahil also mentions: 'they are understandably cagey about their personal philosophies, which probably vary enormously. For instance, the Special Branch have confiscated from Bongie Bibles, prayer books and religious tracts' – a suggestion for the *Sash* readers that this young woman was perhaps not even that 'political' after all.[63] Instead the testimony and cross-examination of another Soweto eleven – the young state witnesses brought from detention to testify on the activities of their peers – were those who spoke as participants during the trial.[64] In contrast to the Cillié Commission of Inquiry into the same events which heard the evidence of only two young women from a list of 563 witnesses, the testimony of young women was central to the depiction of youth politics in the courtroom. The Cillié Commission had in fact displayed a profound scepticism about the value of young witnesses for understanding 16 June and its aftermath. Cillié himself commented on what he saw as the dubious authenticity of young witnesses as part of his understanding of the importance of 'agitators' in provoking and spreading the uprising. For example:

> In one outstanding case, a coloured girl gave very able testimony on grievances before the commission in Cape Town. It subsequently transpired that she had not been expressing her own or local views, but was reciting the contents of a pamphlet that had been drawn up in Soweto and distributed from there. She had learned this pamphlet off by heart. It was later handed in to the commission.[65]

In contrast, at the trial of the Soweto Eleven, young people were treated as windows onto a world.

The young witnesses who appeared had arrived to testify directly from detention, where they had also been held for up to a year. Large numbers of young people were arrested in the aftermath of the first anniversary of 16 June and the commemorative events that were organised.[66] Testifying as accomplices they were at risk of being re-detained after their testimony if they did not satisfy the court that they had given 'full and frank answers'. The trial proceedings record that of those who appeared in the courtroom, even the often-unsympathetic judge, noticed their fear. The following exchanges come from the testimony of Anastasia Zulu, led by Prosecution Advocate Von Lieres:

Adv. V. Lieres: Just a bit slower please, just a bit slower.

By the Court: I know she is a bit nervous, but she must speak slowly and distinctly. She needn't be afraid.

Adv. V. Lieres: (cont.) Even Seth is laughing at you.[67]

This exchange also reveals a little of the social pressures for young people who were testifying in front of their friends. Seth, whom Advocate Von Lieres refers to, was Seth Mazibuko, one of the defendants.

In the trial, the 'domain of the sayable' was shaped by the wider frameworks of interpreting 16 June put forward by prosecution and defence, as well as the very material circumstances of detention that surrounded the young people testifying. During proceedings young women's presence and speech was used as a way of reiterating youth political and/or social space as normatively male. How far this reflected the realities of political or social organising is not straight forward. First, the historian must understand what was 'sayable' for these young women.

A popular house

The evidence of a number of the young witnesses revolved around a particular house, which belonged to the Ngubeni family and its four daughters, two of whom testified in the trial. The nature of student meetings within this house became a point of debate. The representation of this particular domestic space within courtroom testimony also structured the narratives of the young women witnesses and their male counterparts. The Ngubeni house appeared within the courtroom testimony as having been presided over by the mother of the family Maria Ngubeni, with four sisters, two brothers and a cousin living there.[68] One of the sisters, Elizabeth Ngubeni, described how her cousin, Herbert Mabuza, had asked first if two girls named as Baby and Joyce could stay at the house, and had then invited a number of the accused to also stay there.[69] Jon Soske has drawn attention to the place of households within township anti-apartheid political activity. He argues that 'because of the segregated character of black areas and the clandestine nature of organising, anti-apartheid activism often relied on linkages among a series of overlapping, closely knit personal and political networks around prominent township households'.[70] He goes on: 'family networks and households provided meeting spaces, places of refuge, and nodes of transit – for information, material, ideas and individuals'.[71] All of this is borne out in the descriptions of the Ngubeni household that emerged out of the trial testimony.

Elizabeth Ngubeni was asked by the prosecution to describe the meetings that happened in the house: 'What did they used to do when they came to your house? – If I was at home I would give them supper. Yes? – They would close the door and hold a meeting then'.[72] Later the prosecution asked again, 'Could your sisters, or your brothers, or your mother attend these meetings? – No, except Herbert'.[73] Through the Prosecution's questioning, the young female witnesses were thus placed outside the main SSRC grouping. From the outside, looking in, the meetings seemed exclusive and serious. There was, it should be noted, an advantage for these young women witnesses in denying their involvement. Not just as individuals seeking to escape jail but as Helena Pohlandt-McCormick has argued, young women and girls could use their 'invisibility to the eyes of the exclusively male police force to perform some of the movement's most important tasks, such as facilitating communication networks between male activists in hiding'.[74] The 'natural' or normative expectations of gender was something the defence drew upon. Defence advocate Wentzel asked the second of the Ngubeni sisters, Cecelia, about the frequent visits of some of the accused to her house:

> I have also heard the evidence in this court of your sister who has testified already and one [*sic*] listens to the two of you it would seem that there was a lot of coming and going into your house, is that right? – Yes.
>
> We can judge from all the evidence there was your family with the various daughters and you must have had lots of friends? – Yes.
>
> And we have your cousin Herbert Mabuza? – Yes.
>
> I believe that your sister is a very good cook? – Yes.
>
> That in itself makes the house a popular one, doesn't it? –Yes.[75]

In this way Wentzel suggested that these meetings were social gatherings. His implication was that the young women's confinement to the kitchen of their home was unremarkable – a normal arrangement and the result of Elizabeth Ngubeni's special talent. However, it was later during the cross-examination of another accomplice, Nelson Thamondqa Ndwendwa, that Wentzel really emphasised the masculinity of the SSRC as the result of its character as a social grouping. During his evidence, led by the prosecution, Ndwendwa had described activities at the Ngubeni house thus:

> We'd come in, sit down and listen to music, I'd complain of hunger, bread would accompany my tea and so on, I would then hold a conversation with the people I found there, I would talk generally, also amongst other things about girls. I would then, in passing in our conversation, speak to an individual there about matters which we had

> discussed during our meetings at the SSRC and try to find out from this person how he viewed things.[76]

In cross-examining the witness Wentzel picked up on this description for his own purposes:

> For example at this house in Diepkloof, you would discuss politics, girls, soccer, and literature? – That is so.
>
> In other words, to put it very shortly, you were like any group of young folk gathered together? – That is so.
>
> And you disputed amongst yourselves, some of you had this opinion about soccer, some had that opinion, some had this opinion about politics, others had that opinion? – That is so.
>
> I suppose you even differed about the girls? – That is so.
>
> I want to just get away from the idea that we're dealing with a kind of command post at the house in Diepkloof, *that wasn't a house full of a lot of long faced, serious young men talking SSRC, from morning till night was it?* – That is so [emphasis added].[77]

The implications of Ndwendwa's evidence were drawn out by Advocate Wentzel to try to undermine the prosecution's concentration upon the defendants' subversive political identity to the exclusion of all else. The portrayal of the SSRC as a masculine grouping was central to both cases; only its meaning was disputed. What is also worth remarking upon here was the repeated response that Ndwendwa gave each time to Wentzel. 'That is so' was affirmative but did not elaborate in any way – suggestive of Ndwendwa's attempts to draw the process of questioning to a close as quickly as possible.

This line of argument caused problems for the defence when they came up against their own witnesses' extolling of the importance of the youths' political actions. Bishop Manas Buthelezi of the Black Parent's Association, which had been formed in Soweto during the Uprisings, was one of only two witnesses for the defence. Under cross-examination the prosecution chose to confront him with his own words in various newspaper articles, in which he had praised the actions of the students and heralded 16 June as a momentous political event. Advocate for the prosecution Van Lieres put forward the notion of a new generation taking leadership of the liberation struggle. He thus implied, even without any grand conspiracy theories of links with the ANC, that the SSRC should be thought of in the same way.

> **Adv. V. Lieres:** Now one gets the impression Bishop, if one looks historically at the position that in the 1970s apparently the youth has sort of taken over the role of the older people in connection with the

> liberation of the Black people in putting forward grievances and so forth, would you agree with that? –
>
> **Bishop Buthelezi:** Not 'taken over', I took them as having; they tried to do their own thing in the student's pattern.[78]

Buthelezi's argument was to try to contain the importance of this new politics by the description 'student's pattern'. Advocate Van Lieres later read out a section of an article that had appeared in the *Sunday Express* on 15 August 1976. Buthelezi was quoted as saying:

> Black politics was experiencing a birth in the flow of fresh political ideas. In the 50s and 60s, the dominant figures on the political scene were such figures as Chief Luthuli and Dr Moroka. Accused in political trials of those days were usually, 'the old people', but the big new factor in the '70s is that you have the politics of the youth, Dr. Buthelezi explained, it started with SASM, the BPC and now it is the whole student body. It appears as if the grievances which were expressed in the past by the grown-ups, were just not being listened to. You must therefore, see the role of the students in relation to unsuccessful attempts in the past to bring about change.[79]

It was very difficult for Buthelezi to maintain plausibly that he referred only to youth political leadership on the issue of Bantu Education and Afrikaans as a medium of instruction. The prosecution played upon ideas of trials and detention as a marker of political opposition to apartheid. Buthelezi had commented that 'accused in political trials' of the past had been 'the old people'. The implication that was hard to avoid was that the students, by virtue of being on trial fitted into the roll call of ANC leaders, Chief Luthuli and Dr Moroka and should be treated accordingly by the State. The social practices of youth politics were explicitly gendered as male by both prosecution and defence. In the prosecution's case the wider idea of youth politics as a historical phenomena, the Soweto generation, was more implicitly – but also nevertheless quite definitely –male.

Being heard from the margins

The trial evidenced a widespread presence of young women within the world of Soweto student political organising but also partially erased this presence. The testimony of Masabata Loate provides a stark illustration of the domain of the sayable within which young women spoke and were heard. This book began with the judge's comment on her body, coming at the end of her testimony in which she had revealed the weight loss she had suffered in detention.[80] This instance reveals the ways in which young black women had to negotiate multiple discourses, not just those of their peers, which framed their actions and bodies as up for scrutiny, control and judgement. If they were 'invisible' to police as potential political actors, they were hyper-visible in other ways. The judge's comment on Loate's weight followed on from a quite lengthy cross-examination in which Wentzel suggested that Loate was the object of a falling-out between one of the defendants and Herbert Mabuza, another SSRC member (and cousin of the Ngubeni sisters).

> **Adv. Wentzel:** Now I'd like you to look at the eighth accused. Accused no 8 Kgotsietsile Mogami? I don't want to say more than I have to about very personal matters. I see from the smile on your face you know what I am about to say? He was your particular boyfriend was he not? – He is my ex-boyfriend.
>
> And at one time he was very much your boyfriend is that right? I won't put anything personal? – Yes.
>
> Do you know a young man called Herbert Mabuza? – Yes.
>
> Am I right in saying that his nickname was 'Chance Taker'? – I can't say.
>
> You can't say? What chances was Herbert always taking? – Divorcing girlfriends of his friends, making love to . . .
>
> **By the court:** Making love to his friend's girlfriends? Was he a ladies man? – Yes.
>
> **Adv. W:** And in fact Herbert Mabuza was rather interested in you, he found you a very attractive young lady? – He was having a soft spot for me.
>
> The eighth accused wasn't very pleased about this was he? – Yes, he didn't like it.
>
> It led to trouble between him and Herbert did it not? – Yes.[81]

Wentzel did not pursue this line of questioning any further, but the implications of this exchange placed Masabata Loate in a very particular role with regards to the SSRC social grouping. She was one of the 'girls' discussed and disagreed over. This was all part of Wentzel's portrayal of the SSRC as group of young friends rather than serious or dangerous political actors.[82]

It doesn't seem too much of a leap to suggest that the depiction of young women's position employed here in defence of young political activists can, and should, be connected by the historian to the tales told by young men and others about youth politics subsequently. The idea that young women who became involved in political activities might get a reputation that they were sexually available is an issue that young men mentioned in Catherine Campbell's widely cited study of youth politics in 1990s Umlazi township, outside Durban. Campbell was told that a woman who attended political meetings 'gets the reputation of being a woman who goes after men'.[83] One reading of Wentzel's exchanges with Loate might be to see this as further evidence of the sexual control of young women as part of youth sociality and political organising.[84] This interpretation, however, should be resisted. Instead, it should be seen more precisely as evidence of the courtroom as a site for the *reiteration* of such a narrative. The production of such a narrative in this space undoubtedly had effects. In the Soweto Eleven trial Loate appears very much as a peripheral young woman – this peripheral status was confirmed on her release. In 1982 she told another courtroom, this time as a defendant on trial herself, that following her appearance as a state witness, 'politics were never discussed in my presence' and she received a threatening letter and was shot in the leg.[85] The trial thus heard Loate and the other young women witnesses from the margins and placed them there in very real terms on their release.

Sibongile Mkhabela née Mthembu recalled the attitude of Prosecutor Von Lieres during the trial in her 2001 autobiography: 'He had especially focused on the only young woman, the black rose, who stood among men. He, an Afrikaner male of the time could not understand how a black female could be determined to defy the white man's law: after all, black women belonged in the kitchen'.[86] The perception of the judge, prosecution and defence lawyers, as well as the security services, in selecting witnesses all shaped the way in which young women's speech in the courtroom was heard.

The way youth politics was discussed in the trial did not quite capture the nature of young women's involvement, even whilst it registered their presence. The issue was raised in the court that various young women, including the accused Sibongile Mthembu, found it difficult to attend SSRC meetings regularly. In his testimony, Issie Gxluwe, who also attended Naledi high school, explained why his school had four representatives in the SSRC instead of two.

> **Adv. Vo. Lieres:** But all four of them served on the SSRC, that is if I understand you correctly? – Susan Mthembu sometimes didn't attend. Sometimes she didn't attend, most of the time she did not.[87]

Mkhabela mentions in her autobiography that she would sometimes miss political meetings. She saw this as insignificant in contrast to her male comrades who she says felt they *had* to attend to prove themselves political.[88] Other young women's testimony at the trial similarly echoed a constrained commitment – or a different kind of identification with politics. For example, Ayanda Cokile:

> **Von Lieres:** What was your attitude to being elected as a member of the – to represent your school on the SSRC? – I asked the chairman himself when he came to our school . . .
>
> Is that Mr. Sono you asked? – Yes.
>
> What did you ask him? – I asked him that as being in the SSRC some people like myself were having domestic problems, so that I won't be able to attend these meetings regularly. So he said that as long as I am representing the school and I am well informed about what [*sic*] the meetings which were held when I wasn't there and gave the reports back to the students as to what was said at the meetings, that was ok.
>
> Your, perhaps just briefly, your domestic problems, did you have to do the household at home? – Yes.[89]

Another witness, Sarah Makepe, suggested that membership of the SSRC was for her a social choice as much as anything else. After being elected by her school to the SSRC she resigned the following day. The judge intervened to ask her, 'Why did you resign the very next day?' She replied: 'I had to decide whether I was representing my students on the SSRC or whether I should go back to my old procedure, that is being an actress'.[90] These are glimpses of political participation that the trial and its narratives cannot quite erase. It shows us student politics was something that existed alongside housework and drama groups, even during the turmoil of 1977. The gendered dynamics of state repression and prosecution (and the defences this elicited) interrupt young women's voices and interpolate young women's speech to their own ends but they were there, and they did speak.

Silence in court

The trial includes one final form of speech that is neither the coerced talk of state witnesses nor the intimate and internal dialogue of 'My Thoughts', though it exists somewhere in between. Whilst being held in detention, Sibongile Mkhabela née Mthembu wrote letters on tissue paper which were then rolled and sewn into the hem of a skirt and smuggled out of prison.[91] The extraordinary fragility of the letters, written with great difficulty on such thin paper means that had they reached their intended recipients they would not have been easy to preserve and keep, even if this was desired. But the fragility of three of these letters was transformed, when they were intercepted by police. They were transcribed and admitted as evidence. They became the foundation of an additional charge of 'terroristic activities' that was laid against Mkhabela. In defending his young client, the letters were read out in full to the courtroom by Ernest Wentzel, in the hope that it would be clear their content was personal and not, as the prosecution alleged, evidence of terrorism. After reading one, he exclaimed to the court, 'is this letter not just patently the letter of a lonely, unhappy girl, communicating with her family?'[92]

Even at the time Wentzel clearly thought it was extraordinary that the letters could be read as sufficient evidence of incitement to terrorism. In a letter to her younger sister that is full of encouragement to 'try to keep strong' in the face of her ongoing detention, there is also the reflection: 'it has become obvious that a violent struggle is the only hope we cherish'.[93] This was highlighted by the prosecution, as was the observation to her brother, 'should we be scared of the last kicks of a dying horse, that we give it a second chance. I don't give these bastards more than 5 years'.[94] However, in 1970s South Africa many young people were tried and convicted for trying to leave the country to undergo military training or recruiting others to do so, on the basis of casual conversations, even where no action was taken.[95] The line between 'casual talk' and incitement was extremely thin.[96] The danger of speaking about the struggle was very real. In these convictions the State also blurred what was in the realm of private thought and public action, conditions which shaped everyday speech. Reflecting on the way her activism in 1976–7 affected her close relationships, especially with her father, Mkhabela recalled 'growing quieter' over time. Writing in 2001 she remembered:

> As I grew less and less communicative with Baba, I became even less communicative with my own comrades. All conversations I engaged in were of an intense nature; I was finding it difficult to talk about ordinary, day-to-day things. The desire for liberation had gripped me more than I was prepared to admit.[97]

In her own account the pressures and intensity of activism shaped what Mkhabela said in intimate as well as political spaces, breaking down distinctions between them.[98] The incorporation of her letters into the trial did so again. Of the three letters, only two were relied upon by the prosecution as evidence of terrorism. The third was still nevertheless read out to the court by Wentzel. Indeed, he began his arguments with a prison guard W. McPherson with what was, in Wentzel's words, a 'love letter'.[99] He read it to underline its personal nature. Alongside the experience of Masabata Loate during the trial, discussed as a girlfriend and her body scrutinised, here the only young woman amongst the accused was also subjected to an extra level of exposure in the courtroom, her personal letters read in public. Helena Pohlandt-McCormick has argued, drawing on another young woman's anguished letters that were subsequently confiscated by police, that the choice to become involved politically and to stay involved was 'harder and more poignant' for young women and girls because of their caring responsibilities, either for younger siblings or children of their own.[100] In her autobiography, Mkhabela reprints two of the three letters at the back of her book, omitting the love letter. She thus reclaims them.[101] She does not tell us what it was like to hear them read aloud. As with Loate, exposure sits alongside silence.

Exploring Sibongile Mkhabela's autobiographical account of the trial more fully, silence is a recurring theme. Dealt with in one chapter, titled simply 'The Trial', her account focuses on the moment of sentencing in May 1979. It begins in the third person:

> One by one the 11 accused emerged from the holding cells, *Emgodini*, to take their place in the dock. Fists were raised high in power salutes and shouts of *amandla* continued to defy the 'system' that had convicted them and was now going to pass sentence on them. The audience responded with *amandla* and the court orderly shouted 'Silence in Court'.[102]

The silence of the courtroom is something Mkhabela mentions repeatedly and always in contrast to what is going on inside her own head: 'above the noise in my head and the silence of the courtroom the Judge pronounced his sentence'; and then, 'Silence in court, why, I thought, I need silence in my head. What is he going to say?'[103] Mkhabela takes us inside the 'noise' within her head by telling the life story of her mother's sister, whom she called 'Gogo', who was watching that day in the public gallery. She also re-enacts what she calls 'a silent dialogue' she held with the judge as he read his 114-page judgement:

> *Crime 1: The accused were leaders of the South African Student Movement (SASM) a student movement which strived to create political, social and cultural awareness and solidarity among Black schoolgoing students.*
>
> (Surely, Judge, that cannot be a crime. If this was a crime I wondered why the leaders of my church, The African Methodist Church, were not on trial. I further wondered why the Broederbond was not on trial).[104]

Mkhabela thus overwrites her silence in the courtroom with the story of her Gogo's struggles to live under the strictures and repression of the apartheid system and her own view of her actions for which she was being tried: 'you are not dealing with terroristic activities, you are dealing with students who were anxious to preserve their right to an education'.[105] In her autobiography the trial is transformed into a space through which to tell these stories. In doing so her account also points us to what remained unsayable at the time.

On hearing her sentence for six years (four years suspended) Mkhabela recalled being unable to say anything; there was 'a muffled cry from the audience' and she remembered 'I smiled and steered my thoughts beyond the two years' effective prison sentence'.[106] Then, 'Gogo's voice erupted in a scream. She shouted my name'. She described leaving the courtroom: 'I felt the loneliness of being the only woman amongst men and getting convicted. I thought of Ma and Gogo; her scream in the courtroom would not leave me, I heard it loud and clear. I wanted her to know I would be ok.'[107] This moving description of the pain of separation from her family makes clear the limits of what was sayable in the courtroom. Her Gogo's story was not heard there – but her scream was.

Conclusions

There are two Soweto elevens in this chapter – the eleven accused and the eleven who testified during the trial. Asking who spoke, as well as what they said, and how they were heard, uncovers some of the dynamics of speaking about the struggle. In thinking about what was sayable for these young people in the context of this trial and the legal battles (with very real material consequences) over the meaning and nature of youth political action in June 1976 and its aftermath, I argue that we can begin to see some of the ways in which gendered narratives of struggle were made. The portrait of youth politics that was drawn inside the courtroom during the trial of the Soweto Eleven served several different purposes and it also had effects beyond the courtroom. It was an important site for reiterating and amplifying youth politics and youth sociability as male. For Masabata Loate the trial, and her testimony as a state witness, marginalised her (through speech rather than silence) in two ways. In the historical record she is framed and heard as on the edges of the SSRC – one of the girls disagreed and fought over. On the streets of Soweto, after the trial, her talk marginalised her within the ongoing practice of anti-apartheid politics.

Over twenty years later, on the anniversary of the 1976 Uprisings, a special hearing of South Africa's Truth and Reconciliation Commission (TRC) was held, to reconstruct again the events of 16 June. Two of the Soweto Eleven – Dan Montsisi and Murphy Morobe – spoke authoritatively about the march and its aftermath.[108] Other witnesses such as Amelia Molapo gave more jumbled accounts of participation and injury that day: for Molapo the march was 'noise . . . confusion . . . running around . . . running away'.[109] When the TRC again returned to the events of 16 June during a special Johannesburg children's hearing, another witness, Nomande Ntabeni, who had been sixteen in 1976 and shot during the march, was asked repeatedly by one commissioner, Joyce Seroke, about the extent of young women's involvement, specifically in violence: 'I want to establish if the girls were also in a position of fighting back, perhaps fight back with stones or bombs like the previous witness who has told us they would be in possession of explosives. What were the girls up to?'[110] When I first began asking questions myself about young women's political participation, this moment of repeated questioning and the refrain 'what were the girls up to?' resonated loudly with my own frustrations. They *were* there after all. My own view now is that an equally important question is: Why do we not know what they were up to? Why is the historical record so contradictory? Examining the bounds of the sayable within the trial of the Soweto Eleven, it seems clear that young women involved in politics experienced a struggle to speak because speech was so central a site of the struggle. Speaking about the struggle *produced* gendered narratives, narratives forged out of necessity in courtrooms as well as on the street, in moments of protest and reflection. These gendered narratives enable us to see and hear Masabata Loate but they do not help us to unpick who wrote down 'My Thoughts'.

Notes

1. This account is the one Masabata Loate gives within her testimony to the trial of the Soweto Eleven. Supreme Court of South Africa (Transvaal Provincial Division), *State vs. W.W.C. Twala and Ten Others*, case K/P 282/78; WHP: AD1450: Box 5: Record of Proceedings, 1084–7.

2. At her trial in 1982 Masabata Loate told the court that 7798 was her brother Barney's house and that she stayed there with her grandmother, her mother, her sister-in-law Sophia (married to Barney), and three children of her sister. See: *State vs. Mary Masabate Loatse and others*, case: 41/4115/81 Magistrates Court, District of Johannesburg; WHP: AD2021: SAIRR Security Trials 1958–82. Boxes 19–20. Record of Proceedings, 533. Digitised trial proceedings, accessed July 2019, http://www.historicalpapers.wits.ac.za/?inventory/U/collections&c=AD2021/R/.

3. *State vs. W.W.C Twala*, Proceedings, 1087.

4. *WRAB vs. Santam*, SAB WLD 6857/77, vol. 436, accessed June 2024, www.gutenberg-e.org/pohlandt-mccormick/archive/detail/DSCN2877.jpg.html.

5. The papers confiscated from Loate are discussed and available in the digital archive that accompanies Helena Pohlandt-McCormick's e-book. Pohlandt-McCormick, *'I Saw a Nightmare' . . . : Doing Violence to Memory*, accessed June 2024, http://www.gutenberg-e.org/pohlandt-mccormick/archive/.

6. Pohlandt-McCormick, *'I Saw a Nightmare'*, chapter 5, 90.

7. Paul Brunton, *The Hidden Teaching beyond Yoga*, Tenth Impression (London: Rider & Company, 1941).

8. An account of his life is available here: Paul Brunton Philosophic Foundation (blog), 'Illustrated Biography', 19 November 2023, https://www.paulbrunton.org/about-paul-brunton/illustrated-biography/.

9. Brunton, *The Hidden Teaching beyond Yoga*, 348.

10. Daniel R. Magaziner, *The Law and the Prophets: Black Consciousness in South Africa, 1968–1977* (Athens, OH: Ohio University Press, 2010), 48.

11. Magaziner, *The Law and the Prophets*, 48.

12. Brunton, *The Hidden Teaching beyond Yoga*, 345.

13. Brunton, *The Hidden Teaching beyond Yoga*, 345.

14. *State vs. W.W.C Twala*, Proceedings, 1087.

15. *State vs. W.W.C Twala*, Proceedings, 1086.

16. These are details given by Murphy Morobe in his testimony to the Truth and Reconciliation Commission. See: Murphy Morobe, Truth and Reconciliation Commission, Human Rights Violations Committee Public Hearings, Soweto – June 16 Hearings, Day 1, 22 July 1996, accessed February 2024, https://www.justice.gov.za/trc/hrvtrans/soweto/morobe.htm.

17. Michael Lobban, *White Man's Justice: South African Political Trials in the Black Consciousness Era* (Oxford: Clarendon Press, 1996), 220.

18. Lobban, *White Man's Justice*, 220.

19. In 1961 the Urban Bantu Council Act established Urban Bantu Councils as the means by which urban African populations were 'represented' within the system of administration boards that ran African townships. UBCs never enjoyed much legitimacy amongst urban Africans and were nicknamed 'useless boys' clubs'. After the failure of UBCs to intervene in the Soweto Uprisings, this system was replaced by Community Councils. For the role of the UBCs and the subsequent Community Councils within the township uprisings of the mid-1980s see: Franziska Rueedi, *The Vaal Uprising of 1984 and the Struggle for Freedom in South Africa* (Woodbridge, Suffolk: James Currey, 2021), 60.

20. He did so at in his testimony at the Truth and Reconciliation Commission. See: Dan Montsisi, Truth and Reconciliation Commission, Human Rights Violations Committee Public Hearings, Soweto – June 16 Hearings, Day 1, 22 July 1996, accessed February 2024, https://www.justice.gov.za/trc/hrvtrans/soweto/montsisi.htm.

21. 'Orlando Stayaway goes on', *Rand Daily Mail* (Township Edition), 22 June 1977, 1.

22. According to her testimony at her own trial in 1982, *State vs. M.M. Loatse et al.* as discussed in Chapter 3.

23. This moment is discussed at the very beginning of the Introduction to this book, *State vs. W.W.C. Twala*, 1096.

24. Sifiso Mxolisi Ndlovu amongst others notes the discrepancy between photographic images of 16 June 1976 that show the widespread participation of young women and their lack of voice within the historical record and histories of the Soweto Uprisings. See: Sifiso Mxolisi Ndlovu, 'The Anatomy of the Crowd', in *The Road to Democracy in South Africa: Volume 7: Soweto Uprisings: New Perspectives, Commemorations and Memorialisation* (Cape Town: Unisa Press, 2017), 49.

25. 'Inventory of items confiscated by the police (17 June 1976) from Masabatha Loate'. Civil Case WLD 6857 (1977), vol. 413, accessed June 2024, www.gutenberg-e.org/pohlandt-mccormick/archive/detail/DSCN2753.jpg.html and 'Brown envelope

with inventory of documents seized during Masabatha Loate's arrest'. Civil Case WLD 6857 (1977), vol. 436, accessed June 2024, www.gutenberg-e.org/pohlandt-mccormick/archive/detail/DSCN2881.jpg.html.

26. 'Inventory of items confiscated by the police (17 June 1976) from Masabatha Loate', accessed June 2024, www.gutenberg-e.org/pohlandt-mccormick/archive/detail/DSCN2753.jpg.html.

27. Kasonde T. Mukonde, '"If You Belong to My Generation and You Never Read James Hadley Chase, Then You Are Not Educated": Everyday Reading of High School Students in Soweto, 1968–1976', *Journal of Southern African Studies* 49, no. 2 (4 March 2023): 223, https://doi.org/10.1080/03057070.2023.2204782.

28. Between 1955 and 1960 the National Party government removed residents from Sophiatown, a black freehold suburb of Johannesburg. Resistance to these removals, whilst ultimately unsuccessful, were a radicalising moment within the liberation struggle. See: Tom Lodge, 'The Destruction of Sophiatown', *The Journal of Modern African Studies* 19, no. 1 (1981): 107–32; The significance of the destruction of Sophiatown derives in part from the cultural life of the suburb that was home to many writers and artists. See: Paul Gready, 'The Sophiatown Writers of the Fifties: The Unreal Reality of Their World', *Journal of Southern African Studies* 16, no. 1 (1990): 139–64, http://www.jstor.org/stable/2636643.

29. Magaziner, *The Law and the Prophets*, 18.

30. Daniel R. Magaziner, 'Pieces of a (Wo)Man: Feminism, Gender and Adulthood in Black Consciousness, 1968–1977', *Journal of Southern African Studies* 37, no.1 (1 March 2011): 38, http://dx.doi.org/10.1080/03057070.2011.552542.

31. Magaziner, *The Law and the Prophets*, 93–9.

32. Mukonde, '"If You Belong to My Generation and You Never Read James Hadley Chase, Then You Are Not Educated"', 215.

33. *State vs. M.M. Loatse et al.*, Proceedings, 610.

34. Rachel Matteau-Matsha, '"I Read What I Like": Politics of Reading and Reading Politics in Apartheid South Africa', *Transformation: Critical Perspectives on Southern Africa* 83, no. 1 (27 December 2013): 57.

35. Pohlandt-McCormick, *'I Saw a Nightmare'*, chapter 1, 115, 135.

36. Murphy Morobe recalled being taken out of detention and being forced to read statements extracted through torture before the Cillié Commission, but also that he and others later refused to confirm those statements despite the consequences: 'we knew what refusal meant because we were still in detention'. See: Murphy Morobe, Truth and Reconciliation Commission, Human Rights Violations Committee Public Hearings, Soweto – June 16 Hearings, Day 1, 22 July 1996, accessed February 2024, https://www.justice.gov.za/trc/hrvtrans/soweto/morobe.htm.

37. Jeremy Seekings, 'Gender Ideology and Township Politics in the 1980s', *Agenda* 10 (1991); Seekings, *Heroes or Villains? Youth Politics in the 1980s* (Johannesburg: Ravan Press, 1993).

38. For a critique of the ways in which narratives of Apartheid's 'emasculation' of Black men assumes certain constructions of masculinity see: Helen Moffett, 'Sexual Violence, Civil Society and the New Constitution', in *Women's Activism in South Africa: Working Across Divides*, ed. Hannah Britton, Jennifer Fish and Sheila Meintjes (Scottsville, South Africa: University of Kwazulu Natal Press, 2009), 161, 164.

39. Leslie Anne Hadfield, 'Challenging the Status Quo: Young Women and Men in Black Consciousness Community Work, 1970s South Africa', *Journal of African History* 54 (2013): 248, https://doi.org/doi:10.1017/S0021853713000261.

40. For many insightful thoughts on the relationship between violence and politics see: Franziska Rueedi, '"Siyayinyova!": Patterns of Violence in the African Townships of the Vaal Triangle, South Africa.1980–86', *Africa* 85, no. 3 (August 2015): 395–416, https://doi.org/doi:10.1017/S0001972015000261; N. Chabani Manganyi and Andre Du Toit, eds., *Political Violence and the Struggle in South Africa* (London: Palgrave Macmillan, 1990), http://link.springer.com/book/10.1007/978-1-349-21074-9.

41. Peter Delius and Clive Glaser, 'Sexual Socialisation in South Africa: A Historical Perspective', *African Studies* 61, no.1 (2002): 48, https://doi.org/10.1080/00020180220140064; Clive Glaser, *Bo Tsotsi: The Youth Gangs of Soweto, 1935–1976* (Oxford: James Currey, 2000), 189.

42. Judith Butler, *Excitable Speech: A Politics of the Performative* (New York: Routledge, 1997), 133.

43. *State vs. W.W.C. Twala and Ten Others*, Box 4: The Indictment, 3.

44. *State vs. W.W.C. Twala*, 'Schedule F', 25–32.

45. *State vs. W.W.C. Twala*, 'Schedule B', 7.

46. Lobban, *White Man's Justice*, 221.

47. J. R. L. Milton, 'Criminal Law in South Africa – 1976–1986', *Acta Juridica* 1987 (1987): 44.

48. Pam Kleinot, 'SA's first sedition trial in 30 years', *Rand Daily Mail*, 1 May 1979.

49. Lobban, *White Man's Justice*, 225.

50. Lobban, *White Man's Justice*, 225.

51. Lobban, *White Man's Justice*, 226.

52. Lobban, *White Man's Justice*, 232.

53. Lobban, *White Man's Justice*, 230.

54. Enid Fourie, 'The UN Convention on the Rights of the Child and the Crisis for Children in South Africa: Apartheid and Detention Symposium: UN Convention on Children's Rights', *Human Rights Quarterly* 12, no. 1 (1990): 111.

55. *State vs. W.W.C. Twala*, Proceedings, 603.

56. *State vs. W.W.C. Twala*, Proceedings, 1522.

57. South Africa, *Report of the Commission of Inquiry into the Riots at Soweto and Elsewhere from the 16th of June 1976 to the 28th of February 1977* (Pretoria: Govt. Printer, 1980), 357.

58. Ndlovu, 'The Anatomy of the Crowd', 44.

59. Ndlovu, 'The Anatomy of the Crowd', 45.

60. Zwelakhe Sisulu, 'Students face a marathon trial', *Rand Daily Mail* (Township Edition), 31 July 1978.

61. Janet Sahil, 'The Soweto Eleven', *Sash: The Black Sash Magazine*, 1979, 6.

62. Lobban, *White Man's Justice*, 247.

63. Sahil, 'The Soweto Eleven', 6.

64. The prosecution also called as witnesses policemen, several white people who had been in Soweto on June 16, eleven bus drivers and employees of the bus company PUTCO, the Director of Finances at the West Rand Administrative Board, and Dr A. B. Fourie of the Department of Bantu Education. The Defence called only two witnesses – the educationalist Dr Franz Auerbach and Bishop Manas Buthelezi, one of the founders of the Black Parents Association that sought to mediate between the students of Soweto and the authorities. Lobban, *White Man's Justice*, 243–7.

65. South Africa, *Report of the Commission of Inquiry into the Riots at Soweto and Elsewhere from the 16th of June 1976 to the 28th of February 1977*, 279.

66. See for example the report of the arrest of Masabata Loate on 20 June 1977: 'Police detain three more, but release six', *Rand Daily Mail*, 20 June 1977.

67. *State vs. W.W.C. Twala*, Proceedings, 1699.

68. *State vs. W.W.C. Twala*, Proceedings, 692.

69. *State vs. W.W.C. Twala*, Proceedings, 693.

70. Jon Soske, 'The Family Romance of the South African Revolution', in *Love and Revolution in the Twentieth-Century Colonial and Postcolonial World: Perspectives from South Asia and Southern Africa*, ed. G. Arunima, Patricia Hayes and Premesh Lalu, Palgrave Studies in the History of Social Movements (Cham: Springer International Publishing, 2021): 179, https://doi.org/10.1007/978-3-030-79580-1_7.

71. Soske, 'The Family Romance of the South African Revolution', 179.

72. *State vs. W.W.C. Twala*, Proceedings, 694.

73. *State vs. W.W.C. Twala*, Proceedings, 695.

74. Pohlandt-McCormick, *'I Saw a Nightmare'*, chapter 4, 59.

75. *State vs. W.W.C. Twala*, Proceedings, 705.

76. *State vs. W.W.C. Twala*, Proceedings, 993.

77. *State vs. W.W.C. Twala*, Proceedings, 994.

78. *State vs. W.W.C. Twala*, Proceedings, 2461.

79. *State vs. W.W.C. Twala*, Proceedings, 2461–2.

80. *State vs. W.W.C. Twala*, Proceedings, 1096.

81. *State vs. W.W.C. Twala*, Proceedings, 1093.

82. It is worth mentioning Shahid Amin's work on judicial discourses in colonial India here. In discussing the testimony of an 'approver' or accomplice turned witness, Amin comments, 'the prosecution treats the Approver's testimony as a sealed text which derives its meaning from its constitution and not from any context . . . the defence attempts to "socialize" the event, implicate it – and hence the Approver's testimony – into the reality of its milieu'. Shahid Amin, 'Approver's Testimony, Judicial Discourse: The Case of Chauri Chaura', in *Subaltern Studies V*, ed. Ranajit Guha (Oxford: Oxford University Press, 1987), 187.

83. Catherine Campbell, 'Learning to Kill? Masculinity, the Family and Violence in Natal', *Journal of Southern African Studies* 18, no. 3 (September 1992): 625, https://www.jstor.org/stable/2637301.

84. Delius and Glaser, 'Sexual Socialisation'.

85. *State vs. M.M. Loatse et al.*, Proceedings, 498 and 496.

86. Sibongile Mkhabela, *Open Earth and Black Roses: Remembering 16 June 1976* (Braamfontein, South Africa: Skotaville Press, 2001), 83.

87. *State vs. W.W.C. Twala*, Proceedings, 676.

88. Mkhabela, *Open Earth and Black Roses*, 40.

89. *State vs. W.W.C. Twala*, Proceedings, 1241–2.

90. *State vs. W.W.C. Twala*, Proceedings, 735.

91. Mkhabela, *Open Earth and Black Roses*, 63.

92. *State vs. W.W.C. Twala*, Proceedings, 1529–30.

93. Mkhabela, *Open Earth and Black Roses*, 122.

94. Mkhabela, *Open Earth and Black Roses*, 123.

95. A number of such cases in which convictions were justified on the basis of 'mere talk' are discussed in Lobban, *White Man's Justice*, 115–95.

96. Lobban, *White Man's Justice*, 117.

97. Mkhabela, *Open Earth and Black Roses*, 59.

98. Another of the Soweto Eleven, Murphy Morobe, recalled during his testimony to the Truth and Reconciliation Commission what he thought of as a sense of exhaustion, he dated to September of 1976: 'my own emotions had totally run out by then'. See: Murphy Morobe, Truth and Reconciliation Commission, Human Rights Violations Committee Public Hearings, Soweto – June 16 Hearings, Day 1, 22 July 1996, accessed February 2024, https://www.justice.gov.za/trc/hrvtrans/soweto/morobe.htm.

99. *State vs. W.W.C. Twala*, Proceedings, 1527.

100. Pohlandt-McCormick, *'I Saw a Nightmare'*, chapter 4, 63.

101. I have not discussed the third letter, that Mkhabela chooses not to reprint, believing that to do so would be to repeat that act of exposure.

102. Mkhabela, *Open Earth and Black Roses*, 83; The Afrikaner Broederbond was a secret, all-male society that sought to promote the interests of the Afrikaner nation. It was an organisation with close links to the National Party and exerted a 'profound influence at all levels of South African politics'. See: Dan O'Meara, 'The Afrikaner Broederbond 1927–1948: Class Vanguard of Afrikaner Nationalism', *Journal of Southern African Studies* 3, no. 2 (1 April 1977): 156, https://doi.org/10.1080/03057077708707970.

103. Mkhabela, *Open Earth and Black Roses*, 88, 89.

104. Mkhabela, *Open Earth and Black Roses*, 84.

105. Mkhabela, *Open Earth and Black Roses*, 84.

106. Mkhabela, *Open Earth and Black Roses*, 89.

107. Mkhabela, *Open Earth and Black Roses*, 89.

108. Dan Montsisi, Truth and Reconciliation Commission, Human Rights Violations Committee Public Hearings, Soweto – June 16 Hearings, Day 1, 22 July 1996, Available at: https://www.justice.gov.za/trc/hrvtrans/soweto/montsisi.htm and Murphy Morobe, Truth and Reconciliation Commission, Human Rights Violations Committee Public Hearings, Soweto – June 16 Hearings, Day 1, 22 July 1996, accessed May 2023, https://www.justice.gov.za/trc/hrvtrans/soweto/morobe.htm.

109. Amelia Molapo, Truth and Reconciliation Commission, Human Rights Violations Committee Public Hearings, Soweto – June 16 Hearings, Day 1, 22 July 1996, accessed May 2023, https://www.justice.gov.za/trc/hrvtrans/soweto/molapo.htm.

110. Nomonde Ntabeni, Truth and Reconciliation Commission, Human Rights Violations Committee Public Hearings, Johannesburg Children's Hearing, Day 1, 12 June 1997, accessed May 2023, https://www.justice.gov.za/trc/special/children/ntabeni.htm.

Chapter 3

Witnessing, detention and silence: speech as struggle

Introduction

Just three months after the trial of the Soweto Eleven ended, Masabata Loate appeared in the *Rand Daily Mail*, as a winning beauty queen, Miss Mainstay 1979 (Mainstay was a brand of South African sugar cane spirit). On 3 August she was pictured alongside the two runners-up in the contest, and on 28 August carrying out her duties at the first-round draw for the Mainstay Cup, a football competition sponsored by the brand.[1] The only hint that this young woman had a political past, and future, was her natural Afro hairstyle. Three years later she was back in court, on trial herself, charged under the Terrorism Act. What do these two fragments of a life – the beauty queen and the alleged terrorist – say when we hold them alongside one another? At her 1982–3 trial, Loate's defence team suggested these two identities were incompatible. Masabata Loate spoke at her trial, and she spoke of beauty contests. In doing so she transgressed the boundaries as they were being drawn around these two apparently different lives. She spoke, too, of crossing another fiercely maintained distinction, that between a state witness and an anti-apartheid activist. This is even more extraordinary, given the context of intensifying struggles over speech that marked the 1980s.

The trial of Mary Masabata Loate and Sidney Khotso Seatlholo on two counts under the Terrorism Act that began in February of 1982 was all about speech and silence. It was shaped by an uneven compulsion to speak that played out along lines of gender and age.[2] The prosecution alleged that Seatlholo and Loate were members of both the SSRC, banned since 1977, and the South African Revolutionary Youth Council (SAYRCO). According to the prosecution, Seatlholo was the SAYRCO president and Loate the secretary, and SAYRCO recruited students in Soweto to undergo military training in Botswana as part of a conspiracy with other internal black organisations to violently overthrow the State. The trial was marked by three significant maintained silences: that of Khotso Seatlholo himself; the 'silent five' male witnesses who refused to testify for the State; and that of 'Freedom', a young woman friend of both the accused, who once in the witness box also dramatically refused to give evidence against them. Masabata Loate did testify in her own defence. A number of other young detainees appeared as state witnesses. For them, and for Loate, talking was a means of saving oneself and implicating others, if they could convince the magistrate that their talk was authentic. A large part of the defence case rested upon calling into question the motivations of these young witnesses and suggested that for them, testifying *in camera* as many did, the courtroom was an extension of the interrogation room. Unlike the trial of the Soweto Eleven considered in Chapter 2, there was, in 1982, less of an effort on the part of defence or prosecution to portray youth politics a particular way. Instead, the central debate of this trial was not the meaning of youth political action, but rather the meaning and motivation of speech. The defence suggested that the struggle at this time was an all-consuming environment. A 'web' was the metaphor used, which could entangle all young people; unwitting innocents, committed activists and criminal chancers alike. They argued that the prosecution acted cruelly, in failing to distinguish between them, and that how individuals spoke during the trial, was the key to telling them apart.

Jacob Dlamini has noted that state witnesses were at the very centre of South Africa's political show trials and that the 'choice' that many detainees faced was, 'talk and live or refuse and die'.[3] This was a 'choice' faced at every interrogation but also again in court and in the early 1980s more and more chose silence at this moment. The refusal of potential state witnesses to give evidence was noted as an increasingly common feature of security trials in the 1982 Survey of Race Relations annual report. In 1982 at least fifteen people had been sentenced for refusing to testify on behalf of the prosecution. Two other features of Loate's trial were also noted as wider trends by the same report: the holding of potential state witnesses for long periods in detention with release only following their court testimony, and the holding of portions of the trial *in camera* at the request of the prosecution or witnesses fearful that their 'lives would be endangered if the black community was aware they were giving evidence for the State'.[4] Despite being framed as a way of 'protecting' state witnesses, critics argued that *in camera* court proceedings were aimed at linking the moment of interrogation and the moment of testimony as closely as possible in the detainee's mind, maintaining the closed world of detention and its psychological and physical compulsions to talk. These features taken together suggest increasing pressures on detainees in the 1980s, from multiple directions.

In this context silence was valorised by the liberation movement. An article in the August 1983 edition of *Sechaba* celebrated 'voices of protest from the witness box' that were challenging apartheid 'on every front . . . even its own courtrooms'.[5] The author praised those state witnesses who refused to testify, or did so only to 'denounce in court those methods used to pressurise them' into giving evidence as 'the most effective challenge to the courts' credibility'.[6] At the same time that silence was valorised, talking was punished. As the 1980s went on, reprisals against state witnesses became increasingly violent and fatal. The 'necklace', a petrol-soaked tyre that was placed around a person's neck and set alight, was a method used against informers during the period of intense political violence under the States of Emergency declared from 1985 onwards. Between 400 and 700 people were killed in this way during the mid to late 1980s.[7] Whilst the UDF espoused non-violence and the ANC sanctioned the use of disciplined and strategic violence carried out by its armed wing UmKhonto We Sizwe (MK), the leadership of both organisations neither fully condoned, nor fully condemned, necklacing at this time. In what Reidwaan Moosage has named a 'prose of ambivalence', the practice was denounced (often as an 'excess' of violence) but those who carried out the necklacing were not.[8] As Nyasha Karimakwenda has noted, 'vulnerability to accusations of collaborating, and the form of punishment for men and women, were recurrently gender dependant'.[9] The speech and actions of women were subjected to specific controls. Loate and Seatlholo's trial took place at the very beginnings of this intensification of the violent struggle over speech. Loate was released and returned to Soweto when this violence was at its height, with tragic consequences.

Trial by talk

Seatlholo maintained a defiant silence throughout the trial, accompanied by black power salutes to the public gallery.[10] It was an irony, given his reputation as a 'forceful speaker'.[11] In contrast Loate did testify in her own defence and was cross-examined for a whole day. What Loate said whilst on trial makes her status difficult to 'fix' in terms of the clear-cut oppositional narratives of liberation. This was Loate's second time in the witness box. Indeed, her situation as an accused in 1982 was inextricably linked to her first appearance as a state witness in 1979. Loate's defence in 1982 relied upon a portrayal of her position within the struggle community as one that was deeply ambiguous following her appearance as a witness in the trial of the Soweto Eleven. She was, her defence team suggested, not trusted by the Soweto activist community and, in a misguided attempt to redeem herself, she became involved peripherally in SAYRCO through a romantic relationship with Seatlholo. Advocate George Bizos led Loate's evidence regarding the effects of her testimony in 1979 in the following exchanges:

> Now after you gave evidence, what was the attitude of the community that you were living in towards you? – The attitude was quite negative.
>
> How was this negative attitude expressed? – Firstly I received a threatening letter and a two [*sic*] weeks after receiving this letter I was shot in the leg . . .
>
> Were the people with whom you had been associated in the SSRC still keen to speak to you? – Well they used to talk to me, they used to walk with me, I was regarded as having been finished with the court and they held no grudges against me.
>
> Did they continue discussing their political plans with you? – No politics were never discussed in my presence . . . No reason was given by them but the fact that nobody discussed these things in my presence, this was because I had given evidence against them.[12]

The defence argued that having become reacquainted with Seatlholo on a visit to Botswana in February of 1981, Loate and Seatlholo resumed their previous romantic relationship. This was the reason for their communications and for Loate's meetings with other SAYRCO members; meetings that the prosecution alternatively alleged revealed her role as a military recruiter. Loate was with Seatlholo when he was arrested on his return to South Africa in June of 1981. She maintained in her testimony that she was Seatlholo's girlfriend and not a member of SAYRCO. Loate claimed she had not even heard of the organisation before her arrest, and as a result she had mis-spelled the organisation's acronym in a letter she wrote from detention. As she said, 'The fact that I could not even spell its name is evident [*sic*] enough of my ignorance'.[13]

Bizos argued that Loate subsequently found herself on trial alongside Seatlholo, not because of her role in SAYRCO, but rather because, after her arrest, she had managed to smuggle letters out to her family, and to lawyers, including Bizos, that described how she had been tortured whilst in detention. Concurrent with the trial were Supreme Court proceedings launched by Loate's mother against the police to try to prevent her from being assaulted further. Bizos argued that it was in response to this that the police further victimised her.[14] The defence also pointed to her situation in 1981 to argue she had too much to lose by being an activist: she had finished school and passed her matric exams, despite her detention in the aftermath of 1976; she was a successful beauty queen who won competitions; and she had a place at the University of Botswana, funded by a United Nations scholarship. This, and not the organisation of military training, Bizos argued, was the reason for her multiple visits to the country.

Conveying a sense of Loate's vulnerability was central to her defence strategy and it was a successful one to a certain extent. The magistrate expressed 'sympathy' for her position, but found her guilty, nonetheless. Perhaps in part because the idea of Loate as an exploitable girlfriend, who had been socially cast out and wanted a way back in, was not a role fully embraced by Loate in the courtroom. When under cross-examination it was put to her that 'you thought you were unfairly regarded as a sell-out', she replied:

> Well I would not say it was unfairly said by the people because I did give evidence against my people and that is being a sell-out . . . I would not say I was forced, even if my mother had encouraged me to give evidence, that if I personally did not want to, that she could not force me to talk.[15]

She thus laid claim to her earlier decision 'to talk'. Later when Loate was asked if her political views were the same before and after the Soweto Eleven trial, she replied:

> I do have political views, one stays in such a society where one cannot ignore politics . . . I would say I am aware that a black man in this country is oppressed but because I have suffered this period of 18 to 19 months in detention, that does not mean I ignore the fact that the black man is oppressed in this country. I then decided that in order to help my society I will have to be involved with its cultural objection rather than getting myself involved in politics.[16]

Loate thus both lays claim to an awareness of black oppression, that she did not 'ignore', and puts some distance between herself and liberation politics by gendering that oppression. It is 'a black man' who is oppressed. She later made this admission: 'I did not deny that I am a person who is politically minded, I am in possession of banned literature'.[17] This last statement in particular points to a certain level of involvement in political circles. To read and possess banned literature was, as Matteau-Matsha has argued, to belong to an alternative public. As Chapter 2 outlined, to acquire, to possess, to hide banned literature, and perhaps most interestingly of all, to identify as a person who does so, places Loate, however marginally, within a circle of radical readers who through their reading practices 'created a new social order'.[18]

During the trial Loate also admitted membership of AZANYU and the specific charges laid against her detailed that she had arranged for SAYRCO members from Botswana to contact the AZAPO national organiser (and one of the Soweto Eleven) Thabo Ndabeni and subsequently for two AZANYU executives, Alex Selani and Carter Seleke, to contact SAYRCO. AZANYU was described by Loate during the trial as 'a non-political organisation, it is a youth cultural movement'.[19] Loate claimed to have left membership of the organisation after her third visit to Botswana since she thought she would not have the time to dedicate herself to it once she began her studies. AZANYU was in fact established in Soweto in 1981 by the PAC as an internal youth wing that would build its underground presence and recruit military volunteers. However, it did present itself publicly as a cultural movement. It is an understudied organisation and Loate's role within it is unclear – for example, the extent to which she knew of the organisation's 'real' purpose.[20] At this moment it is worth dwelling on the intricacies of the political landscape in Soweto in the late 1970s and early 1980s, as those who had been involved in the 1976 Uprisings found various routes to maintain their political participation. Whilst many young activists who fled the country joined the ANC and the ranks of MK in exile, some joined the PAC, or continued to adhere to Black Consciousness through AZAPO. Others resisted being incorporated into any of the existing liberation organisations. Alongside Tsietsi Mashinini, Loate's co-accused Khotso Seatlholo worked in this vein to establish SAYRCO as an alternative political home for students in exile and, they hoped, back in South Africa too.[21] Loate appears on one reading of the evidence to have been involved from the very beginnings of AZANYU in creating dialogue between the organisation and SAYRCO, whilst eventually choosing to place her loyalties with Seatlholo and SAYRCO. This is perhaps evidence of what Jon Soske has called 'the internal heterogeneity and the interlacing histories of the various currents in the liberation struggle' that studies which use organisations as their primary subject and organising principle can fail to capture.[22] Organisational histories of AZANYU and SAYRCO are very recent and based on 'scant' knowledge.[23] When he began working on AZANYU, Tshepo Moloi encountered a 'reluctance, if not outright refusal, by the former members of AZANYU to be interviewed',[24] a reluctance he was able to overcome through a slow process of winning trust. Within these existing histories of AZANYU and SAYRCO, Loate's presence is barely registered. Toivo Asheeke's history of SAYRCO describes Seatlholo as 'working closely with a woman named Loate'.[25]

Recollecting the trial in an interview with Thomas Karis and Gail Gerhart in October 1989, George Bizos remembered Loate as 'a young, inexperienced, enthusiastic woman' and later as 'really a somewhat embittered and confused young woman'.[26] Gerhart questioned him about Loate's 'curious' simultaneous involvement with AZANYU and SAYRCO. It was something Bizos dismissed, stating 'I think that she was probably rejected, as sometimes happens. We have instances where people are not welcome in the Charterist movement, sometimes for good and sometimes for bad and irrational reasons, where you have to rely on who you think is an informer or who is reliable, this sort of thing can happen'.[27] For Bizos, Karis and Gerhart, who posed particular questions about the trial to him, the trial's importance centred around the refusal of certain witnesses to give testimony, not the ambiguities of Loate's story.

According to Bizos, Loate '*for no apparent reason*, took people who had come from outside and established contact with her, to Zwelakhe Sisulu' (emphasis added). Zwelakhe Sisulu, son of Walter and Albertina and thus a member of an important ANC family, was a journalist and then president of the Media Workers Association of South Africa. This meeting was perhaps not quite so random as Bizos seemed to think. We can recall one of the profiles of the Soweto Eleven published in the *Rand Daily Mail*, written by Sisulu, that appeared in Chapter 2 of this book. Loate also established contact with Thami Mazwai, another prominent Black journalist. The students and the SSRC had, during the years of the uprisings, a close relationship with journalists, particularly at *The World*. SAYRCO, Seatlholo and Loate might have reasonably thought such contact could prove useful in establishing recruiting channels for their organisation. However, according to Bizos,

> Zwelakhe for all practical purposes didn't know Loate and didn't know the people, and as would be expected, he was probably suspicious of the whole situation and turned the people away. Well, when she was detained she told them that she had taken people to Zwelakhe Sisulu and this led to Zwelakhe's detention. He, of course, would have found it most embarrassing to give evidence in a trial. And John Coker, who was for the man, Seatlholo, and I persuaded the prosecutor, who was acting quite professionally, that we don't really recquire the evidence against Sisulu to prove anything and it really isn't your function to put Sisulu up for the purposes of getting him a term of imprisonment. The

> court is really used for the proving or disproving of offenses. He accepted the argument and he caused Zwelakhe to be released. But he was a decent prosecutor, and I think the moral pressure that we put on him was successful; but it doesn't always happen that way. That provision is used to punish people.[28]

Evidently in Bizos's recollections those who did not speak during the trial of Loate and Seatlholo were deemed the more important story, than that of Loate the 'confused' young woman. This echoed the contemporary valorisation of silence in the courtroom that surrounded the trial. In his 2007 autobiography, Bizos again emphasised the story of Zwelakhe Sisulu's involvement as the most significant aspect of the trial. In this later version of events, he described SAYRCO as 'a little known' and 'off-beat organisation'.[29] He wrote of Loate that, she 'had no defence on the merits. Not only did some of her friends give evidence against her, she was also found in possession of incriminating evidence. The case against her was watertight'.[30] Given this, it is even more extraordinary that Loate gave testimony and did not stay silent, as her co-accused did, and as the Soweto Eleven had done a few years earlier.

Silent witnesses

The silence of one of the potential state witnesses who refused to testify against Loate reveals further the ways in which age and gender mediated the contradictory pressures to talk and to remain silent. The defence team suggested that the witness known as 'Freedom' (Innocentia Nonkululeko Mazibuko) was the female activist who was recruiting young Sowetans to join the underground and that the prosecution was framing Loate instead, as punishment for her mother's legal action against the police. Freedom was a friend of both Loate and Seatlholo and was, according to Loate, the one who told her that Seatlholo was returning to South Africa and asked her to help arrange accommodation for him. There was much discussion during the trial over the events of a particular afternoon in June 1981 following the 1976 commemoration service that year which the two young women attended together. The service was broken up by the police firing teargas into Regina Mundi Church and Loate and Freedom gathered, along with other young people, in a nearby house to escape the fumes. It was there that Loate took the names of some of those young people, she said at the instruction of Freedom for an unknown purpose. She claimed to have assumed it was for a drama project. The prosecution alleged Loate was knowingly recruiting volunteers for military training and a few of the young men on the list testified in support of this. After the testimony of several other witnesses who had described Freedom as a member of SAYRCO who was involved in recruiting members, she herself appeared in court on 8 February. The *Rand Daily Mail* reporter, John Majapelo described her appearance:

> A state witness broke down and cried in the witness box after refusing to take the oath and give evidence against two Soweto student leaders . . . She told the magistrate that she was afraid to give evidence . . . she would rather go to jail than give evidence for the state.[31]

On February 13 she was jailed along with six others for their refusal to testify. In sentencing her to twelve months, the magistrate described her as 'an actress of rare ability', a comment that was also reported in the press.[32] He suggested 'I think she is able to turn on and off the tears and everything that accompanies that at will and that she can do so most convincingly', although he also claimed that 'I do not hold that against her'.[33] The magistrate's comments, and the press reporting of them, point to perceptions of women as capable of emotional manipulation. In contrast, the reporting of male silence was accompanied by statements of principle. Five of those sentenced for refusal to testify that day were men and given eighteen months each. They included Thami Mazwai, at the time the former news editor of *The Sowetan* newspaper, Carter Seleke, the National President of AZANYU, Alex Selani AZANYU's National Chairman and Thabo Ndabeni, AZAPO National Organiser.[34] Mazwai's lawyer explained his position: 'if Mazwai gave evidence he would lose his credibility as a journalist in the black community'.[35] Where Freedom was 'afraid' to give evidence, Mazwai's silence was presented as based on principle and integrity. The five men, who were subsequently referred to by the press as 'the silent five' (Freedom disappeared from their story) lodged an appeal against their sentences at which their stance was reiterated: 'they were prisoners of conscience who fully realised they would go to jail if their appeal failed. They chose to face prison rather than give evidence'.[36] Their appeal was unsuccessful.

In a further twist to Freedom's story, before her twelve-month sentence for silence was completed, she was put on trial herself, answering terrorism charges alongside three young men. All four were eventually acquitted because of 'unreliable and unsatisfactory evidence' from state witnesses.[37] This was a case that was noted as a victory for the 'voices of protest' undermining the apartheid justice system in *Sechaba*.[38] In her own trial, Freedom denied all charges against her including membership of SAYRCO, and she told the court that what had been a 'very good relationship' with the security police during her initial detention, had 'changed drastically' when she refused to testify at Loate's trial. Thereafter she was threatened with imprisonment and that she would be 'turned into a jailbird' with repeated arrests until she left South Africa.[39] For individuals to circle through the system as detainee, witness, trialist and back again was not unusual. As Micheal Lobban has argued, from the perspective of the security services 'it did not strictly matter who was the defendant and who the state witness' in any given trial since 'both could be neutralised: the one gaoled, the other discredited' through the process.[40] Freedom's pathway through the system echoed that of Loate herself. I do not know what happened to Freedom once she was acquitted. The fragments we have of her story are even more sparse than those we have for Loate.

'Well, I decided to talk'[41]

In defence of Loate, Bizos focused upon the demeanour and authenticity of those testifying against her to establish that they spoke to save themselves and to satisfy their interrogators. Some were quick to bring up their circumstances. One young woman pleaded with Bizos, 'I am asking the council for defence to exercise some patience with me because my mind is full of the cell'.[42] For most, this involved suggesting that they were motivated by fear of their interrogators and that they had a prepared statement from which they could not deviate. The cross-examination of Dipalesa Catherine Thamae was extensive and saw Bizos using this strategy, asking questions outside of the witness's original testimony and using these answers to sow confusion until Thamae protested: 'I thought I was to give the evidence according to what I was questioned about'.[43] Later when she forgot a previous answer to a repeated question and Bizos asked why, she admitted: 'This is because I have been sitting for a very long time and I have forgotten my statement'. Bizos retorted, 'You know that is perhaps the truest statement you have ever made, you are there really to repeat word for word what was in your statement irrespective of what the truth may be'.[44]

Bizos's tone was often slightly mocking. There was a distinct lack of sympathy for these young witnesses in contrast to the Soweto Eleven trial during which state witnesses, Loate included, had been cross-examined quite gently. At one point, Bizos pushed Thamae to clarify her memory of a meeting between herself and Loate, in which Loate allegedly revealed her role as a SAYRCO recruiter: 'Can you explain to His Worship why she would have exposed herself in this way by making herself guilty, if what you have told is true, by using the very words of the Internal Security Act and the Terrorism Act in a hurried conversation?'[45]

As the cross-examination went on Bizos commented: 'You are now speaking so softly that even the interpreter standing next to you has difficulty in hearing you'.[46] Fear, tiredness, a slow dawning that she had not delivered her statement as expected, all we can presume weighed on this witness and caused her voice to falter. In their final set of exchanges Bizos returned again to Thamae's account of meeting with Loate on the latter's return from Botswana when she alleged that she tried to recruit her for SAYRCO. He commented on her 'very feminine interest' in Loate's clothing over her reading material and pushed her on the credibility of herself and Loate as military recruits: 'did you ever ask accused number one but what is this business of military training for women?'[47] This question ignored the reality, that as early as the late 1960s the ANC in exile was developing 'a rich visual rhetoric' of militarised motherhood and drawing women into the ranks of MK.[48] Military training was more unusual for young women but not unheard of. Thandi Modise, one of the most famous female MK guerrillas of the 1976 generation, recalled that after crossing the border to Botswana amongst a group of twenty young people, girls and boys, she was the only young woman who chose to undertake military training: 'girls were encouraged to continue their schooling' in exile.[49] However, by 1980 Radio Freedom had a half-hour programme called 'Dawn Breaks: The Voice of the ANC Women's Section' which aimed specifically to recruit women for MK, as the ANC became more interested in mobilising women within South Africa.[50] In her interviews with Soweto COSAS activists of the 1980s, Emily Bridger has noted that young women were much less likely to be recruited into the underground or offered MK training but this was not necessarily due to a lack of interest amongst young women.[51] During the trial, comments like those of Bizos on 'this business of military training for women', deliberately evoked normative gender boundaries around militarised political action in a way that placed Thamae and Loate firmly as outsiders to politics and rendered young women's speech about politics as unreliable. Loate's identity as a beauty queen was drawn into these arguments.

Beauty queens and the struggle

An important plank of the defence case for Masabata Loate was to present her identity and status as a beauty queen as incompatible with that of a political activist. However, the relationship between popular consumer cultures and the politics of the liberation struggle was one of proximity and tension. Focusing on this point of friction we can see that though Loate's trial conveyed the beauty queen and the activist as inhabiting separate worlds, this was a porous and performative separation that had to be actively made and maintained. Loate's straddling of both worlds was at the centre of her ambiguity and her vulnerability.

Beauty contests were to be found in the South African print media from as early as the 1920s and 1930s and were ubiquitous from the 1960s, especially within publications aimed at a 'township' audience.[52] Nakedi Ribane, herself a former model during the late 1970s and early 1980s, has recalled that during the peak time of beauty pageants: 'You had Miss Hospitals, Miss Football Associations, Miss Soccer Teams, Miss Brigades, Miss Lucky Legs, Miss Creams and Soaps, Miss Different Months, Miss Boxing Associations, Miss Teenagers, three different Miss South Africas, Miss Mini Universe . . . I am Telling you! Miss Anything-you-can-think-of!'[53] Pin-up cover girls and beauty queen models were central to the successful commercialised black urbanity that magazines like *Drum* emerged from and sold back to their readers.[54] According to Van Kessel, a 'feasibility survey' conducted in 1991 to explore the possibility of continuing production of the politically radical community newspaper *Grassroots* 'found that people were interested in reading a local paper, but it should feature a picture of the Spring Queen rather than Nelson Mandela'.[55] As well as making for diverting pictures, these beauty contests were presented through newspapers and magazines as serious propositions for young black women looking for professional and financial success, albeit always only in the years *before* marriage when such a career would end. This was a model of femininity and success that was highly visible in townships. The very spaces which were the site of political mobilisation were very often also used for staging such contests. For example, in February 1977 successive articles in the *Rand Daily Mail* show that DH Williams Hall in Katlehang, Germiston was used to stage a beauty contest amongst residents of a local female hostel and just days later was the venue for the launch of the Katlehang Students Representative Council.[56]

The politics of beauty contests were pliable. Beauty queens could be read as examples of Black urban modernity that contradicted apartheid ideology and could carry cultural pride. As Sisonke Msimang has noted when discussing the beauty and glamour of Winnie Madikizela-Mandela, 'the subject of beauty and desirability in African women has always been about more than lines and proportions and whatever is in the eye of the beholder – it has been about whether or not Africans are fully human'.[57] An aesthetic of Black pride was central to Black Consciousness philosophy. So, as Dan Magaziner discusses, the Black Renaissance Convention in late 1974 organised by Catholic priest and 'Black Consciousness fellow traveller' Smangaliso Mkhatshwa had a planned beauty contest to crown 'Miss Black'.[58] The awkward collision of Black as a political philosophy with the objectifying gaze of a beauty contest was made clear in Mkhatshwa's announcement that: 'Those who may have lighter skins than the "darkies" ought not to be disheartened. The criterion will not be the *colour* of the skin, because our definition of *Black* does not refer primarily to the colour of the skin!'[59] Beauty contests could also be tied, perhaps more neatly, into conservative political agendas. In May of 1977 DH Williams Hall was host to another competition, this time the 'first-ever Transkei National Independence Party (Transvaal region) beauty contest'.[60] TNIP was the ruling party of the Transkei, the first of the 'homelands' given independence in 1976, and closely aligned with the State's Bantustan project. This beauty contest sat alongside various other trappings and performances of nationality that were supposed to bolster the legitimacy of these pseudo-nations: flags, parliaments and anthems.

The few studies which have begun to focus on those who participated in beauty contests demonstrate that their politics could be multivalent. Peter Alegi has argued with reference to the Spring Queen contest, held annually amongst garment workers in the Cape Flats from 1980, that whilst beginning as an initiative of factory managers to distract and control their workforce, over time the women participating transformed the contest into 'a partially autonomous space for proletarian women's sociability and power'.[61] Ribane recalls that those contests that were established as Black-led ventures in a predominantly white world, such as the Miss Soweto contest, which first ran in 1979, 'received a lot of support from the public and sponsors'.[62] However, Ribane also notes that commercial beauty contests and modelling brought young black women into a predominantly white world of capitalist consumption which carried dangers. As she puts it, describing models in the 1980s 'even though their communities were proud of them, they were under constant suspicion of going out with white men'.[63]

This association with commercial culture made beauty queens an oppositional figure within youth politics as it developed over the course of the 1970s and 1980s. That such women might be a particular target for youth activism was signalled early on in the resurgence of protest following 16 June 1976. In the run-up to Christmas 1976, as the students sought to impose a ban on celebrations and focus on mourning within township communities, Pat Malagas, a well-known fashion model, was attacked by 'youths' and her home set on fire after accusations that she was an informer. She told the *Cape Times* she was accused of 'mixing with white people'.[64] Similarly in July 1977 the *Rand Daily Mail* reported an incident involving 'Bubbles' Mpondo, a beauty queen and model who was in a controversial relationship with an Afrikaans bodybuilder, Jannie Beetge. It was a relationship that saw them arrested several times, as contravening the Immorality Act but also brought Bubbles into conflict with 'the youth':

> Three beauty queens on their way to a contest at the Diepkloof Hotel had a narrow escape when youths began stoning their cars along a funeral route yesterday. Bubbles Mpondo who was involved in a much publicised romance with white muscleman Jannie Beetge, and two of her friends were involved . . . one of the people in the car behind Bubbles' vehicle said 'I heard a shout from the students who stopped Bubbles, "here's the sell-out to the black community"'. When youths started hurling stones at the beauty queens car it took off at high speed . . . Meanwhile at the hall where Bubbles was competing, the crowd was hostile to her. There were jeers and boos. She was not placed in the competition.

Faith 'Bubbles' Mpondo's story is a tragic one – she was eventually murdered in 1978 by Jannie Beetge, who shot her before he killed himself, reportedly due to her infidelity.[65] Such attacks, accusations and killings reiterated ideas of women as carriers of culture and as representative of the health and 'purity' of 'the community', be that national, or as in the report above, a racial one. These are ideas that have been foundational to nationalist projects in many contexts. They also point to the ways in which anti-apartheid politics was entangled with the control and disciplining of women's bodies and relationships, particularly sexual relationships, in a context in which, as Beetge's murder of Mpondo shows, this was violently controlled across South African society.

Xaba has argued that 'struggle masculinity' was characterised by promiscuity and violent aggression towards women.[66] These tendencies were particularly prevalent in youth political movements and the 'comrade' culture of the mid-1980s. According to Clive Glaser, a township gang culture in which young men viewed sexual control over young women's bodies as an extension of territorial control over streets, found its way into the practice of youth anti-apartheid politics during the mid-1980s, at the height of the 'politics of confrontation'.[67] He and Peter Delius have suggested that 'schools could offer girls some protection from marauding youth gangs, and the form of masculinity that emerged among the leadership of these schools was less physically aggressive and more respectful of women's sexual choices'.[68] However, even in the 'more respectful' student political organisations young women were often perceived as in need of control and/or protection. For example, Seekings, Van Kessel and Neihaus have all put forward the argument that COSAS campaigns against teachers' sexual harassment of female students were primarily motivated by young men's resentment and jealousy over such relationships.[69] Certainly the framing of young women by COSAS's predominantly male leadership was that of a constituency that needed paternalistic guiding and protecting. A COSAS document titled 'Women's Participation for Victory' set out the leadership's stance upon mobilising female school students. It began, 'in our last Congress a resolution was taken to ensure an all-sided attempt to draw our women fold into our organisation'.[70] It highlighted the position of young women within the family: 'female students are drawn into domestic work at an early age'.[71] Consequently their 'performance in school work is pathetic' and:

> What they become interested in, in their school life is nothing else but events in our schools, your 'Miss Orlando High' and 'Miss Freshette' etc. It is this situation which forces students to strike a 'deal' with your wielding teachers. A love affair notes that you will sometimes be exempted from punishment. This is why in our schools we have sugar daddies and sweet sixties!!! . . . It is therefore our task to organise our women students into COSAS, to mobilise them against the problems they experience. We must educate them about the nature of our society.[72]

For COSAS the beauty contest was a symbol for all that was wrong with young women's social position and behaviours from which they consequently needed to be saved and educated. No wonder then that Bridger, and others, have noted that the figure of the female comrade of the 1980s that emerges through contemporary oral history is a 'tomboy'; 'to be accepted into [comrade] culture and to take up arms alongside young men, female comrades needed to erase outward signs of femininity and adopt many of the defining characteristics of struggle masculinity'.[73]

However, commercial beauty culture was not separate from the worlds of anti-apartheid politics. Bridger heard one story of politicisation from a former COSAS comrade that demonstrates this. Florence recalled seeing a photograph of Winnie Madikizela-Mandela in a newspaper in 1977: 'she was so pretty . . . and I started reading because then, the only pictures that we'd seen in the newspapers, they were adverts . . . and the prettiest ladies would be advertising Lux, the soaps, the creams'.[74] Florence asked her family about Madikezela-Mandela but 'nobody could explain because they are scared of explaining'. Florence recalled this silence as triggering a curiosity about politics that led to her involvement. That the world of politics offered the possibilities of its own sort of glamour comes across from Bridger's interviewees, both male and female. Another female comrade remembered the excitement of attending their first political rally: 'there were these people who were taking videos, taking photos and things. And being young I didn't know what that was. For my side I was just happy that I will appear on newspaper . . . If you appear on the

Soweto News, the local newspaper, you were like, a big thing'.[75] As Bridger notes, far from being superficial, such motivations show participation in politics as a social and cultural phenomenon and as containing 'the pleasure of agency'.[76]

Masabata Loate, as she emerges from her trial, appears to transgress the boundary between beauty queen and activist, standing in direct contradiction to the 'tomboy' comrade.[77] At her trial she confirmed that she had been able to earn money whilst still at school by entering and winning beauty contests.[78] Loate's prize as Miss Mainstay in 1979 was reported as R200 – by 1981 the winner of the same title received R35,000.[79] The contest was run by a Mrs Christine Mguni and in the first few years was linked to the Soweto Cultural Club (for the Advancement of African People). In the year that Loate won, the proceeds raised by the contest were to be put towards the establishment of 'a recreational and cultural club house'.[80] One of the opportunities on offer to the winner of this contest was to present the trophy at the final of the National Professional Soccer League's (NPSL) Mainstay Cup. The Mainstay Cup was a project of the Football Council of South Africa, which had been formed in October of 1976. Peter Alegi and Chris Bolsman have described the formation of the Council as part of the National Party government's plans to 'ameliorate apartheid', situating the Council alongside policies like the 'independence' being offered to the Bantustans, and the legalisation of black trade unions.[81] The Football Council pursued the establishment of mixed elite sport, not the non-racial sport being advocated for by, for example, the anti-apartheid South African Council on Sport (SACOS). Its politics were conservative. The Mainstay League cup was launched in 1977, but the competition was not completed in this first year, hampered by 'ineffective management, high travel costs, spectator violence, police intervention, and the constraints of residential segregation' that restricted fans' freedom of movement in attending games.[82] Mainstay was a brand of South African sugar cane spirit, owned by the Stellenbosch Farmer's Winery. The Winery put R70,000 into the Cup in its first year, a figure that went up to R100,000 in 1978.[83] That year the competition was completed, with Wits University winning the final against the Kaiser Chiefs. The motives for the Winery were articulated clearly by its public relations officer: 'There's a definite spin-off from black consumers. They identify your product with the game and support it. Football's helped us retain our market share in a competitive industry'.[84] The politics of Miss Mainstay, whilst not overtly pro-apartheid were certainly not identifiably anti-apartheid either. Loate was also a runner-up in the Miss Sona (Soweto Netball Association) contest in 1979, entered the more famous Miss Soweto contest in June of 1980, and was a winner of a regional heat of Miss Benson and Hedges in October that same year.[85]

Loate's trial testimony suggests that she sought to keep her life as a beauty queen separate from whatever political involvement she had – even whilst she spoke about it. She told the court of her relief that the police were unable to find her diary when they searched her house. Asked by Bizos what was in the diary she replied: 'I took part in beauty contests and I had the addresses of boyfriends, other contestants, my ambitions, all such things'. Bizos continued, 'Did you use to write down your innermost feelings?' 'That is correct', Loate responded.[86] Whether these 'innermost feelings' bore any resemblance to 'My Thoughts, which were explored in Chapter 2, and this was the reason for Loate's relief, we cannot know, but given her experience of exposure and scrutiny during the trial of the Soweto Eleven we can understand why she was glad the diary was not found. What little evidence we have from inside the world of beauty contests points to a desire to maintain an apolitical stance from contest organisers, sponsors and modelling agencies. Nikedi Ribane comments on one fellow beauty queen, Miss Africa South of 1974, Evelyn Williams: she 'had a somewhat tougher time in the industry as she was outspoken and something of an activist. She was always speaking out about racism in beauty pageants and the modelling arena. It was particularly tough for her because she was a lone voice at the time!'[87] Ribane herself recalls getting a reputation as 'always being angry'. Her own career in modelling began when she was expelled from Ngoye University where she had been studying law, and was detained for a year, for her part in student protests on campus in 1976.[88] In both the worlds that Loate inhabited – that of politics and beauty contests – young women's silence was preferred.

Conclusions

In his very lengthy judgement on Loate and Seatlholo's trial, the magistrate argued that Loate's claim to be socially involved with Seatlholo but unaware and ignorant (or kept ignorant) of his political activities, was simply not credible, especially given that she admitted she still held the political beliefs that had first led her to be involved in the activities of the SSRC in 1976. He concluded:

> dan is dit na my mening bo alle twyfel duidelik dat wat Beskuldigde Nr. 1 hier probeer vermag is om die beste van twee wêrelde te hê of soos die Engelse spreekwoord dit baie korrek en gepas uitdruk, sy wil haar

> koek beide hê en dit eet. Ek dink nie dat dit moontlik is dat sy hierdie dinge in dieselfde asem oortuigend kan beweer nie. [it is, in my opinion, beyond any doubt that what Accused No 1 is trying here, is to have the best of two worlds, or as the English proverb expresses it very appropriately, she wants to have her cake and eat it. I don't think it's possible that she can claim these things in the same breath].[89]

Was Loate deeply involved politically, or was she simply in the wrong place, at the wrong time, because of her romantic entanglements and because she and her mother had the audacity to try to protect her from police brutality? The ambiguity of her status was either her strength as a political operator, or her vulnerability as a scapegoat, or both. She was certainly not a helpless victim. We can say with certainty that it was her refusal to submit to the discipline of the Apartheid State, either as an activist, or a defiant detainee, that resulted in the trial.

This young woman continually evades clear historical judgement and, to my mind, therein lies her importance to struggle history. She is a 'mediated and unstable subject' of the kind that social historians of the liberation struggle have not always acknowledged.[90] Shrouded by assumptions based on gender and youth, it is, even now, hard to hear her clearly. Her life, as we know it, was marked by moments of silence and speech in which she pushed against the expectations of talking and not talking and she suffered for speaking when she should not. The gendered entanglement of speech *as* struggle were such that, even when they were compelled to speak, young women were at particular risk of being punished by both state security forces and comrades as women who talked too much. On her release from prison in 1986, Loate was murdered, apparently for speaking up against the use of violence against suspected informers. Chapter 4 considers this final act of silencing in Loate's life, and what it might mean, that it is through her death that she is remembered in the post-apartheid present.

Notes

1. *Rand Daily Mail* (Township Edition), 3 August 1979, 16, and 28 August 1979, 26.

2. *State vs. Mary Masabate Loatse and others*, case: 41/4115/81 Magistrates Court, District of Johannesburg; WHP: AD2021: SAIRR Security Trials 1958–82. Boxes 19–20. Digitised trial proceedings, accessed July 2019, http://www.historicalpapers.wits.ac.za/?inventory/U/collections&c=AD2021/R/.

3. Jacob Dlamini, *Askari: A Story of Collaboration and Betrayal in the Anti-Apartheid Struggle* (Johannesburg: Jacana Media, 2014), 171, 70.

4. South African Institute of Race Relations, 'Survey of Race Relations in South Africa 1982' (Pietermaritzburg, 1982), 235–6.

5. L. O., 'Voices of Protest', *Sechaba: Official Organ of the African National Congress South Africa*, 1983, 12.

6. O., 'Voices of Protest', 13.

7. Riedwaan Moosage, 'A Prose of Ambivalence: Liberation Struggle Discourse on Necklacing', *Kronos* 36, no.1 (2010): 137.

8. Moosage, 'A Prose of Ambivalence'.

9. Nyasha Karimakwenda, 'Safe to Violate: The Role of Gender in the Necklacing of Women During the South African People's War (1985–1990)', *Journal of Southern African Studies* 45, no. 3 (4 May 2019): 561, https://doi.org/10.1080/03057070.2019.1642646.

10. Mike Louw, 'Charges laid before a Johannesburg Regional Magistrate', *Rand Daily Mail*, 2 December 1981.

11. Seatlholo was described as such by Gail Gerhart. As quoted in Tiovo Tukongeni Paul Wilson Asheeke, *Arming Black Consciousness: The Azanian Black Nationalist Tradition and South Africa's Armed Struggle*, African Studies Series (Cambridge: Cambridge University Press, 2023), 149. For more on Khotso Seatlholo and his own absence from the historiography of the struggle see endnote 14 to the introduction of this book; Lynn Schuster who interviewed Seatlholo for her book on the Mashinini family, described him as 'an intense, articulate youth'. Lynn Schuster, *A Burning Hunger: One Family's Struggle Against Apartheid* (Athens, OH: Ohio University Press, 2006), 42.

12. *State vs. M.M. Loatse et al.*, Proceedings, 496–8.

13. *State vs. M.M. Loatse et al.*, Proceedings, 526.

14. *State vs. M.M. Loatse et al.*, Proceedings, 529.

15. *State vs. M.M. Loatse et al.*, Proceedings, 550.

16. *State vs. M.M. Loatse et al.*, Proceedings, 600–601.

17. *State vs. M.M. Loatse et al.*, Proceedings, 610.

18. Rachel Matteau-Matsha, '"I Read What I Like": Politics of Reading and Reading Politics in Apartheid South Africa', *Transformation: Critical Perspectives on Southern Africa* 83, no. 1 (27 December 2013): 57.

19. *State vs. M.M. Loatse et al.*, Proceedings, 528.

20. For one exception see: Tshepo Moloi, 'Youth Politics: The Political Role of AZANYU in the Struggle for Liberation: The Case of AZANYU Tembisa Branch, 1980s to 1996', Research Report, University of the Witwatersrand, 2005. https://core.ac.uk/download/pdf/39664456.pdf.

21. The fullest account of SAYRCO in existing literature is within Asheeke, *Arming Black Consciousness*, 3–4 and 146–59.

22. Jon Soske, 'Open Secrets, Off the Record: Audience, Intimate Knowledge, and the Crisis of the Post-Apartheid State', *Historical Reflections/ Réflexions Historiques* 38, no. 2 (2012): 60, https://doi.org/10.3167/hrrh.2012.380205.

23. As described in Asheeke, *Arming Black Consciousness*, 4.

24. Tshepo Moloi, '"Oral Testimonies by Former Members of the Azanian National Youth Unity (AZANYU): The Sayable and Unsayable in an Oral History Interview"', in *Oral History: Representing the Hidden, the Untold and the Veiled'. Proceedings of the Fifth and Sixth Annual National Oral History Conference*. (Pretoria: Research Institute for Theology and Religion, University of South Africa, 2013), 1, https://www.sahistory.org.za/sites/default/files/archive-files/ohasa_2008-2008-22-05-2013_oral_history_conference_papers.pdf.

25. Asheeke, *Arming Black Consciousness*, 158.

26. 'Memoirs of George Bizos, as related to Thomas Karis and Gail Gerhart' (New York, 1989), 97–8, accessed 14 March 2023, https://www.jstor.org/stable/al.sff.document.gerhart0018.

27. 'Memoirs of George Bizos', 97–8. 'Charterist' refers to those organisations that declared their allegiance to the Freedom Charter and were therefore aligned with the African National Congress.

28. 'Memoirs of George Bizos', 97.

29. George Bizos, *Odyssey to Freedom* (Johannesburg: Penguin Random House South Africa, 2011), 438.

30. Bizos, *Odyssey to Freedom*, 439.

31. 'Terror trial witness won't give evidence', *Rand Daily Mail*, Township edition, 9 February 1982.

32. *State vs. M.M. Loatse et al.*, Proceedings, 265.

33. *State vs. M.M. Loatse et al.*, Proceedings, 266.

34. Moloi notes that after this moment AZANYU moved underground. See: Moloi, 'Youth Politics', 106.

35. *Rand Daily Mail*, 'Six Jailed for Court Silence', 13 February 1982.

36. 'Six Jailed for Court Silence'.

37. O., 'Voices of Protest', 12–14.

38. O., 'Voices of Protest'.

39. Evidence of Accused Number Four, *State vs. Stanley Radebe, Ephraim Mthuthuzele Madalane, Ernest Lebana Mohakala and Innocentia Nonkululeka Mazibuko*, Case: SH 635/82, Regional Court for the Regional Division of the Southern Transvaal (Kempton Park), WHP AD2021: SAIRR Security Trials 1958–82. Boxes 40–44, Proceedings, 2505–6, Digitised Trial Proceedings, accessed July 2019, http://www.historicalpapers.wits.ac.za/?inventory/U/collections&c=AD2021/R/.

40. Lobban, *White Man's Justice*, 13.

41. *State vs. Stanley Radebe et al.*, Proceedings, 425.

42. *State vs. Stanley Radebe et al.*, Proceedings, 470.

43. *State vs. Stanley Radebe et al.*, Proceedings, 155.

44. *State vs. Stanley Radebe et al..*, Proceedings, 169.

45. *State vs. Stanley Radebe et al.*, Proceedings, 162.

46. *State vs. Stanley Radebe et al.*, Proceedings, 181.

47. *State vs. Stanley Radebe et al.*, Proceedings, 206–8.

48. Kim Miller notes that a 1968 *Sechaba* front cover that featured a woman simultaneously carrying a spear and a baby appeared at a time when women members of MK were excluded from active combat and 'forbidden' from falling pregnant, in some cases through the forcible fitting of IUDs. Kim Miller, 'Moms with Guns: Women's Political Agency in Anti-Apartheid Visual Culture', *African Arts* 42, no. 2 (2009): 68 and 74, http://www.jstor.org/stable/20626992; For more on the experience of motherhood and exile see: Rachel Sandwell, '"Love I Cannot Begin to Explain": The Politics of Reproduction in the ANC in Exile, 1976–1990', *Journal of Southern African Studies* 41, no. 1 (2 January 2015): 63–81, https://doi.org/10.1080/03057070.2015.991988.

49. Thami Mkhwanazi, 'Thandi Modise: The Knitting-Needles Guerilla', *Weekly Mail*, March 23–30, 1989.

50. Kameron Hurley, 'The Voice of Women? The ANC and the Rhetoric of Women 's Resistance, 1976–1989' (MA thesis, Durban, University of Natal, 2003), 8.

51. Emily Bridger, *Young Women against Apartheid: Gender, Youth and South Africa's Liberation Struggle* (Woodbridge, Suffolk; Rochester, NY: James Currey, 2021), 142–3.

52. Lynn M. Thomas, 'The Modern Girl and Racial Respectability in 1930s South Africa', *The Journal of African History* 47, no. 3 (2006): 461–90, https://doi.org/10.1017/S0021853706002131. Lynn M. Thomas, *Beneath the Surface: A Transnational History of Skin Lighteners* (New York: Duke University Press, 2020).

53. Nakedi Ribane, *Beauty: A Black Perspective* (Scottsville: University of KwaZulu-Natal Press, 2006), 45.

54. Rachel Johnson, '"The Girl About Town": Discussions of Modernity and Female Youth in Drum Magazine, 1951–1970', *Social Dynamics* 35, no. 1 (1 March 2009): 36–50, https://doi.org/10.1080/02533950802666899.

55. Ineke Van Kessel, *Beyond Our Wildest Dreams: The United Democratic Front and the Transformation of South Africa* (Charlottesville: University Press of Virginia, 2000), 280; for a discussion of the long-running beauty contest amongst garment workers in the Western Cape, The Spring Queen see: Siona O'Connell, 'The Spring Queen Pageant and the Postapartheid Archive', *Safundi* 18, no. 2 (3 April 2017): 168–76, https://doi.org/10.1080/17533171.2016.1272239; Peter Alegi, 'Rewriting Patriarchal Scripts: Women, Labor, and Popular Culture in South African Clothing Industry Beauty Contests, 1970s–2005', *Journal of Social History* 42, no. 1 (2008): 31–56, https://doi.org/10.1353/jsh.0.0070.

56. *Rand Daily Mail*, 11 February 1977; *Rand Daily Mail*, 14 February 1977.

57. Sisonke Msimang, 'Winnie Mandela (1936–2018)', 4 June 2016, https://jacobinmag.com/2018/04/winnie-mandela-south-africa-obituary-anc.

58. Daniel Magaziner, *The Law and the Prophets: Black Consciousness in South Africa, 1968–1977* (Athens, OH: Ohio University Press, 2010), 57.

59. Magaziner, *The Law and the Prophets*, 58.

60. *Rand Daily Mail*, 30 May 1977.

61. Alegi, 'Rewriting Patriarchal Scripts'.

62. Ribane, *Beauty*, 93.

63. Ribane, *Beauty*, 89.

64. *Cape Times*, 24 December 1976.

65. Nakedi Ribane discusses the case of Bubbles Mpondo in Ribane, *Beauty*, 56.

66. Thokozani Xaba, 'Masculinity and Its Malcontents: The Confrontation Between "Struggle Masculinity" and "Post-Struggle Masculinity" (1990–1997)', in *Changing Men in Southern Africa*, ed. Robert Morrell (London: Zed Books, 2001), 116.

67. Clive Glaser, *Bo Tsotsi: The Youth Gangs of Soweto, 1935–1976* (Oxford: James Currey, 2000), 189.

68. Peter Delius and Clive Glaser, 'Sexual Socialisation in South Africa: A Historical Perspective'. *African Studies* 61, no. 1 (2002): 48, https://doi.org/10.1080/00020180220140064.

69. Jeremy Seekings, 'Gender Ideology and Township Politics in the 1980s', *Agenda* 10 (1991): 77–85, https://doi.org/10.1080/10130950.1991.9675138; Kessel, *Beyond Our Wildest Dreams*; Isak Niehaus, 'Towards a Dubious Liberation: Masculinity, Sexuality and Power in South African Lowveld Schools, 1953–1999', *Journal of Southern African Studies* 26, no. 3 (September 2000): 387–407, https://doi.org/10.1080/713683581.

70. 'Women's Participation for Victory', undated, SAHA: AC2457: N3.2 COSAS.

71. 'Women's Participation for Victory'.

72. 'Women's Participation for Victory'.

73. Emily Bridger, 'Soweto's Female Comrades: Gender, Youth and Violence in South Africa's Township Uprisings, 1984–1990', *Journal of Southern African Studies* 44, no.4 (4 July 2018): 560, https://doi.org/10.1080/03057070.2018.1462591; See also: Janet Cherry, '"We Were Not Afraid": The Role of Women in the 1980s Township Uprising in the Eastern Cape', in *Women in South African History: They Remove Boulders and Cross Rivers*, ed. Nomboniso Gasa (Cape Town: HSRC Press, 2007), 281–314.

74. Bridger, *Young Women against Apartheid*, 48.

75. Bridger, *Young Women against Apartheid*, 59.

76. The term 'the pleasure of agency' is taken from the work of Elizabeth Jean Wood on insurgents in El Salvador. See discussion in: Bridger, *Young Women against Apartheid*, 60–61.

77. She was not the only beauty queen turned activist noted by the press: Lydia Johnstone, former Miss Africa South was arrested at a protest march in Kraaifontein in September 1976 and subsequently charged with public violence, *Cape Times*, 16 October 1976.

78. Loate mentions winning prizes of R100, R250 and a refrigerator, see *State vs. M.M. Loatse et al.*, Proceedings, 617.

79. See reports in the *Rand Daily Mail*, 1 August 1979, 15, and 3 July 1981, 14.

80. *Rand Daily Mail*, 1 August 1979, 15.

81. Peter Alegi and Chris Bolsmann, 'From Apartheid to Unity: White Capital and Black Power in the Racial Integration of South African Football, 1976–1992', *African Historical Review* 42, no. 1 (1 June 2010): 7, https://doi.org/10.1080/17532523.2010.483783.

82. Alegi and Bolsmann, 'From Apartheid to Unity', 9.

83. Alegi and Bolsmann, 'From Apartheid to Unity', 9.

84. Alegi and Bolsmann, 'From Apartheid to Unity', 9.

85. See reports in the *Rand Daily Mail*, 4 July 1979, 16; 5 June 1980, 14; 10 October 1980, 10.

86. *State vs. M.M. Loatse et al.*, Proceedings, 520.

87. Ribane, *Beauty*, 77.

88. This is discussed in the Author's Note that precedes the main text – another sign perhaps of the (self)disciplining of Ribane's voice: Ribane, *Beauty*, xiii–xv.

89. *State vs. M.M. Loatse et al.*, Judgement, 97. My thanks to Ruhan Fourie for producing a translation of the entire 148-page judgement.

90. Jenny Robinson, '(Dis)Locating Historical Narrative: Writing, Space and Gender in South African Social History', *South African Historical Journal* 30 (May 1994): 150, https://doi.org/10.1080/02582479408671788.

Chapter 4

Stories of life and death: the struggle to speak

Introduction

Masabata Loate was a young woman who spoke too much. After her appearance as a witness in the trial of the Soweto Eleven, Loate was shot in the leg; on her release in 1986 after serving half of her sentence for terrorism, she was murdered. This was an act of silencing. She apparently spoke up openly in opposition to the use of necklacing and was killed by a large group of men at a moment of heightened violence in Soweto. This is one way of interpreting her death. As this chapter will detail, there are others. Hermonie Lee has noted that within biography, or what might be more broadly termed 'life writing', 'we are all fascinated by the manner of the subject's death . . . [it] plays a part in the meaning of the life'.[1] What does Loate's death, just before her twenty-sixth birthday, tell us about her life? Of the many public stories of her death none deals with the personal loss that it must have represented for her family and friends. Masabata Loate was a daughter, granddaughter and sister. She told the court during her 1982–3 trial that her sister Paulina was her closest confidant. It was with her that she had discussed her plans to enrol at the University of Botswana to study business administration – plans which her arrest put a stop to, and which she was never able to pursue. The fact that Masabata's mother, Maria Loate, was a member of a burial society, the 'good hope society' – a detail which emerged at Masabata's trial – takes on a new poignancy after her death.[2]

Burial societies were critical in enabling the adaptations of funereal and mourning practices necessitated by life within apartheid's urban townships. Amidst the dislocations wrought by migrant labour and the pass laws that separated families and wider kinship networks, 'burial societies became surrogate families'.[3] Rebekah Lee has argued that whilst burial societies had their origins within mining compounds, as a means of ensuring migrant miners could return home after their death, by the late twentieth century African women's burial society membership was a means of 'consolidating women's position *in town*' (emphasis in original).[4] Maria Loate's membership of the 'good hope society' was mentioned during her daughter's trial because the police asserted that it was a political organisation, something Loate denied. A political organisation it almost certainly was not, but this belied the reality that burial had become highly politicised in 1970s South Africa. After 1976, funerals became sites of mobilisation, and often, when they were disrupted by security forces, moments of further loss.[5] The Soweto Uprisings wrought 'dramatic' changes in funerary practices within Soweto, by overturning the exclusion of children from participation in mourning rituals.[6] From the funeral of Hector Pieterson onwards, it was youth who led the burials of their fallen comrades with songs, slogans, dances and political eulogies.[7] Those who lost loved ones in the struggle had to negotiate the pain of personal loss alongside powerful public narratives that sought to shape the meanings of these deaths.[8] For those killed under suspicion of being an informer or collaborator there were few spaces or possibilities of public mourning for their families; instead, grief was experienced alongside a lack of community support and shame.[9]

The story of Loate's murder is harrowing. She was attacked at night by a crowd of around twenty men, from whom she escaped several times, before being stabbed to death.[10] Some reports detailed that the final assault that killed her was on her grandmother's doorstep. Maria Loate offered this summation of her daughter's life: 'that she had to die this way, after dedicating all her life to the cause of freedom and justice, is heartbreaking'.[11] This gives us some sense of personal loss, but already her life and death were contained within the framework of the struggle. Maria Loate was also quoted as explaining her daughter's death as the result of her opposition to the use of violence; Masabata 'totally abhorred the "necklace" executions taking place in the townships, and always voiced her opposition to the wanton stoning of people's cars and the burning down of their homes'.[12] In contrast Casper Venter, spokesman for the Bureau of Information, the official source of news from unrest areas under the State of Emergency, stated that 'the police don't regard this as unrest-related. It's being investigated as a crime'.[13] Amongst the most chilling details in these initial reports are the lines that describe the public nature of her death: 'family members said people in the vicinity saw the crowd kill Miss Loate, but no one went to her aid'.[14] The manner of her death remains the same in all the versions that follow. What does change are the meanings and the place within broader struggle narratives that her death is given.

There has been much more written about Masabata Loate's death than about her life. It is through her death that she appears within two of the principal post-apartheid sites for retelling the past: the Truth and Reconciliation Commission (TRC) and autobiographical memoir. Listening to Loate's silencing by tracing the circulation of stories of her death enables us to hear the effects of the sanctions on speech that existed for young women within the confrontational and polarised politics of the townships in the late 1980s. The post-apartheid afterlives of the stories of her death show us how the gendered boundaries of speech within the struggle were contested and reshaped during the transition. While Loate was silenced, women's voices, and amongst them some of her contemporaries, were being heard in new spaces and in new ways. The second half of this chapter considers the stories of three women who came to political activism during June 1976, and how, when and where it is, that their lives in the struggle have been told. Within these moments of voicing, silence remains an important part of their stories.

Speaking up

In her mother's explanation, Loate was killed because she espoused non-violence within the struggle. How and why might this have led to her death? The initial stories of Loate's death take us to the heart of speech as an increasingly violent terrain of struggle during the 1980s. One of the central aims of the States of Emergency, declared in 1985 (partial) and 1986 (national) was to halt the circulation of information. Journalists were not allowed to report on the actions of the state security forces and the only information that could be published about declared 'unrest areas' was that supplied by the Government Bureau of Information. At the same time the security forces attempted to improve their own access to information from within the struggle. The Detainee Parent's Support Committee (DPSC), an organisation established, as its name suggests, to support the parents and families of the increasing numbers of people, activists and non-activists alike that were being detained, produced a report on 'repression trends in the Transvaal area between June and September 1986'.[15] It noted that, 'what has emerged is a vast increase in the numbers of people held, especially rank and file membership, as well as an increase in the time period for which people are being held'.[16] The report goes on to make the argument that 'information coming into the DPSC office suggests' that following a concerted attack within township communities on those seen as 'collaborators' in 1984–5 the security forces were 'using the [1986] State of Emergency in an attempt to reconstruct its informer network'.[17] The report highlights testimony suggesting police attempts to coerce 'less experienced and less politicised detainees' into becoming informers and noted a rise in forced confessions,[18] finally commenting that:

> The attempt to coerce people to inform isn't only designed to get information about the democratic movement and activities in the townships. It is also designed to create divisions by sowing suspicion that detainees have agreed to inform. The State wants people to believe that there is a vast network of informers. In this way it hopes to undermine the people's confidence in their ability to build strong organisation or wage effective struggle.[19]

Speaking in 1986 was potentially extremely dangerous. A period in detention, talking as a state witness in court, connections of friendship or family: all could be grounds for suspicion. The edges of the struggle to control speech were messy and dangerous, where police surveillance and activist efforts to resist it percolated into everyday life. Jon Soske has emphasised the 'relationship between uncertainty and proximity in this period' and a 'generalised illegibility of people, of events, of ongoing developments'.[20] Within the politics of struggle speech, as in daily life in apartheid townships, there were what Karimakwenda has called 'unique precarities' that black women had to navigate.[21] Necklacing was a form of violence which varied. It often involved the placing of a burning tyre around a person's neck – hence its name – but those who were necklaced could also be killed in other ways. Such murders were ritualistic and enforced group solidarity.[22] According to the findings of the TRC, incidents of necklacing reached their peak in 1986 – the year of Loate's death.[23] Karimakwenda has argued that necklacing was a deeply gendered practice with three categories of women often targeted: women accused of appearing haughty or cheeky; women accused of not being sexually available to the comrades; and women who were attacked as proxies for men accused of collaborating who could not be found.[24] Karimakwenda examines cases of necklacing that happened. The daybooks of the DPSC, who ran advice offices taking statements from detainees and their families, show us something of the ways in which the *threat* of violence, and particularly necklacing, was employed against women whose speech or silence was deemed inappropriate.

In August 1986, Thompson Ramanala came to the DPSC to report the detention of three women, Catherine (24), Kgomotso (30) and Nomsa (24). All were unmarried and unemployed. They had been detained on 17 June 1986. This was how their story was recorded: 'According to Thompson the three [arrested] ostracised a woman friend who became friendly with a policeman. She motivated the policeman to take action. The three are accused of intending to 'necklace' the woman friend. He is thought to be one of the arresting police'.[25] The ostracising of a woman friend for getting close to a policeman was undoubtedly a politicised if not a directly political act in a township in 1986. The threat of necklacing was a fate reserved for enemies of the struggle. Arrest and detention was a fate reserved for enemies of the State. This was an incident deeply entangled with the forms of the township struggle, yet none of the women are mentioned as having political ties, a detail the DPSC was usually keen to find out. It is also a personal falling-out amongst friends and this is how it appears in the DPSC daybooks. Incidents like this hint at the multiple logics by which violence was enacted, often simultaneously.

A fear of getting caught-up in the violence of necklacing is something that pervades the stories of life in Soweto written by the journalist Nomavenda Mathiane, published during the 1980s in the magazine *Frontline*. In one story, 'Waiting for the knock on the door' published in August/September 1987, Mathiane recounts the experiences of a friend, Thoko, who some years earlier had returned home after a period in detention (she had been arrested for her participation in a street committee) and found an altered atmosphere in her home.[26] Mathiane and eventually Thoko became aware of tensions within her family and circle of friends based on a rumour that another close friend, Dimakatso and Thoko's mother, had 'betrayed her' in order to 'get at Thoko's father who adored her over all her other children'.[27] Mathiane explains what she thought lay beneath this rumour: 'Dimakatso was riding on the crest of fame being a member of the Soweto Parents Crisis Committee. It was quite obvious to me that there were certain personalities who felt jealous of her success and recognition'.[28] Thoko rejects the rumour and publicly embraces Dimakatso, thereby neutralising the danger. Yet, Mathiane wonders: 'How many people have fallen victim to such slander and been necklaced? . . . in times of necklaces who dared question people telling stories?'[29] This kind of fear of speech is omnipresent in the archives of the Emergency years.

In April of 1986, a father came to the DPSC to report the arrest of his son Ike. He described the way in which the police came to the family home, asked for Ike and started to physically beat him. His sister Rebecca intervened, telling them they should arrest him, not beat him, so they turned their sjamboks on her, forcing her to throw her nine-month old baby onto the bed to prevent the child from being hurt. The report from the father adds, 'They then said that Rebecca taught Ike all these things and that she was cheeky'.[30] Rebecca also made a separate statement on the incident:

> After they beat me up one of them who I thought was a senior came to me and said 'Ousi next time you must keep quiet because we, the police are going to necklace you', not the students because I talk too much. I asked him whether he was serious and he said he meant it.[31]

Women activists have spoken about the dangers of being read as a 'cheeky' woman by police: that there was a particular violence that such women would be subjected to when they did not conform to expectations of feminine weakness or submissiveness.[32] In the threats levelled at Rebecca Maleka in the spring of 1986 it is also clear that all forms of violence, be they state or resistance, could be called upon to discipline women who 'talked too much'. That this violence and its ever-present threat served to constrain what was sayable for young women should be no surprise. The idea that Loate might be killed for speaking up against the use of necklacing is entirely plausible in this context.

In her study of a necklace murder, the psychologist Pumla Gobodo-Madikizela offers some thoughts on the dynamics of what she terms 'speaking out' within instances of group violence. She suggests,

> A person who does not depend much on the group's approval for a favourable evaluation of his or her self-esteem could take the liberty to do something that challenges the group's perceived solidarity . . . Speaking out to voice opposition to the violence of one's group is likely to come from such a person . . . those who speak out in a crowd therefore are likely to be extraordinary people whose moral sense exceeds the needs that can only be satisfied by being associated with a particular identity.[33]

Gobodo-Madikizela offers the example of Archbishop Desmond Tutu and his intervention in an incident in 1986 in which he prevented a young woman from being necklaced. We might have Masabata Loate in our minds when she also notes that, 'people who have the courage of their convictions often sacrifice their self-preservation'.[34]

Parade of violence

The violence of Masabata Loate's death was what all the initial newspaper reports focused upon. The most graphic story appeared in the *Cape Times*, under the headline 'Anti-necklace ex-beauty queen murdered'.[35] That Loate's past as a beauty queen was recalled alongside a violent description of her death gives this report a sensationalist edge. This tone is one that Emily Bridger and Erin Hazan have identified as marking the descriptions of violence against women within media targeted at township audiences, from at least the 1930s onwards.[36] They note the frequency with which reports of rape objectify and sexualise the, mostly, unnamed women victims, with references to 'shapely' or 'curvaceous' 'dolls'.[37] Most newspaper reports did not refer to Loate as a beauty queen, emphasising instead her identity as a political activist. Beyond its headline, the *Cape Times* also detailed that Loate was a member of the Soweto Youth Congress and was killed by her 'undisciplined' comrades. This story quoted an unnamed family member who revealed she had been 'on the hit list for some time' and that she had evaded a previous attempt to find and kill her.[38] In these stories, and those told within activist publications, Masabata Loate's death was widely regarded as an example of the growing problem of *youth* violence. In a 1987 issue of *APDUSA Views*, the publication of the African People's Democratic Union of Southern Africa (APDUSA), Loate's murder was discussed in an article on youth violence, titled 'Freedom fighters or plain killers?'[39] The author describes the appearance of what they termed the 'Fake Comrades' under the States of Emergency: 'an anti-social criminal element' who 'kill in the name of the liberatory movement' but who in fact were uneducated, 'power-drunk' youth led astray by the forces of reaction.[40] APDUSA represented an older political generation who viewed the heightened township mobilisation of young people in the 1980s largely through what Seekings has termed the 'apocalyptic stereotype' of youth.[41] In this analysis Loate's murder is listed as an example of a 'political murder' and evidence of the wayward actions of the youth. The report detailed simply that, 'Miss Masabata Loate was brutally hacked to death by some 20 youths'.[42]

Moving further away from her death in time and location, the violence it was seen to represent became less specific. Where Loate's death was reported in the international media it came as part of a commentary on the scale of violence engulfing South Africa. *Time* magazine concluded a report which included her death: 'the appalling parade of violence is one more sign of a people in agony'.[43] Very often Loate's death was listed as part of a catalogue of incidents; its power to shock came from its position as one of many. United Press International news noted that her death 'pushed the death toll to 326' since the countrywide State of Emergency had been introduced on 12 June.[44] In all these stories her past was foreshortened. For APDUSA she became 'a well-known freedom fighter'. In *Time* she was 'a leader of the 1976 anti-apartheid student uprising'. In the *Financial Mail* she was described as 'one of the best-known student activists during the Soweto 1976 upheavals'.[45] What all these recollections of her role in the events of 1976 do, is suggest that her death signalled something wider had changed within the liberation struggle – that there was a distance that had opened up between 1976 and 1986 in South Africa. The subtext was that the violence of 1986 was destroying the 1976 generation. None of the reports recalled her appearance as a state witness in 1979.

Breaking silence

In 1989 another version of Loate's death would be told, the only one to be recounted by a woman.

Nomavenda Mathiane, whose story 'Waiting for the knock on the door' we considered above, worked as a journalist during the 1970s and 1980s, writing for the *Voice* before it was closed. She was one of the founders of *Frontline*, a magazine that began publishing in 1978 and has been later self-described as 'one of the zillion home-made efforts to contribute to the ending of South Africa's apartheid system'.[46] The magazine situated itself as 'on the side of change, very substantial change. But it does not set out to speak only to those who also want change, it wants to speak as well to those who don't'.[47] *Frontline* was a part of a wider proliferation of voices and spaces within South African print media during the 1980s, often described as the growth of an 'alternative press'.[48] These were spaces that were nevertheless significantly structured by hierarchies of race and gender. Mathiane testified at the TRC's special hearing on the media, in Johannesburg in 1997, and there described the ways in which black female journalists were offered even fewer opportunities than their male counterparts within the white-dominated world of South African print journalism.[49] Black women reporters were 'hired to report on domestic affairs such as cookery pages, fashion, health, horoscopes, Dear Dolly columns and church businesses. When major stories in these bits broke out, who would be sent to cover that? Male journalists'.[50] Mathiane's reporting for *Frontline* challenged this in more than one respect. Dennis Beckett, editor of *Frontline*, described Mathiane as 'unconventional', since she would 'say out loud the things everybody else only mumbles quietly among consenting adults in private'.[51] Mathiane is credited with breaking the story of the Mandela United Football Club (MUFC) and Winnie Mandela's alleged involvement in violence and murder, which occurred amidst the call to render the townships 'ungovernable' in the mid-to-late 1980s.[52] This was a time when, as Hassim puts it, 'the ethical line between violence that enables the end of repression and violence that exists in and of itself was constantly breached'.[53] The MUFC was, it seems, formed as a social club for youths that morphed into the personal bodyguard of Winnie Mandela and became involved in the brutal disciplining of those perceived as state informers. Mathiane wrote the first article discussing the MUFC's behaviour within Soweto. According to Jon Soske, the MUFC tried to necklace her for this but 'she was protected by her neighbours'.[54]

In a story titled, 'Living a lie, reaping a whirlwind', published in March 1989, Mathiane recounts the story of the killing of 'Masabatha' as she calls her, as one of the many incidents in which the MUFC were involved, and which bred an air of impunity around their activities:

> Another story began back in the days of street committees, when Masabatha was killed near her house on a Friday afternoon by a gang of 21 males, who were openly seen and known to many residents. Masabatha was a model and beauty queen who had also been an activist who had served five years. She was prominent in street committee work and it is widely believed that her committee had aroused jealousies among others who had believed that her street was meant to be part of their territory.
>
> Sometime later a youth, Tholi Kenneth Dlamini, son of a well-known Phomolong family, defected from the comrades he had been associating with to return to school and his previous hobby of ballroom dancing. His brain was blown out a la Al Capone style with a Makaroff machine gun. People around Orlando West were distressed about this whilst also saying 'while we feel sorry at his death, we have not forgotten that he was one of those who killed Masabatha'.[55]

There is an echo in this story. The suggestion that Dlamini was killed for leaving the comrades to return to 'his previous hobby of ballroom dancing' recalls Sarah Makepe's tale, heard during the trial of the Soweto Eleven, of being elected to the SSRC only to resign, in order to 'go back to my old procedure that is being an actress'.[56] Also, Loate's own claims that, after that trial, and her time in detention, she sought to 'help my society' by being 'involved in its cultural objection'.[57] In Dlamini's death we can see the struggle's increasingly jealous and violent claim to the bodies of young men, not just young women. We also hear that Loate's death was remembered.

This is the least sensational of the stories of Loate's demise and connects it to patterns of violence that engulfed Soweto during the Emergency years. In contrast to the futility that would later be attributed to her death, Mathiane argues that 'Masabatha' and others she recalls 'did not die in vain'. She goes on:

> They may have taught us lessons: that when we live lies, we reap whirlwinds, and if there is to be order in our land, it will come when the leaders can be called to account by the ordinary decent people who are currently battling to preserve their morality through the disasters which white rule produces.[58]

This version of Loate's death was published at a time in which women's voices and writing were 'emergent' within reconfigured national public discourses both within and beyond South African borders.[59] Writing in 1990, a feminist literary critic, Cherry Clayton, looked back on the previous decade and argued that 'the cultural transformation which is achieved in black (South African) women's writing in the eighties is the transformation of the black woman as object, interpreted only in the liberal gaze, and previously obscured by guilt or projection, and sheer ignorance, into a speaking subject'.[60] This was a 'process of self-announcement, the breaking of the silence of a very marginalised group'.[61] Included in Clayton's survey was the anthology *Women in South Africa: From the Heart*, as well as the work of Miriam Tlali, the first black woman to publish a novel in South Africa, and Ellen Kuzwayo, author of *Call Me Woman*. The publishers of the works she discusses are instructive. *Women in South Africa: From the Heart* was published by Seriti Sa Sechaba, the first book to come from this Black feminist South African publishing house that operated briefly in the late 1980s. Miriam Tlali was published by Ravan Press, a white-owned radical oppositional publisher of literature (poetry and prose) as well as historical and socio-political research, founded in 1971. Ellen Kuzwayo's autobiography was produced by The Women's Press, a London-based feminist publisher. Taken together, these various publishing outlets show the contours of the spaces in which women's voices were being heard in the 1980s – spaces opened up by both internal South African political struggles and wider global social movements. That Loate died at the moment these spaces opened shows us the uneven and partial nature of the opportunity to voice. There is also an irony here: at a time when 'emergent' voices were expanding the boundaries of what was sayable in the struggle for women, a series of silences and new prohibitions on speech were beginning to surround Winnie Mandela – and by extension

Masabata Loate and her death. Staying with these emergent voices we can hear that they too contain silences within them, which are audible when we consider the ways and means by which women's voices came to be heard at this time.

Emergent voices

Gillian Whitlock has argued that Ellen Kuzwayo's *Call Me Woman* was 'germinal . . . both chronologically and conceptually' to a 'threshold moment' for black women's autobiographical writing in South Africa.[62] This threshold was constituted by the links between that writing and 'woman centred campaigns in the anti-apartheid movement both within and outside South Africa and the beginnings of the reform movement'.[63] In 1985 *Call Me Woman* was the first of a number of black South African women's autobiographies published by The Women's Press. In 1981 a South African political exile Ros de Lanerolle had taken over as managing director of The Women's Press and for the next ten years 'presided over an important reorientation of the press' identity towards writing from the developing world'.[64] In this, it has been argued, The Women's Press was responding to criticisms that black women (along with working class and lesbian women) were being marginalised within global feminist politics.[65] As part of this project The Women's Press aimed to adopt a more collaborative approach to commissioning, editing and marketing.[66] The editor of *Call Me Woman*, Marsaili Cameron, has said of the multiple rewrites that produced the final manuscript that editing had been, in this case, a 'truly shared project'.[67] In this attention to the dynamics of editing, part of the aim was presumably to avoid the experience of publication becoming one of appropriation that was particularly acute when publishing marginalised authors. By the mid-1980s Miriam Tlali had already begun to speak of her relationship with her publisher Ravan Press with 'anguished accusations of excision and betrayal'.[68]

After *Call Me Woman*, The Women's Press went on to publish another four autobiographies written by black South African women: Caesarina Kona Makhoere's *No Child's Play* (1988), Emma Mashinini's *Strikes Have Followed Me All My Life* (1989) and Sindiwe Magona's two volumes *To My Children's Children* (1991) and *Forced to Grow* (1992). The archives of The Women's Press frustratingly do not contain papers on *Call Me Woman* but its influence is evident in the decision making on, and promotion of, subsequent autobiographies of South Africa women that the press published. For example, the editorial file for Cesarina Kona Makohere's *No Child's Play* contains the initial impression that the manuscript had 'All the potential Ellen K's book had, and more'.[69] It was de Lanerolle's aim to encourage new writers through its promotion of black women's writing: 'our readers are our writers and our writers are our readers!'[70] In considering the pathways by which Ellen Kuzwayo, Emma Mashinini, Cesarina Kona Makohere and Sindiwe Magona came to be published by The Women's Press, the link was not quite this straightforward. As Lewis, Whitlock and others have all noted, Kuzwayo's book was written directly to readers 'outside the closed world of apartheid' and to a certain extent this is also the case with Makohere and Mashinini.[71] However, Dorothy Driver suggests that 'when Emma Mashinini came out of detention, thinking, "Now, what is left of me?", she read Kuzwayo's *Call Me Woman* and felt inspired to write her own story.'[72]

Reading the acknowledgements offered by all of these authors, together with the correspondence in The Women's Press archives, points to the significance of the personal connections of white feminist South African exiles, as well as those of the more official links between the ANC in exile and the anti-apartheid movement to the publication of Kuzwayo, Mashinini and Makohere. Magona's publication by The Women's Press came about through links with internal oppositional publishers, in her case David Philip, and thus represents a coming together of what were, during the 1980s, relatively separate circuits of publication. For Mashinini and Kuzwayo the link to The Women's Press came through the film-maker Elizabeth Wolpert – the networks of white South African (feminist) exiles. For Makohere this network was active too through the artist Judy Seidman but also the ANC's arts and culture department in the person of Barbara Masakela. While The Women's Press was publishing black South African women's stories internationally there were initiatives from within the broad-based politics of the UDF and its affiliates to create spaces specifically for women within the internal liberation movement. The cultural wings of the resurgent black trade unions in the 1980s were important spaces for the cultural participation of women and led to the organisation of several women's initiatives, some of which were explicitly feminist. In 1987 *Agenda*, a feminist academic/activist journal was established by a collective of women in Durban. Its name signified its stated desire to put 'women's issues on the agenda'. The same year Dinah Lefakane left the Black publishing collective Skotaville to found Seriti Sa Sechaba, a Black feminist publishing house.

Feminism as an ideology, or feminist as a label of self-identification, had an uncomfortable relationship with the anti-apartheid movement.[73] It was conceived by many anti-apartheid activists, male and female alike, as a challenge to women's loyalty to the primacy of the national struggle. It was also considered by many black South African women as a white, Western, and imperialist framework for defining women and their issues that was irrelevant, or at worst damaging, to the analysis of black women's societal position and the advancement of their interests. Shireen Hassim has described this as a situation in which feminism as a set of ideas was 'dismissed rather than engaged' by the leadership of the national liberation struggle.[74] She goes on to suggest however, that this was not the same thing as 'the absence of feminist consciousness and analysis among the rank and file of the movement'.[75] There were South Africans who increasingly in the late 1980s and early 1990s began organising as feminists.[76] These projects, like *Agenda*, were marked by hierarchies of race and class and were ongoing spaces of dynamic engagement over what, and who, women were, and what they wanted.

It was in response to critiques of the racial exclusions of feminism that The Women's Press looked for black women writers to publish. What kind of inclusion did this represent? Whilst the publication of black women writers by The Women's Press was intended to offer a rejoinder to the whiteness of feminism, this was not an aim explicitly articulated through the marketing of these books. One particular edit of the suggested cover for Sindiwe Magona's second book, a volume of short stories, *Living, Loving and Lying Awake at Night* saw the Press step back from a framing of a black South African woman's stories as a challenge to white voices, although this was clearly a challenge that Magona herself had in mind:

> 'My great hope for African Women is that one day they will come into their own. (We suffer from a triple burden, that of class, race and sex. Writers in South Africa are white, therefore the history that will be handed down to our children is a white reality. Even when it is supposed to be a black reality it is through a white perspective.) That is why I chose to write.' Sindiwe Magona.
>
> 'Jacqui: Blurb Cut! – see above'.[77]

Everything contained within the brackets above was cut, excising the racial context for Magona's choice to write. Nor were the autobiographies published by The Women's Press framed as 'breaking silences'. Indeed, by the 1990s they were being seen by various reviewers, particularly those reading as feminists, as *maintaining* significant silences around gendered discrimination or abuse within the liberation struggle. In a 1991 review Dorothy Driver argued that 'Mashinini pulls back. Like Kuzwayo before her, she specifically refuses to "expose dirty linen in public", a metaphor which neatly conflates women's domestic and social roles (women in charge of the laundry, women in charge of the secrets of male abuse)'.[78] Writing a little later, Whitlock argued that 'Kuzwayo's silence could be read as strategic but she apparently desires to speak'.[79] There were tensions between a desire for speaking subjects and the boundaries of the sayable within struggle speech. The experience that all the South African women's autobiographies published by The Women's Press in the 1980s *did* speak about, was detention and imprisonment.

Speaking of detention

As Daniel Roux has identified, prison has enjoyed a 'privileged status' within the autobiographical life writings of anti-apartheid activists,[80] containing as it does 'an encounter between the life narrative of the individual and the more collective voicing of dissent against an oppressive regime'.[81] Whilst, and perhaps because, this genre of writing was dominated by heterosexual black men, prison was an important 'authorising' experience for marginal figures within anti-apartheid activism. Paul Gready has argued detention gave white anti-apartheid activists the authority to write.[82] It was in detention awaiting trial for treason that Simon Nkoli came out as a gay man to his UDF comrades. In doing so he challenged prevailing ideas of 'homosexuality being separate from political identity'.[83] Whilst he never wrote an autobiography, his prison letters have been an important means by which he has been incorporated into narratives of the anti-apartheid struggle.[84] For black women in the 1980s, imprisonment was a gendered struggle experience about which women could speak. It enabled women to speak as confrontational subjects. It also tells us about the difficulties of speaking about anything else. During the 1980s a publication like *A Woman's Place Is in The Struggle Not Behind Bars* shows how detention and imprisonment was an experience through which women activists' stories became accessible to an international audience. *A Woman's Place* was jointly produced by the DPSC and FEDTRAW and, after being banned in South Africa, was picked up and published in the USA by The Africa Fund and the United Nations Centre Against Apartheid.[85] The publication contains various stories and testimonies, both direct and indirect, of women active within the liberation struggle and their experiences of detention, torture and imprisonment. There are sections titled, 'The Women Speak: Being Detained' and 'The Women Speak: A Mother's Cry'. Another section tells the story of Deborah Josephine Marakalla under the heading: 'A Voice Silenced'. Marakalla was a member of the Tembisa DPSC and worked at the Tembisa Black Sash Advice Office. She was apparently detained for this work; a family member commented: 'They didn't like what she was doing at the advice office. They don't like anyone who speaks for themselves. They think locking them up will keep them quiet'.[86]

Writing an introduction to the USA edition, Jennifer Davis described the publication as a kind of direct line to South African women: 'Through its pages it broadcasts the voices of South African women themselves, providing a graphic description of the pain and the power of their struggle. Here is the voice that Pretoria has unsuccessfully tried to quell'.[87] It was through detention and imprisonment that these stories were collected.

Pointing to the way detention enabled the speech of women as activists is not to diminish the difficulties of talking about imprisonment, and the physical and mental abuse suffered by women prisoners. As Emma Mashinini recalled, the trauma of detention was a story she struggled to tell:

> For a long time I didn't talk to my family about my prison experiences. Neither Dudu nor Molly knew about many of the things I had been through until they saw me in *Mama I'm Crying*, telling of the terrible time I could not remember Dudu's name. They kept saying, 'Mom, you never told us about this.' They didn't even know about my forgetting Dudu's name. This book will serve as a living memory of the evil of the apartheid regime. It is an opportunity for me to speak to my children.[88]

In addition to the challenge of articulating trauma verbally, Mashinini's framing of her book as 'an opportunity for me to speak to my children' is an indication of the barriers women faced when speaking about the struggle within their families. Motsemme has suggested that silence within the activist family was about protection; not knowing something meant not being able to talk under pressure. The silence of mothers could also be about trying to assert normality in the face of the intrusions of apartheid repression.[89] For Mashinini a space outside the everyday, first the film interview and then the writing of the book, allowed her to communicate what she had otherwise been unable to say.

Makhoere in 'mid-air'

Caesarina Kona Makhoere was twenty-one in 1976, living and studying in Mamelodi (north-east of Pretoria). During the Soweto Uprisings she sought to undertake military training. Despite being arrested before she could leave the country, she was, like many others during 1976–7, tried and imprisoned for the attempt.[90] On her release, after serving five years, she became involved in the Black Sash advice offices. Makhoere's autobiography is strikingly reminiscent of the testimonies of former detainees in the DPSC daybooks – it is, like these testimonies, an instance of speaking out. Makhoere documents her imprisonment as a series of confrontations with the prison authorities in which she can assert her sense of self-worth, which was violently assaulted in detention. Prison writing is often read, as Carli Coetzee has noted, as a 'mode of resistance testimony' and 'an attempt at controlling (through narrative) the hostile prison environment'.[91] That Makhoere's was a 'prison story' was used by The Women's Press as a selling point of the narrative. The press release issued on the book's publication described 'this amazing account of a woman's battle to retain her fighting spirit and her pride, even when helpless in the hands of a powerful enemy' as 'destined to become a classic of prison literature'.[92] This was a framing picked up by all the initial reviews of the book. The Women's Press linked the promotion of the book to events and campaigns around political prisoners, particularly the International Defence and Aid Fund's (IDAF) campaign on children in detention.[93]

In their May 1996 submission to the TRC, Beth Goldblatt and Sheila Meintjes argued that 'where women were abused in the [ANC] camps, this needs to be acknowledged and condemned by those involved'.[94] They wrote that:

> We were unsuccessful in our attempts to speak to women about their experiences in the camps. In an interview with Caesarina Kona Makhoere she expressed an unwillingness to speak about the camps but intimated that her experience had been terrible. She said, 'At least in prison I knew I was in the enemy camp'.

The retrospective clarity of Makhoere's prison experience, reiterated here in contrast to her experience of MK camps is, I think, a clue as to the tight focus of her autobiography on her period of detention.

At the stage of publication at which The Women's Press commissioned readers' reports, various silences within Makhoere's text were picked up on, and to an extent endorsed. Her experience within ANC camps was not one of them. One reviewer described by de Lanerolle as 'a very experienced English editor, who is well read but does not . . . know South Africa' who 'represent[ed] the reader we'd hope to reach with the book' noted that the account of Makhoere's imprisonment was set 'mid-air'.[95] She went on, 'I think that most readers would like to know rather more about the author of this remarkable work than they do at present'. In particular, the reviewer wanted more on Makhoere's family relationships:

> Several episodes cry out to be written . . . one example is the rather disappointing description of her first visit in over 2 years from her mother. She fails to describe her mother or the visit . . . she also suddenly mentions her son! . . .
>
> . . . her FATHER, the black policeman, this rather startling information is treated very matter of factly. Given the present attitude in South Africa towards black collaboration, Caesarine [*sic*] needs to write more on this subject – both in relation to her own political evolution (she hints at this) and also in relation to her family's position in the community.[96]

In contrast the 'silence' around Makhoere's torture in prison was judged 'a very powerful one'. In sending the reports on to Barbara Masekela and Makhoere, Ros de Lanerolle herself commented: 'some of the information required is more personal, and Caesarina and you will have to decide what you feel is appropriate. I had rather hoped that she would decide to tell the full story of how/why she was imprisoned . . . is this possible, or is it not?'[97] The published version of *No Child's Play* does include the story of Makhoere's arrest, and her father's role in this, and some explanation of her family life and relationships, but relatively brief – only six pages of the book focus on her life before her period of imprisonment. Her trial, which the same reviewer said 'begged to be described more fully', is not discussed in detail, beyond describing her father's reaction.

No Child's Play 'sold very well' but was not published separately in the United States or Canada as had been expected. By 1993, when Makhoere wrote to The Women's Press about the possibility of a reprint, their enquiries as to the possible market in South Africa met with this response from David Phillip publishers: 'No Childs' Play. Difficult to project large sales unless Caesarina is prepared to assist in some form of promotion. Subject matter something many South Africans are wanting to forget – we're finding it increasingly difficult to sell back list of similar titles'.[98] Makhoere's tight focus on her period of detention thus marked it as of a particular moment and her story was no longer guaranteed an audience less than a decade later, despite the emphasis on voices and testimony that the TRC would bring.

From repression to expression

A particular onus upon women to speak up about the past, for the future, was embedded at the beginnings of South Africa's transition to democracy. The year 1990 saw, in February, the unbanning of the liberation organisations and, in May, the ANC's statement on the emancipation of women in South Africa. Together, these two public statements marked a new climate for, and indeed called for, the voicing of the political concerns of women. The 'emancipation of women' urged, mandated and demanded women themselves take the initiative in leading a national debate on a Charter of Women's Rights, 'so that in their own voice women define the issues'.[99] Such an initiative, the statement claimed, would be 'a major agency for stimulating women to break the silence imposed on them'. Exactly who had imposed this silence on women was left unsaid. The framing of women's stories of struggle as 'breaking a silence' or 'speaking up/out' is ubiquitous from the 1990s onwards across a range of spaces. What work does this framework do in placing women's stories within broader national narratives of becoming? The critiques that emerged during this period make clear that black women's struggles to claim voice were formed in pushing back against men's control over narratives of the liberation struggle *and* elite, mostly white, women's control over women's stories. This was a control, firstly over the spaces within which black women could speak, and secondly, of white women's virtual monopoly as analysts of the meaning of black women's stories. In talking back to these two interlocutors, women's speech often focused on gendered and racialised oppressions separately. Stories of Masabata Loate's life and death are only glimpsed during this moment of opening.

Within the internal discussions of the newly unbanned liberation organisations the call for women's voices included criticisms of the masculinity of liberation organisations. In a number of spaces, especially *Horizon*, the magazine of the re-launched African National Congress Youth League (ANCYL) the position of young women within the national liberation struggle was articulated explicitly, by young women. In the early summer of 1991 *Horizon* included an article titled 'Isolating Sexism'. It began: 'The ANC Youth League is strongly committed to fighting sexism. It is committed to affirmative action to ensure that women are able to take their rightful place as equals in the organisation. But we still have a long way to go'.[100] Five women members of the ANCYL Johannesburg branch were invited to speak about their experiences. The comments made by the young women, only identified by their first names as Mpho, Ayesha, Zandi, Hazel and Fikile were frank and damning. For example: 'Ayesha: Some men think that because we *say* we are fighting sexism, sexist practices don't exist in the organisation'; 'Zandi: What makes me angry is when guys *say* that women must be liberated, but they don't even bring their girlfriends to meetings. Sometimes they even have other girlfriends in the meetings!'; 'Hazel: And men *say* "you don't discuss anything important in your meetings. All you do is *gossip* and drink tea"'; 'Fikile: They think that they must push women to take leadership positions . . . They don't realise it's because women don't have the necessary skills or confidence'; 'Mpho: It's always the women who do the cleaning and catering' (emphases added).[101] It is also clear from their comments that these were not just issues that they faced in the past. Hazel told one anecdote that suggested attitudes had hardened following the unbanning: 'The other day I was talking to a male comrade. I told him that if my husband 'jolled' [cheated], I would 'jol' too. The comrade's reply was, 'Mm, it's because the new South Africa is coming that *women are saying such things*'. (emphasis added)'[102] The centrality of speech in almost all of these comments is striking. Permission or ability to speak, and political and personal freedoms were intertwined. Also apparent is the treachery of speech. Men can say one thing and do another. The final comment on the enabling atmosphere of the new South Africa contains the idea of women's speech as disruptive, conditional and momentary, reminding us that a certain degree of 'backlash' was present even at this moment of 'opening doors'.[103] Indeed, as Helen Moffett, Shireen Hassim and others have argued, the nature of the processes by which women won political rights within the post-apartheid settlement created a strong disjuncture between a public sphere that accorded women full citizenship, and a private sphere in which many were, and are, subordinated and controlled by sexual violence.[104]

The early 1990s also saw the vocalising of tensions amongst South African women as they began mobilising to meet the opportunities of the political transition. These tensions erupted into outright confrontation between women at various academic/activist conferences organised in the early 1990s. As Emily Cooper-Hockey has explored, these conflicts over the racial hierarchies within women-led and feminist projects like *Agenda* were captured and re-circulated through those very spaces. Accounts by various participants at the Women and Gender in Southern Africa conference held at the University of Natal in 1991, and the Women in Africa and the African Diaspora conference held in Nigeria in July 1992, were published in *Agenda* as competing responses to the conference. In the latter case this took the form of a debate between individuals who came down on different sides of the argument over the participation of white women in a conference on, and in the view of the African-American delegation, what should have been a conference *for*, (Black) African women. As Cooper-Hockey puts it: '*Agenda* . . . provided an arena for the translation of heated debates over race, access to knowledge and representation'.[105]

Following on from the immediate transition period, Njabulo Ndebele described the public hearings of the TRC's Human Rights Violation committee as 'confirmation of the movement of our society from repression to expression'.[106] He went on: 'Where in the past the state attempted to compel the oppressed to deny the testimony of their own experience, today that experience is one of the essential conditions for the emergence of a new national consciousness'.[107] The TRC hearings that began in 1996, however, revealed that women's silences were loud and insistent. After five weeks of public hearings it became apparent to some of those watching and participating that whilst the majority of the witnesses who came before the commission were women, they were not testifying to human rights violations they had suffered personally but were instead talking largely about the suffering of (usually male) relatives or friends.[108] In March 1996 the Centre for Applied Legal Studies at the University of the Witwatersrand held a workshop entitled 'Gender and the Truth and Reconciliation Commission'. From this workshop there emerged an official submission to the TRC on the importance of integrating a gendered approach to South Africa's past into the Commission's work. The submission argued that the TRC was not doing enough to solicit women's own stories of oppression when they came to testify.[109] It was argued that with improved questioning, statement takers could uncover women's stories, and that in closed women's hearings, testimonies would be given.[110] In all of this there was a particular concern that women's experiences of sexual violence at the hands of the State and liberation movements had not been heard.

In response the TRC re-trained statement takers to ask more 'probing questions', the human rights violations protocol was modified to include the reminder to women to 'tell us what happened to yourself if you were the victim of a gross human rights abuse', and in June of 1996 the women's special hearings were instituted.[111] Further along in the process of the Human Rights Violation hearings the TRC came to a similar realisation as to the lack of 'youth' voices that were being heard. In this the Commission was guided by the principles of the United Nations Convention on the Rights of the Child (CRC), which the South African government had signed in 1995.[112] In light of the CRC's instruction of 'honouring the voice of children', the TRC decided to give children and youth 'the opportunity to express their feelings and relate their experiences as part of the national process of healing'.[113] Four children and youth special hearings were held in 1997. As Fiona Ross argues however, these measures assumed 'testimony would follow naturally' should the conditions in the hearings be right. What they did not consider was that the reasons for the silences in women's or youth's speech may have lain outside of the immediate space of the hearings.[114]

Ross has argued that following the changes made to the TRC's processes of statement taking and the institution of special women's hearings, 'sexual violence was represented in the hearings and in public discourse as a defining feature of women's experiences of gross violation of human rights'.[115] As Meg Samuelson puts it, 'woman's story' and the story of sexual violence became conflated.[116] Women's silences around experiences of sexual violence are not unique to South Africa, and, as the archives of the DPSC make clear, had a long history. The DPSC themselves acknowledged, in ways similar to the TRC, their problems with getting women to testify to instances of sexual assault by security officials whilst being held in detention. The DPSC prefaced one statement it did receive with the following: 'Sexual assault and rape of women in detention is known to be a common occurrence. It is extremely difficult to get statements from women on their release. Women are sometimes told that if they tell anyone they will be re-detained, even killed'.[117] Yet, we can also hear through the TRC the ways in which women negotiated this conflation and maintained long-held silences. Thenjiwe Mtintso appeared as the first witness at the Johannesburg Women's hearing on 28 July 1997 and explained that she herself chose to maintain her silences:

> The logic, the politics, everything was very clear, Chairperson, but the emotion was not clear. There was that conflict. Even as I tried to draft the other day when your statement-taker came to me, I tried to fill those forms and I said: can I face the consequences? The consequences which I could not imagine had happened, Chairperson because they are known to me.
>
> What I know is that I have sat for years, I have built an armour around that pain. I have nursed that pain, I have owned that pain. I seem to refuse to move away from that pain. I seem to gain strength from the fact that it is my pain.
>
> The women today have gone beyond that stage that I'm still fighting to get beyond.[118]

For Mtintso it was silence not speech that was a source of her strength and even subjectivity itself. Mtintso reminds us of the emotive intensity of silence itself. She presents her decision to maintain certain silences as an emotional one. For other women, most famously Winnie Madikizela-Mandela, silence appears to have been a political decision – if it is possible to make this distinction. Madikizela-Mandela refused to speak about the accusations levelled against her in connection with the MUFC, before the TRC, in what Ntombizikhona Valela has called 'silence as self-censorship', as an 'intellectual tool of resistance'.[119] Shireen Hassim argues that in the 1990s '[Madikizela-Mandela] chose silence and refusal, and justified these in the language of radical refusal, of questioning the very terms of the TRC and the post-Apartheid State'.[120] The TRC should then lead us to problematise any straightforward understanding of the ending of apartheid bringing about the end of restrictions on women's speech and make clear that women might chose to maintain their silences for both personal and political reasons.

Just over a decade after Loate was killed, a new telling of her death surfaced at the hearings of the TRC's Human Rights Violation committee. It was one in which her death was told, in passing. The following exchange is from a transcript of the 1997 TRC Special Hearings into the MUFC in which a one-time member of the club, Lerothodi Andrew Ikaneng, was questioned by Piers Pigou, a member of the TRC's investigating team:

> **MR PIGOU:** Thank you Chair. Mr Ikaneng, I just want to go back to the context of the formation of the football club and ask you whether you agree or disagree with what I put forward to you. Do you recall the death of a Masabata Luate [*sic*], the sister of Wilson Sebuwane who was also known as Magojo? Was the death of this woman – did this result in tension and fighting within SAYCO [*sic*], the Soweto Youth Congress Movement of which I believe you were a member at the time?
>
> **MR IKANENG:** Yes, I do remember.
>
> **MR PIGOU:** And was it as a result of this fight that the football club came together, that there was a decision to bring people together and find some activities for these people to undertake and that a decision was taken at a meeting that you would play football?
>
> **MR IKANENG:** Yes, that is true.[121]

Commissioner Dr Randera later summarised this particular 'foundation story' for the MUFC, which was one which emphasised its origins as a conflict resolution but omitted the cause of the conflict:

> . . . there's a situation where there's a clash between SOYCO and other young people and out of this Mrs Madikizela-Mandela intervenes, tries to get people together, opens her house and her office up because she's a social worker and people are allowed to go and stay in the back of her house and there's a football club that plays football, okay?[122]

In the TRC's final report the story was further pared down: 'In late 1986 [Winnie Madikizela-Mandela] was instrumental in the resolution of an internal conflict within the Orlando West branch of the Soweto Youth Congress, which resulted in the formation of the MUFC'.[123] Loate's death thus appeared briefly on the stage of the retelling of the nation's history, only to disappear in the final analysis, displaced by the narrative of another woman, Winnie Madikizela-Mandela. A story that was, itself, about the maintenance of silence.

Lists of death

Within the post-apartheid boom in autobiographical writing, Loate's death has been retold again. There is a brief account of her demise in Rian Malan's best-selling memoir of his life as a journalist, *My Traitor's Heart*.[124] In 2003 Loate was included in an online AZAPO list of Black Consciousness Movement Heroes and Heroines 'who died in the fight against Boer oppression'.[125] Her death was recalled by Andile Mngxitama in 2004 as a 'brutal necklacing' which 'devastated' Khotso Seatlholo, her co-accused in her 1982 trial.[126] This is perhaps the clearest expression of the emotional impact of her death. According to Mngxitama, Seatlholo also spoke out against the necklacing of collaborators on his own release from prison in 1990. There still appears to be confusion over her political affiliation. Whilst AZAPO claims Loate as one of its own, Mngxitama recalls her as active within the UDF at the time of her death. What does it mean for Loate to be in so many lists of death? For her own demise to always be a part of a catalogue of horrors and for its specificity to be largely forgotten or confused?

For Rian Malan, Loate's death is one of those that he wants to 'pound' into his reader's brain. Her death comes in the memoir at the moment of Malan's dissolution, when he is 'sick' of South Africa and has no certainty to hold onto anymore. It comes after an oft-quoted passage in which Malan addresses his reader: 'Am I upsetting you, my friend? Good. Do you want to argue? . . . Let's open my bulging files of tales of ordinary murder. You choose your weapons and I'll choose mine, and we'll annihilate the certainties in one another's brains'.[127] The second 'ordinary murder' Malan relates in this 'frenzied catalogue' is that of Loate.[128]

> We're in Orlando West Soweto, outside the home of the lovely Masabata Loate, a beauty queen in a more light-hearted era. She's what the Western press would call an anti-apartheid activist. She's just spent five years locked in prison for agitating for the downfall of the apartheid state. She expected to be welcomed home as a heroine, but her politics are out of fashion these days. Here she comes now, running for her life, with a pack of rival 'anti-apartheid activists' on her heels. She falls, is stabbed, rises and runs on again, screaming for help. She

> pounds on the doors of neighbours, but they're too scared to let her in. She goes down for the last time on her grandmother's doorstep, where she's hacked to pieces with pangas.[129]

In Malan's story she is the 'lovely Masabata Loate'. Not only does she belong, as a beauty queen, to a 'more light-hearted era' but her politics are 'out of fashion'. There is a hint in these details that Malan regards Loate as somehow not serious enough, certainly not violent enough, for politics in 1986. Malan withholds his own description of her; she is 'what the Western press would call an anti-apartheid activist' killed by a 'rival pack' of 'anti-apartheid activists'. Malan's use of quotation marks seems to suggest that these labels are not meaningful or at least do not convey the truth of these relationships.

Malan's work was as controversial as it was successful. *My Traitor's Heart* has been described by Osinubi as 'an abusive narrative' in which Malan 'deliberately and systematically performs violence on his readers'.[130] Whilst many have construed Malan's 'melodramatic performance of his guilty white self' as ultimately victim blaming, Osinubi more generously argues that 'the diverse forms of violence enacted through and upon narrative articulate the complex coming to terms with the discursive formations unleashed by apartheid's cultures of violence'.[131] Another reviewer writing in 1991 put it like this: 'In South Africa at present, there are some words one does not mention in polite conversation. VAT, negotiation, Winnie Mandela, violence, negotiation, and Rian Malan'.[132] *My Traitor's Heart* provoked 'an outcry of scorn, admiration, brutal dismissal and silent envy'.[133] That Loate's death made it into South African public discourse in connection with two of these words that should not be spoken – Winnie Mandela and Rian Malan – is indicative of the uncomfortable space her life and death occupied. Masabata Loate was silenced but not quite forgotten – her death has been seen to speak for itself although quite what it says is unclear. In death, as in life, she was at the boundaries of what was sayable.

'The documentary history of the youth by the youth'[134]

The 'proliferation of life histories at a dizzying rate' within post-apartheid South African public discourse has had gendered dimensions.[135] Elaine Unterhalter's count of autobiographies written by participants within the anti-apartheid liberation struggle puts the number published between 1948 and 1999 at sixty-six.[136] Of these, forty-two were written by men, with African women authoring only nine. Another study, this time of biographies since 1990, notes that of 225 works of political biography the authors identified, only nine biographies focused on women anti-apartheid activists who were not also activists' spouses.[137] Biographies or autobiographies of the 1976 generation have also been rare. Of the Soweto Eleven only Sibongile Mkhabela née Mthembu has written a full-length autobiography. In 2001 Sibongile Mkhabela published an autobiography with Skotaville Press, the Black publishing collective with its roots in the cultural politics of the 1980s. Mkhabela's story is framed as that of a woman and of youth. The quote above describing the book as 'the beginning of the documentary history of the youth by the youth', comes from a letter written by Dan Sechaba Montisisi – former President of the SSRC and one of the Soweto Eleven, that is printed at the back of Mkhabela's text.[138] The subtitle of the book is 'Remembering 16 June 1976'. Yet Mkhabela also marks the text as a woman's narrative. The title, *Open Earth, Black Roses* refers to the book's final chapter, which is written as a tribute to her mother's sister, whom she called Mawe, who raised her after her own mother's death. The 'open earth' is that of the grave of Mawe, and Ma before her, and the 'black roses', are Mkhabela herself, her sisters and her daughters. Recalling the women's autobiographies of the 1980s, the book is framed as a conversation between generations.

The strange clarity of imprisonment is revisited in *Open Earth, Black Roses* but for Mkhabela the contrast is with the township politics of the 1980s. She describes her arrival in prison after being sentenced for sedition:

> As I walked into the prison, following a stern wardress, there had been shouts of 'Amandla! Comrade!' from women behind closed doors. I felt at home. Home was now a strange world, because at that moment I did not think of home as being in the outside world, but thought of the time I had spent at John Vorster Square, the police station that had claimed many lives and forced detainees to unite.[139]

Mkhabela recalls herself as having been 'protected' in the all-female prison environment from the increasingly acrimonious struggles between liberation organisations that marked the politics of confrontation in the mid-1980s.[140] At this point remembering Loate's fate reminds us of the menace which lies behind Mkhabela's description of herself lying awake at night fearing 'a knock on the door' from UDF aligned comrades (after her marriage to Ishmael Mkhabela, a member of AZAPO, in 1981 she was considered to 'belong' to Black Consciousness). As in Nomavenda Mathiane's story, 'the knock on the door' which usually referred to the arrival of security forces, is inverted and it is Mkhabela's 'own comrades' that she is afraid of: 'I had no position on the matter. I was pregnant and a mother of a three year old who lived in fear. I had not developed the means or the will to fight my own comrades who had become dangerous'.[141] It is in this context that she comments on the detention of her husband:

> Ironically, the 12 June 1986 State of Emergency almost provided some relief to the families of activists and leaders for a short time. While Ish was in prison that year, I felt strangely at ease, not because I trusted the 'system' more, no, I knew that if anything happened to him, I would know who to blame and who to confront . . . If he were to fall into the bloodstained hands of comrades, I would never know what actually happened to him.[142]

What emerges from Mkhabela's writing are the difficulties of finding a language and a political framework for understanding the violence of what she calls the 'dark 1980s'.[143] Her own comments on the strange clarity of imprisonment as a space of simple confrontation with apartheid articulates openly what is implicit in the focus of earlier autobiographies upon the experience of detention.

Yet there are also changes over time in the meaning of detention, and for those detained during the 1980s there appears to be a different configuration of the sayable surrounding violence and imprisonment. This is a dynamic that may be seen in Emily Bridger's recent interviews with former Soweto COSAS activists. Bridger discusses the striking difference between women activists who spoke to her openly about their participation in political violence on Soweto's streets, including in the necklacing of informers, and male activists who 'kept obvious secrets' about their own involvement.[144] Bridger suggests that this is because women 'cannot keep silent about their past involvement in violence and have their roles as comrades publicly acknowledged'.[145] She also argues that action on the street may have in fact offered more scope and space for the expression of young women's political commitment than political meetings in which they were 'silenced'.[146] The relationship between speech, silence and violence is thus inverted here.

Jon Soske has described contemporary South African politics as characterised 'by public struggles for historical visibility' and notes the ubiquity of the 'recuperative gesture' of claiming space in the powerful mainstream narrative of the liberation struggle.[147] For Bridger's interviewees this is a gesture performed through laying claim to the street and their role in political violence. Conversely, for this group of women comrades, prison and detention were more difficult experiences to talk about. Bridger describes the way her interviewees created 'redemptive narratives of their time spent in prison' but which were visibly interrupted by 'stalls, silences or stuttering'.[148] She argues that detention was an experience marked by these activists' gender, and as such, 'directly challenged' their identities as comrades and their 'espousal of struggle femininity and the feelings of empowerment that came with it'.[149] As one interviewee put it, when they were detained and held separately from their male contemporaries: 'that was when it dawned for the first time ever that I'm a woman'.[150] These changes over time in the silences surrounding violence and detention point us to the ways in which the boundaries of struggle speech and the sayable are reiterated anew in different contexts: how, why and where women speak about the struggle reveal ongoing struggles to talk. These complex and dynamic relationships between speech, silence and violence can also be seen in the changes over time in the stories told by individual activists.

'Modise has spoken out'

Thandi Modise was seventeen in 1976. She left her home in the Northern Cape after the Uprisings and became an MK guerrilla. Thandi Modise was an MK soldier, commander, political prisoner and, in the post-apartheid period, as an ANC politician she has been Premier of the North-West Province, Chairperson of the National Council of Provinces, an MP, and between 2019 and 2022 she was Speaker of the National Assembly. In a series of interviews with journalists and academics Modise has described her life as an MK recruit in military training camps in exile as well as her arrest, trial and imprisonment for sabotage. Her account of the gender relations in MK camps shifted dramatically between interviews conducted in 1989 and 1990 and one conducted in 2000. Raymond Suttner has noted this shift, arguing:

> The latter version is more likely to represent Modise's experience. Having just emerged from prison and instilled in tight military discipline, when she did the first interview (1989/1990), Modise may well have suppressed negative experiences. Given the elapse of a decade before the Curnow interview (2000), she may well have felt greater freedom to speak of what she previously concealed.[151]

Here we will explore how changing one's story is read against, or instead of, changes in the spaces and hearings accorded to women's voices. Are the changes in Modise's stories really about the feeling of 'greater freedom to speak'? Were her earlier silences about 'concealment'? This is not to suggest that Modise did not have personal political reasons for changing the stories that she told, nor that military discipline did not have a role to play, but rather to draw attention again to the notion of the 'sayable'. The sayable asks us to think about the conditions of Modise's speech and the subjectivities she could lay claim to within different spaces and moments. In between the interviews she gave there was an important context that both precipitated, and in part constituted, a change in the way women's stories of struggle were heard. This change was the result of their own struggles to talk and have their political demands recognised, struggles that intersected with the remaking of South Africa in the 1990s. It is important to note that it was in *Agenda* – the explicitly feminist academic/activist journal founded by a collective of women in Durban – in which Modise's 'changed story' was published. *Agenda* was both the result of women's struggles to be heard within the context of South Africa's transition and a space in which that struggle continued (and continues) to unfold.[152]

The first public interview that Thandi Modise gave about her life as an activist and guerrilla was to the journalist Thami Mkwanazi and published in the *Weekly Mail* upon her release from prison in 1989. The profile was published in two parts in March of 1989 and began with the following set-up: 'this remarkable account gives a face and personality to that *shadowy* stereotype which we so often read about and fear, and which we understand so little: the ANC guerrilla' (emphasis added).[153] The coincidence of language here in the description of the MK guerrilla as a 'shadowy stereotype' reminds us that where the light falls changes over time – for the *Weekly Mail*'s readers in 1989, exile and the guerrilla camp was largely an unknown story. For us, Modise can be seen as a 'shadowy' figure in another sense entirely than that meant by Thami Mkwanazi in 1989. Even though she is a high-profile politician in the post-apartheid period, what we know about her political participation in the liberation struggle has been shaped in the shadows of struggle speech.

In 1989 she told Mkwanazi that 'the male comrades respected us for having the courage to be soldiers. They did everything to make us feel their equals.'[154] There were also stories of the ways in which she retained certain ideals of femininity – usually through the wearing of clothing.

> On occasions like Women's Day, the women in the camps wore special uniforms. One was an olive green jacket and a skin with a slit at the back; the second was a grey dress worn above the knee. The latter outfit was nearly discontinued, she said, as it incited 'wild stares from the male comrades'. But both uniforms 'gave us a feminine touch', and the

> women liked to wear them. 'We drilled in the short dresses on women's occasions and we felt like women. The men whistled, but we ignored them'.[155]

This picture of 'mild' sexual harassment within the camps is what undergoes the most dramatic change in Modise's stories over time. In 2000 Modise spoke to South African Broadcasting Corporation (SABC) journalist Robyn Curnow for an interview published in *Agenda*. Curnow introduced Modise's biography as revealing 'more than just the struggles of one woman fighting an unjust system . . . In her experience she was a *woman* soldier and a *woman* political prisoner' (emphasis in original).[156] Curnow wrote that, 'her narrative touches on a social reality that many South African women have experienced. The difference is that whilst most have remained silent about their apartheid experiences, Modise has spoken out'.[157]

At the time of the interview in 2000, as well as being an ANC MP, Modise was deputy president of the ANC Women's League. The treatment she described in the camps was compounded by what she saw as a continuing stigmatisation of women who fought in the struggle by their male comrades in post-apartheid South Africa. Modise talked of her time at a camp in Tanzania, as one of six women amongst a hundred men.

> Right there in Tanzania there had been an incident, there had been a terrible fight, something, I mean, which *before 1990 we had been keeping quiet about*. But there had been a fight one night over girls . . . because there had been a feeling among some men that because there are these five, six women there, 'why should they be sex starved?' and there were others who said, 'No, they are not here to be sex slaves, if they want to have affairs they will have affairs, if they don't want to, then you are there to protect them' (emphasis added).[158]

While Modise located women's silence as existing before 1990 she described men's silence on the issue of sexual harassment in the camps, as a continuing one. She related an incident in which the women cadres at one camp confronted and chased a night-time intruder in their barracks. He was hidden by his male cadres. Thereafter the women were not spoken to by the men, in what was known as the 'anti-muhlere campaign' ('muhlere' means woman in Portuguese).[159] The men were apparently angered that the women had not 'dressed properly before going after the suspect'. Modise commented that, 'up to today, you still can't find an ANC male in that camp to talk frankly about that incident'.[160] This statement is an interesting reversal of the mantra of the TRC-era that women would not speak about their experiences of sexual abuse. Instead Modise located the silence in male cadres' narratives. This is an extremely important point. Modise's comment on men's continued silence shifts the burden of speech away from women.

There is at least one more layer to this narrative of Modise's changing stories. The journalist Modise spoke to in 1989, Thami Mkwanazi subsequently became her husband. This was a relationship that Modise revealed in 1995 was an abusive one. An article in the *Mail & Guardian* reported that Modise 'is speaking out' about her experiences despite the fact that a television interview she had given, 'Women Overcoming Abuse', was pulled from a scheduled screening by the SABC when Thami Mkwanazi threatened court action.[161] Modise told the paper that 'Women must learn to speak up. People must know that those problems exist, even for former Umkhonto WeSizwe commanders.' When asked, 'how can a former soldier, a powerful woman like herself become an abuse victim?', she replied,

> It is very simple. Even if we have some success in life, we are taught to keep quiet. Even women are sometimes not sympathetic to other women who open their mouths.
>
> I find that people are ashamed on my behalf that I opened my mouth, because I am a leader and leaders are not supposed to acknowledge problems.[162]

At this point, Modise described the MK camps as a 'happier' space than that of her marriage: 'At the beginning it was difficult for the men to treat us equally, but as the training progressed we proved that we deserved equality. I became an officer and did not have problems with the men under me.'[163] Silences and 'speaking out' thus move through Modise's narratives of the struggle, shifting location as the spaces available for speech changed. The instability of her account of the camps reveals how the act of speaking about the struggle is reshaped by struggles to speak gendered subjectivities – for both men and women.

Conclusions

Masabata Loate's death is the 'sort of death that South African history knows so well' and yet her life is not.[164] As Dan Magaziner has argued with regards to another's untimely and tragic end, this is perhaps in part because 'deaths such as [this] are so compelling that they exert tremendous power over our capacity to grasp life'.[165] Although many have found something to say in her death, exactly what that may be has changed over time and place. We can see certain patterns. A tendency for her killing to become less a specific violent act and understood more as part of a general horror or turmoil, that whilst it implicates young men, does not necessarily uncover the logics of gender that resulted in Loate's murder. Her death is seen. It is often recounted in spectacular terms. It was watched, we know, by her neighbours. It is remembered. Emily Bridger and Erin Hazard have noted a combination of 'surfeit and silence' within the archive when looking for sexual violence against women under apartheid. They argue that 'the historian is confronted with an excess of sources about the violence committed to women's bodies but stifling silences about their identities and subjectivities'.[166] This holds for Loate's death except that certain details of her life are repeated, that is, that she was an activist of 1976 and that she was a beauty queen. In Rian Malan's account, the inclusion of these two identities suggests the death, along with Loate, of the possibility of their combination.

The TRC pinpoints her death in an unfolding narrative of the birth of the MUFC and then removes her from its final version of this story – in itself, a deeply controversial one that threatened to tear apart the fragile bargains of the transition period. In this way, killing Loate was an act of silencing an individual but was also part of a wider culture of silence surrounding the violence of the 1980s and perhaps in particular 1986. Nomavenda Mathiane has recalled 'I found my whole body shaking when reading about the year 1986, which to me was the bloodiest year of my life'.[167] Sibongile Mkhabela similarly describes one night in October 1986 on which Ntate Lengane was killed as 'the hardest night of our lives'.[168] Ntate Lengane was father of Jefferson Lengane, another of the Soweto Eleven, but Mkhabela recalled, 'he was our father too . . . During the trial he had kept us going, giving unselfishly of himself and his family'.[169] His death occurred two nights after that of Loate.

Reading the stories of Masabata Loate's death alongside the life stories of three of her contemporaries, Caesarina Kona Makhoere, Sibongile Mkhabela and Thandi Modise, enables us to see the shifts in the sayable that continued after her demise. In 2001 Sibongile Mkhabela was able to write what Loate was seemingly killed for saying in 1986. However, it is not that the silences within struggle speech have disappeared – only that they have been reconfigured. This chapter has argued that women's struggles to claim a voice within the anti-apartheid movement were marked initially by the prominence of imprisonment and detention as an authorising experience. This has continued to shape the public spaces available to women in post-apartheid South Africa. The Women's Jail, a part of the Constitution Hill complex that was opened in 2005 and houses the newly built Constitutional Court on the site of a former prison, is the only museum space within the vast and expanding South African heritage landscape that is exclusively concerned with telling women's narratives of struggle. The containment of women's stories within the jail thus reiterates the longer history of women's struggles to speak.[170] It is obvious that no narration of the past is complete – be that individual or collective – but the patterns of silence within women's voices point to specific pressures on their speech within the struggle. That women's voices have been heard as speaking up from the margins has had fragmentary effects on the voices that do emerge.

Notes

1. Hermione Lee, *Virginia Woolf's Nose: Essays on Biography* (Princeton, NJ: Princeton University Press, 2018), 11, https://doi.org/10.1515/9780691188607.

2. *State vs. Mary Masabate Loatse and others*, case: 41/4115/81 Magistrates Court, District of Johannesburg; WHP: AD2021: SAIRR Security Trials 1958–82. Boxes 19–20, Proceedings, 523. Digitised trial proceedings, accessed July 2019, http://www.historicalpapers.wits.ac.za/?inventory/U/collections&c=AD2021/R/.

3. Garrey Michael Dennie, 'The Cultural Politics of Burial in South Africa, 1884–1990' (PhD, Maryland, The Johns Hopkins University), 235, accessed 16 April 2024, https://www.proquest.com/docview/304348729/abstract/16FF58AFF3F34936PQ/1.

4. Rebekah Lee, 'Death "On the Move": Funerals, Entrepreneurs and the Rural-Urban Nexus in South Africa', *Africa: Journal of the International African Institute* 81, no. 2 (2011): 228–9, https://www.jstor.org/stable/41485275.

5. Dennie, 'The Cultural Politics of Burial in South Africa, 1884–1990', 234.

6. Dennie, 'The Cultural Politics of Burial in South Africa, 1884–1990', 239.

7. Dennie, 'The Cultural Politics of Burial in South Africa, 1884–1990', 239.

8. This is captured by the headstone erected on the grave of Hector Pieterson in 1981, by AZANYU, which read: 'Deeply mourned by his parents, sisters, and a nation that remembers'. Khangela Ali Hlongwane, 'Bricks-and-Mortar Testimonies: The Interactive and Dialogical Features of the Memorials and Monuments of the June 16 1976 Soweto Uprisings', in *The Road to Democracy in South Africa: Volume 7: Soweto Uprisings: New Perspective, Commemorations and Memorialisation* (Cape Town: Unisa Press, 2017), 208; For an example in which the processes of public commemoration ran up against the wishes of the deceased's family see the discussion of Neil Aggett's funeral in Dennie, 'The Cultural Politics of Burial in South Africa, 1884–1990'. Neil Aggett was a trade union activist and one of the very few white South Africans to die in police custody.

9. In her in-depth study of a necklacing murder, that of Nosipho Zamela in Mlungisi in December 1985, Gobodo-Madikizela explains that Nosipho's funeral 'was attended only by her mother and a few relatives' and was 'held almost in secrecy' in the very early hours of a Saturday morning. After her daughter's killing, Nosipho's mother moved away with the rest of her family. When Gobodo-Madikizela met Mrs Zamela she realised that, 'the trauma of her daughter's death was still very much on the surface, so much so that I could not pursue the interview'. Pumla Phillipa Gobodo-Madikizela, 'Legacies of Violence: An In-Depth Analysis of Two Case Studies Based on Interviews with Perpetrators of a "Necklace" Murder and with Eugene de Kock' (PhD, South

Africa, University of Cape Town (South Africa)), 112 and 258–9, accessed 18 June 2024, https://www.proquest.com/docview/304663465/abstract/2F0BA56C5C8F463APQ/1; Sabine Marschall calls necklace victims the 'most significant group of ambivalent victims' in post-apartheid South Africa. She notes that no public memorial has been installed or proposed to commemorate victims of the necklace. Sabine Marschall, *Landscape of Memory: Commemorative Monuments, Memorials and Public Statuary in Post-Apartheid South-Africa* (Leiden: Brill, 2010), 90–94.

10. For a summary drawing on the stories published in various South African newspapers see: Laurinda Keys, 'Woman Activist Slashed to Death', *AP News*, 19 October 1986, accessed July 2019, https://apnews.com/0c77c01ccad449910d3a-2fa2a4fa97a1. Site inactive on 30 September 2024. Screenshot available from author.

11. Maria Loate gave an interview to *The Sunday Star*, see 'Woman Activist Slashed to Death'.

12. 'Woman Activist Slashed to Death'.

13. 'Woman Activist Slashed to Death'.

14. 'Woman Activist Slashed to Death'.

15. 'Repression Trends in the Transvaal Area between June and September 1986', WHP AG2523, Box F.1.2.1–20, 3

16. 'Repression Trends in the Transvaal Area', 3.

17. 'Repression Trends in the Transvaal Area', 31.

18. 'Repression Trends in the Transvaal Area', 31–2.

19. 'Repression Trends in the Transvaal Area', 33.

20. Jon Soske, 'The Family Romance of the South African Revolution', in *Love and Revolution in the Twentieth-Century Colonial and Postcolonial World: Perspectives from South Asia and Southern Africa*, ed. G. Arunima, Patricia Hayes and Premesh Lalu, Palgrave Studies in the History of Social Movements (Cham: Springer International Publishing, 2021), 189–90, https://doi.org/10.1007/978-3-030-79580-1_7.

21. Nyasha Karimakwenda, 'Safe to Violate: The Role of Gender in the Necklacing of Women During the South African People's War (1985–1990)', *Journal of Southern African Studies* 45, no. 3 (4 May 2019): 560, https://doi.org/10.1080/03057070.2019.1642646.

22. Karimakwenda, 'Safe to Violate', 560–61.

23. In 1986, of 1,352 deaths the TRC found to be political violence, 306 were necklacings or burnings. Truth and Reconciliation Commission of South Africa, *Truth and Reconciliation Commission of South Africa Report*, 1998, 2: 389.

24. Karimakwenda, 'Safe to Violate', 561.

25. Thompson Ramanala, DPSC daybook July–September 1986, WHP, AG 2523, Box G4–G8, 92.

26. Nomavenda Mathiane, *Beyond the Headlines: Truths of Soweto Life* (Johannesburg: Southern Book Publishers, 1990), 36–41.

27. Mathiane, *Beyond the Headlines*, 40.

28. Mathiane, *Beyond the Headlines*, 40.

29. Mathiane, *Beyond the Headlines*, 40.

30. Matthews Maleka, DPSC Daybook, November 1985–May 1986, WHP, AG 2523, Box G4–G8, 84.

31. Rebecca Maleka, DPSC Daybook, November 1985–May 1986, WHP, AG2523, Box G4–G8, 87–88.

32. See for example, Thenjiwe Mtintso who recalled a parallel between the treatment of police and comrades when women did not conform to gendered expectations: 'you get worse treatment from the Boers because they don't want you to behave in that manner and you get still worse treatment from your own comrades because they don't expect you to perform better [than them]'; quoted in Beth Goldblatt and Sheila Meintjes, 'Gender and the Truth and Reconciliation Commission', May 1996, https://www.justice.gov.za/trc/hrvtrans/submit/gender.htm.

33. Gobodo-Madikizela, 'Legacies of Violence', 92–3.

34. Gobodo-Madikizela, 'Legacies of Violence', 93.

35. 'Anti-necklace ex-beauty queen murdered', *Cape Times*, 20 October 1986.

36. Emily Bridger and Erin Hazan, 'Surfeit and Silence: Sexual Violence in the Apartheid Archive', *African Studies* 81, no. 3–4 (2 October 2022): 286–305, https://doi.org/10.1080/00020184.2023.2212606.

37. Bridger and Hazan, 'Surfeit and Silence', 290.

38. 'Anti-necklace ex-beauty queen murdered', *Cape Times*, 20 October 1986.

39. APDUSA had been formed in 1962, as a non-racial mass-based organisation affiliated to the Non-European Unity Movement, intended to harness the spirit of resistance unleashed by the Pondoland revolts and Sharpeville. Decimated by arrests during the early 1970s it was revived during the early 1980s as activists began to be released from Robben Island. However, it was by the 1980s a small organisation, and many of its activists were absorbed by the UDF in the second half of the 1980s.

40. 'Freedom Fighters or Plain Killers?', *APUDSA Views* 16 (February 1987): 4.

41. Seekings, *Heroes or Villains? Youth Politics in the 1980s* (Johannesburg: Ravan Press, 1993), xi.

42. 'Freedom Fighters or Plain Killers?', 3.

43. John Greenwald, 'South Africa The War of Blacks Against Blacks', *Time Magazine*, 26 January 1987, https://time.com/archive/6708166/south-africa-the-war-of-blacks-against-blacks/.

44. Brendan Boyle, 'Two dead in racial violence', *UPI Archives*, Oct 19, 1986, accessed June 2024, https://www.upi.com/Archives/1986/10/19/Two-dead-in-racial-violence/8743530078400/.

45. *Financial Mail*, 24 October 1986, 57.

46. See description 'About Frontline' at an online archive of the magazine's stories, accessed June 2024, https://www.coldtype.net/frontline.html.

47. Dennis Beckett, 'Facing the Future as One Society', *Frontline*, December 1979, accessed June 2024, https://www.coldtype.net/frontline/Frontline.Editorial.pdf.

48. See the two important collections: Keyan G. Tomaselli and P. Eric Louw, eds., *The Alternative Press in South Africa* (London: James Currey, 1992); Les Switzer and Mohamed Adhikari, *South Africa's Resistance Press: Alternative Voices in the Last Generation Under Apartheid* (Athens, OH: Ohio University Press, 2000).

49. Nomavenda Mathiane, Truth and Reconciliation Commission, Special Hearings: Media, Session 4, 17 September 1997, accessed April 2024, https://www.justice.gov.za/trc/special/media/media04.htm.

50. Nomavenda Mathiane, Special Hearings: Media, Session 4, 17 September 1997.

51. Dennis Beckett, Foreword to Mathiane, *Beyond the Headlines: Truths of Soweto Life*, vii–ix.

52. Winnie Mandela rose to public prominence after her marriage to Nelson Mandela in 1958, during the ongoing Treason Trial in which Nelson was a defendant. Prior to

1996 she was known as Winnie Mandela. After her divorce from Nelson that year she changed her name to Madikizela-Mandela. I have used these two names before and after this date. As Nelson Mandela's spokesperson when he was banned and imprisoned, Winnie Mandela built a role for herself as 'Mother of the Nation', becoming 'the voice and image of the ANC itself', see: Shireen Hassim, 'Not Just Nelson's Wife: Winnie Madikizela-Mandela, Violence and Radicalism in South Africa', *Journal of Southern African Studies* 44, no. 5 (3 September 2018): 898, https://doi.org/10.1080/03057070.2018.1514566; Winnie Mandela became an important political actor in her own right, and with an independent and loyal following, particularly among the youth; this was a connection that had first emerged during the 1976 Soweto Uprisings. See: Helena Pohlandt-McCormick, 'Controlling Woman: Winnie Mandela and the 1976 Soweto Uprising', *The International Journal of African Historical Studies* 33, no. 3 (2000): 585–614, https://doi.org/10.2307/3097436. During the 1960s and 1970s she was banned, imprisoned, detained (in solitary confinement) and tortured, to an extent few other women were. In 1977 she was banished to Brandfort for eight years, returning to her Soweto home in 1985. A year later the MUFC was formed. The violence enacted by the MUFC troubled the leaders of the internal and exiled liberation movement and a Mandela Crisis Committee was formed to curb their activities, but the deaths of young people continued. In 1988 four boys were abducted from the Methodist manse in Soweto, amongst them 'Stompie' Seipei, a thirteen-year-old activist. Whilst Mandela alleged that the boys were being sexually abused at the manse and the abduction was for their safety, Seipei was later found dead. In 1991 Mandela was convicted of Seipei's abduction and the coach of the MUFC Jerry Richardson was convicted for his murder. For more on the trial and the homophobia invoked by Winnie Mandela's defence team see: Rachel Holmes, 'Queer Comrades: Winnie Mandela and the Moffies', *Social Text*, no. 52/53 (1997): 161–80, https://doi.org/10.2307/466738; The 1991 trial also concerned the death of Dr Abu Baker Asvat, known as 'the people's doctor', who was murdered in his surgery the month after Seipei's death. Whilst the 1991 trial found insufficient evidence to link Mandela to Asvat's murder, 'many people –including some who knew them both well – continue to insist on her involvement to this day'. See: Jon Soske, 'Open Secrets, Off the Record: Audience, Intimate Knowledge, and the Crisis of the Post-Apartheid State', *Historical Reflections/ Réflexions Historiques* 38, no.2 (2012): 61, https://doi.org/10.3167/hrrh.2012.380205. All of this has made Winnie Madikizela-Mandela a controversial and much debated political figure. For more see: Emily Bridger, 'From "Mother of the Nation" to "Lady Macbeth": Winnie Mandela and Perceptions of Female Violence in South Africa, 1985–91', *Gender & History*, 1 August 2015, https://doi.org/10.1111/1468-0424.12133; Shireen Hassim, 'The Impossible Contract: The Political and Private Marriage of Nelson and Winnie Mandela', *Journal of Southern African Studies* 45, no. 6 (2 November 2019): 1151–71, https://doi.org/10.1080/03057070.2019.1697137; and most recently, Jonny Steinberg, *Winnie and Nelson: Portrait of a Marriage* (Johannesburg: Jonathan Ball, 2023).

53. Hassim, 'Not Just Nelson's Wife', 900.

54. Soske, 'The Family Romance of the South African Revolution', 189–90.

55. Mathiane, *Beyond the Headlines: Truths of Soweto Life*, 132.

56. *State vs. W.W.C Twala*, Proceedings, 735.

57. *State vs. M.M Loatse*, Proceedings, 601.

58. Mathiane, *Beyond the Headlines: Truths of Soweto Life*, 133.

59. The term 'emergent' is used by Clayton, whose analysis is discussed further in what follows. Cherry Clayton, 'Radical Transformations: Emergent Women's Voices in South Africa', *English in Africa* 17, no. 2 (1990): 25–36, https://hdl.handle.net/10520/AJA03768902_330.

60. Clayton, 'Radical Transformations', 32.

61. Clayton, 'Radical Transformations', 26–7.

62. Gillian Whitlock, *The Intimate Empire* (London: A&C Black, 2000), 148.

63. Whitlock, *The Intimate Empire*, 147.

64. Simone Murray, *Mixed Media: Feminist Presses and Publishing Politics* (London: Pluto, 2004), 6, 45, 71.

65. Murray, *Mixed Media: Feminist Presses and Publishing Politics*, 45.

66. Murray, *Mixed Media: Feminist Presses and Publishing Politics*, 76.

67. Marsaili Cameron, 'What the Hell Is Feminist Editing?', in *In Other Words: Writing as a Feminist*, ed. Gail Chester and Sigrid Nielsen (London: Hutchinson, 1987), 125.

68. Elizabeth le Roux, 'Miriam Tlali and Ravan Press: Politics and Power in Literary Publishing during the Apartheid Period', *Journal of Southern African Studies* 44, no. 3 (4 May 2018): 433, https://doi.org/10.1080/03057070.2018.1450007.

69. 'New Title Information', Editorial File Cesarina Kona Makoere: London School of Economics (LSE), The Women's Library (TWL), The Women's Press: 6/TWP/Survey/14.14, Box 14.

70. Murray, *Mixed Media: Feminist Presses and Publishing Politics*, 76.

71. Whitlock, *The Intimate Empire*, 149.

72. Dorothy Driver, 'Imagined Selves, (Un)Imagined Marginalities', *Journal of Southern African Studies* 17, no. 2 (1991): p.345, https://doi.org/10.1080/03057079108708281.

73. For a recent reappraisal of this relationship see: Zine Magubane, 'Attitudes towards Feminism among Women in the ANC, 1950–1990: A Theoretical Re-Interpretation', in *The Road to Democracy in South Africa: Volume 4, Part 2*. (Cape Town: Unisa Press, 2010), 975–1033.

74. Shireen Hassim, 'Democracy's Shadows: Sexual Rights and Gender Politics in the Rape Trial of Jacob Zuma', *African Studies* 68, no.1 (1 April 2009): 61, https://doi.org/10.1080/00020180902827431.

75. Hassim, 'Democracy's Shadows', 61.

76. Whilst the politics of feminism in the book are complex, Diana Russell interviewed some women who laid claim to being feminist in: Diana E. H Russell, *Lives of Courage: Women for a New South Africa* (New York: Basic Books, 1989).

77. 'Cover blurbs for Living, Loving, Lying awake at Night', Editorial File Sindiwe Magona: LSE, TWL, 6/TWP: 39, Box 39, 39.4.

78. Driver, 'Imagined Selves', 348.

79. Whitlock, *The Intimate Empire*, 168.

80. Daniel Roux, 'Jonny Steinberg's the Number and Prison Life Writing in Post-Apartheid South Africa', 2009, 231., http://hdl.handle.net/10019.1/12473.

81. Roux, 'Jonny Steinberg', 231.

82. Paul Gready, *Writing as Resistance: Life Stories of Imprisonment, Exile, and Homecoming from Apartheid South Africa* (Lanham, MD: Lexington Books, 2003), 274.

83. Yasmina Martin, '"Now I Am Not Afraid": Simon Nkoli, Queer Utopias and Transnational Solidarity', *Journal of Southern African Studies* 46, no. 4 (3 July 2020): 680, https://doi.org/10.1080/03057070.2020.1780022.

84. Andy Carolin has explored how the marginalised history of Simon Nkoli is represented. In a discussion of the 2003 play, 'Your Loving Simon', he highlights the inclusion of display cases at the original performances of the play that contained 'handcuffs, passbook, a strip of toilet paper documenting prison conditions and a

letter (to his lover Roy) stamped by Modderbee Prison': Andy Carolin, 'Locating Sexual Rights in the Anti-Apartheid Movement: Simon Nkoli and the Making of Post-Apartheid Protest Theatre', *Critical Arts* 32, no. 5–6 (2 November 2018): 43, https://doi.org/10.1080/02560046.2018.1560342.

85. Federation of Transvaal Women, *A Woman's Place Is in the Struggle, Not Behind Bars* (Reprinted by The Africa Fund, New York, 1988).

86. *A Woman's Place Is in the Struggle*, 32

87. *A Woman's Place Is in the Struggle*, Introduction to the U.S. Edition.

88. Emma Mashinini, *Strikes Have Followed Me All My Life: A South African Autobiography* (London: Women's Press, 1989), 110.

89. Nthabiseng Motsemme, 'The Mute Always Speak: On Women's Silences at the Truth and Reconciliation Commission', *Current Sociology* 52, no. 5 (2004): 918–23, https://doi.org/10.1177/0011392104045377.

90. For a discussion of some examples see: Michael Lobban, *White Man's Justice: South African Political Trials in the Black Consciousness Era* (Oxford: Clarendon Press, 1996), 195.

91. Carli Coetzee, *Written under the Skin: Blood and Intergenerational Memory in South Africa* (Woodbridge, Suffolk; Johannesburg, South Africa: James Currey, 2019), 62.

92. Press Release, Editorial File Cesarina Kona Makhoere: LSE, TWL, 6/TWP: 14.14, Box 14.

93. For more on this campaign see: Emily Bridger, 'Functions and Failures of Transnational Activism: Discourses of Children's Resistance and Repression in Global Anti-Apartheid Networks', *Journal of World History* 26, no. 4 (2015): 865–87.

94. Goldblatt and Meintjes, 'Gender and the Truth and Reconciliation Commission', 29.

95. Readers Reports for No Child's Play, Editorial File Cesarina Kona Makhoere, LSE, TWL, 6/TWP: 39, Box 39.

96. Readers Reports for No Child's Play.

97. Letter from Ros de Lanerolle to Barbara Masekela 29 July 1987, Editorial File Cesarina Kona Makhoere: LSE, TWL, 6/TWP: 39, Box 39.

98. Fax from Bridget Company – David Philip to Mary Hemming Women's Press, 6 April 1993, Editorial File Cesarina Kona Makhoere, LSE, TWL, 6/TWP: 39, Box 39.

99. 'Statement of the National Executive Committee of the African National Congress on the Emancipation of Women in South Africa', *Agenda* 6, no. 8 (1 January 1990): 23, https://doi.org/10.2307/4065629.

100. *Horizon*, May/June 1991.

101. *Horizon*, May/June 1991.

102. *Horizon*, May/June 1991.

103. Indeed, Helen Moffatt has argued that the new political rights extended to women during the transition to democracy occurred without 'revising their social subordination' and thus created a new disjuncture between the public and private realms. This disjuncture, she argues, underpins the increased rates of gender-based violence in post-apartheid South Africa – as men across South African society seek to discipline women's behaviour in private, intimate spaces. See: Helen Moffett, '"These Women, They Force Us to Rape Them": Rape as Narrative of Social Control in Post-Apartheid South Africa', *Journal of Southern African Studies* 32, no. 1 (1 March 2006): 129–44, https://doi.org/10.1080/03057070500493845.

104. Moffett, 'These Women, They Force Us to Rape Them'; Hassim, 'Democracy's Shadows'.

105. Emily Cooper-Hockey, 'Whose Agenda? The Negotiation of Gender, Race and "Difference" in a Feminist Journal in South Africa, 1987–1993'. (BA Honours Dissertation, University of Durham, 2017), 39.

106. Njabulo Ndebele, 'Memory, Metaphor and the Trumph of Narrative', in *Negotiating the Past: The Making of Memory in South Africa*, ed. Sarah Nuttall and Carli Coetzee (Oxford: Oxford University Press, 1998), 20.

107. Ndebele, 'Memory, Metaphor and the Trumph of Narrative', 20.

108. After five weeks the TRC had heard 204 witnesses, 6 out of 10 were women. Whilst three quarters of their testimony and 88 per cent of male witness testimony concerned abuses to men, only 17 per cent of the female witnesses and 5 per cent of the male witnesses were about abuses to women. Fiona Ross, 'Existing in secret places: Women's testimony in the first five weeks of public hearings of the TRC'. Paper presented at the Fault lines Conference, July 4–5, 1996, Cape Town, 1–32.

109. Goldblatt and Meintjes, 'Gender and the Truth and Reconciliation Commission', 17.

110. Goldblatt and Meintjes, 'Gender and the Truth and Reconciliation Commission', 34.

111. Fiona Ross, 'Linguistic Bearings and Testimonial Practices', in *Discourse and Human Rights Violations*, ed. Christine Anthonissen and Jan Blommaert (Amsterdam: John Benjamins, 2007), 109. Three women's hearings were held in Cape Town on 8 August 1996, in Durban on 24 October 1996 and in Johannesburg on 29 July 1997.

112. Karin Chubb, *Between Anger and Hope: South Africa's Youth and the Truth and Reconciliation Commission* (Johannesburg: Witwatersrand University Press, 2001), 22.

113. Truth and Reconciliation Commission of South Africa, *Truth and Reconciliation Commission of South Africa Report*, vol. 4 (Cape Town: Truth and Reconciliation Commission, 1998), 249.

114. Ross, 'Linguistic Bearings and Testimonial Practices', 110.

115. Fiona Ross, *Bearing Witness: Women and the Truth and Reconciliation Commission in South Africa* (London: Pluto, 2002), 24.

116. Meg Samuelson, *Remembering the Nation, Dismembering Women? Stories of the South African Transition* (Scottsville, South Africa: University of KwaZulu-Natal Press, 2007), 121.

117. Introduction to Rose Dimpa, April 1986, WHP, AG2523, Box G24.3.2.4.

118. Thenjiwe Mtintso, Truth and Reconciliation Commission, Special Hearings, Women's Hearing, Johannesburg, Day 1, 28 July 1997, accessed June 2024, http://www.justice.gov.za/trc/special/women/masote.htm.

119. Ntombizikhona Valela, '"I Am 22 Million": Reading Winnie Madikizela as the Intellectual Face of Anti-Apartheid Popular Struggle' (MA thesis, Rhodes University, 2017), 55.

120. Hassim, 'Not Just Nelson's Wife', 905.

121. Lerothodi Andrew Ikaneng, Truth and Reconciliation Commission, Special Hearings, Mandela United Football Club Hearing, Day 7 Second Session, 30 November 1997, accessed July 2019, http://www.justice.gov.za/trc/special/mandela/mufc7b.htm.

122. Lerothodi Andrew Ikaneng, Truth and Reconciliation Commission.

123. Truth and Reconciliation Commission of South Africa, *Truth and Reconciliation Commission of South Africa Report*, 1998, 2: 555.

124. Rian Malan, *My Traitor's Heart* (London: Vintage, 1991).

125. 'List of BCM Heroes and Heroines', AZAPO, last updated 5 January 2003; accessed June 2024, https://web.archive.org/web/20190511202049/http://azapo.org.za/azapohistory/azanian-peoples-organisation/.

126. Andile Mngxitama, 'June 16, 1976 in Perspective: Tsietsi and Khotso, brothers in arms', black opinion, first posted 21 January 2004; reposted 15 June 2016; accessed June 2024, https://web.archive.org/web/20160618051602/http://blackopinion.co.za/2016/06/15/june-16-1976-perspective-tsietsi-khotso-brothers-arms/.

127. Malan, *My Traitor's Heart*, 330.

128. The phrase 'frenzied catalogue' comes from Paul Gready, 'The Witness: Rian Malan's "My Traitor's Heart" and Elsa Joubert's "Poppie"', *Current Writing* 7, no. 1 (January 1995): 88–104, https://doi.org/10.1080/1013929X.1995.9677949.

129. Gready, 'The Witness', 330.

130. T. A. Osinubi, 'Abusive Narratives: Antjie Krog, Rian Malan, and the Transmission of Violence', *Comparative Studies of South Asia, Africa and the Middle East* 28, no. 1 (1 January 2008): 115, https://doi.org/10.1215/1089201x-2007-059.

131. Osinubi, 'Abusive Narratives', 123.

132. Patrick Fish, 'Malan, the Movie: The BBC Version of Rian Malan's "My Traitor's Heart"', *South African Theatre Journal* 5, no. 1 (January 1991): 98, https://doi.org/10.1080/10137548.1991.9688031.

133. Fish, 'Malan, the Movie', 98.

134. Sibongile Mkhabela, *Open Earth and Black Roses: Remembering 16 June 1976* (Braamfontein, South Africa: Skotaville Press, 2001), 129.

135. Nancy J. Jacobs and Andrew Bank, 'Biography in Post-Apartheid South Africa: A Call for Awkwardness', *African Studies* 78, no. 2 (3 April 2019): 165, https://doi.org/10.1080/00020184.2019.1569428.

136. Elaine Unterhalter, 'The Work of the Nation: Heroic Masculinity in South African Autobiographical Writing of the Anti-Apartheid Struggle', *European Journal of Development Research* 12, no. 2 (December 2000): 160, https://doi.org/10.1080/09578810008426770.

137. Jacobs and Bank, 'Biography in Post-Apartheid South Africa'.

138. Mkhabela, *Open Earth and Black Roses*, 129.

139. Mkhabela, *Open Earth and Black Roses*, 95.

140. Mkhabela, *Open Earth and Black Roses*, 103.

141. Mkhabela, *Open Earth and Black Roses*, 115.

142. Mkhabela, *Open Earth and Black Roses*, 114.

143. Mkhabela, *Open Earth and Black Roses*, 119.

144. Emily Bridger, *Young Women against Apartheid: Gender, Youth and South Africa's Liberation Struggle* (Woodbridge, Suffolk; Rochester, NY: James Currey, 2021), 157.

145. Bridger, *Young Women against Apartheid*, 159.

146. Bridger, *Young Women against Apartheid*, 147.

147. Soske, 'Open Secrets, Off the Record', 65.

148. Bridger, *Young Women against Apartheid*, 165.

149. Bridger, *Young Women against Apartheid*, 168.

150. Bridger, *Young Women against Apartheid*, 170.

151. Raymond Suttner, 'Women in the ANC-Led Underground', in *Women in South African History: They Remove Boulders and Cross Rivers*, ed. Nomboniso Gasa (Cape Town: HSRC Press, 2007), 253.

152. See, for example, the important issue of *Agenda* that documents the role of womxn activists within the Fallist movements: 'Feminisms and Women's Resistance within Contemporary African Students Movements', vol. 31, Issue 3–4, (2017).

153. Thami Mkwanazi, 'Thandi Modise: The knitting needles guerrilla', *Weekly Mail*, March 23–30, 1989. Part Two of the interview was published as, 'The life story of Thandi Modise, guerrilla', *Weekly Mail*, 31 March–6 April 1989.

154. Mkwanazi, 'Thandi Modise'.

155. Mkwanazi, 'Thandi Modise'.

156. Robyn Curnow and Thandi Modise, 'Thandi Modise, a Woman in War', *Agenda* 43 (2000): 36.

157. Curnow and Modise, 'Thandi Modise, a Woman in War', 36.

158. Curnow and Modise, 'Thandi Modise, a Woman in War', 37.

159. Curnow and Modise, 'Thandi Modise, a Woman in War', 39.

160. Curnow and Modise, 'Thandi Modise, a Woman in War', 39.

161. Stefaans Brummer, 'MP abused but not beaten', *Mail & Guardian*, 11 August 1995, accessed April 2024, https://mg.co.za/article/1995-08-11-mp-abused-but-not-beaten/.

162. Brummer, 'MP abused'.

163. Brummer, 'MP abused'.

164. Daniel R. Magaziner, 'Two Stories about Art, Education, and Beauty in Twentieth-Century South Africa', *The American Historical Review* 118, no. 5 (1 December 2013): 1406, https://doi.org/10.1093/ahr/118.5.1403.

165. Magaziner, 'Two Stories about Art, Education, and Beauty', 1406.

166. Bridger and Hazan, 'Surfeit and Silence', 288.

167. Mathiane was describing re-reading the stories she had published in *Frontline* for inclusion in the book: Mathiane, *Beyond the Headlines: Truths of Soweto Life*, xi.

168. Mkhabela, *Open Earth and Black Roses*, 117.

169. Mkhabela, *Open Earth and Black Roses*, 116.

170. See Annie Coombes for the way in which the jail represents the narratives of former prisoners in ways in which 'we are never allowed to suspend our distance' from their experiences: Annie E. Coombes, 'The Gender of Memory in Postapartheid South Africa: The Women's Jail as Heritage Site', in *Museum Transformations*, The International Handbooks of Museum Studies Volume 4, ed. Annie E. Coombes and Ruth B. Phillips, (Chichester: John Wiley & Sons Ltd, 2015), 221.

Conclusion: shadow histories

In Bessie Head's foreword to Ellen Kuzwayo's 1985 autobiography, *Call Me Woman*, she reflects that:

> At the end of the book one feels as if a shadow history of South Africa has been written; there is a sense of triumph, of hope in this achievement and that one has read the true history of the land, a history that vibrates with human compassion and goodness.[1]

Head was, I think, referring to Kuzwayo's autobiography as one that shadowed the then mainstream narratives of South African history which underpinned Afrikaner nationalism, the rule of the National Party and apartheid. Yet, Kuzwayo's book is also an assertion of a gendered claim to voice. As we explored in Chapter 4, *Call Me Woman* is recognised as a hugely important intervention within public articulations of a woman's place within the liberation struggle. Gillian Whitlock refers to it as 'germinal, both chronologically and conceptually' to a threshold moment in the 1980s when black women's writing was emergent.[2] From its very title – framed as a reply to Mtutuzeli Matshoba's 1979 collection of short stories *Call Me Not a Man*, Kuzwayo addresses her audience directly and invokes herself as a gendered being.[3] In doing so *Call Me Woman* brings to the fore a potential shadow history of the liberation struggle and the making of the 'new' South Africa, a history of the shadows that this once oppositional national narrative casts and the stories not quite obscured in darkness.

The distance with which we now stand in time from the years of the struggle after 1976 is an uneasy one. We are close enough to talk with many of those who were there, but far enough away that historians have begun to search for the ability to view that time with a new, often more comprehensive, perspective.[4] Some historians have framed this as a need to move *beyond* voices or *beyond* silences.[5] In contrast I have sought insights that might emerge from focusing *within* voices or on the making of silences. In this conclusion, I want to reflect on the challenges that the life and death of Masabata Loate pose to our understanding of the liberation struggle: in particular to methodological questions of visibility and audibility in the archives of the struggle – written and oral. Masabata Loate is a young woman who can be both seen and heard in the archives. Yet the various contexts that compelled her to speak and preserved her words and image were all coercive in multiple ways. She is not reducible to the fragments we have of her. I argue that uncovering the ways in which these fragments were made, provides us with a way of seeing her, as a shadow. This is an impression of her, caused by the way light fell upon her body. It is not her, fully lit. Seeing shadows is a way of recognising the uneasy combination of knowing and not-knowing Masabata Loate that South Africa's anti-apartheid liberation struggle has left us with.[6]

I have used the word 'uneasy' twice in the preceding paragraph, when describing historians' relationship with the past and our inheritance of it. Seeing shadows is my way of staying in a state of uneasiness with the past. In part this discomfort is the inherent awkwardness of biography.[7] It is the result of my own positionality. But it also resides in the necessary partiality of knowledge about Masabata Loate – a partiality that is necessary, because her story and that of South Africa's national liberation struggle criss-cross without aligning.

Image and word

Silences and shadows are often thought of as representative of one another. A shadow is a silent presence. In *The Combing of History*, David W. Cohen argued that 'there are critical areas in the shadows, critical silences in the social worlds we study' and urged historians to pay attention to the 'quiet eddies of potentially critical materials that form' at the same time, and through the same processes by which the 'visible wake of the past' is made.[8] There can be few more obvious examples of the 'visible wake' of the apartheid past than the photography that captured moments of protest and the responses of security forces. Sam Nzima's photograph of 16 June 1976, and the circulation and afterlives of this image, offer one example of the processes Cohen describes. Critical reflection on photography within the history of the struggle can offer a way into exploring the simultaneous making of voices and silences.

Gary Minkley and Ciraj Rassool have urged historians to interrogate our use of photography and not simply accept images as 'filling the gaps' left by history's absences.[9] Taking photographs of struggle during the struggle was not a neutral act of observation – just as talking about the struggle was not. Indeed, many of the same dangers were attached to 'seeing too much' as 'speaking too much'. Santu Mofokeng, the South African artist who worked as a photojournalist during the mid-1980s for *New Nation*, recalled in 2000: 'I was once nearly "necklaced" by comrades at a night vigil in Emndeni (Soweto) after being branded an informer simply by asking permission to make pictures of the proceedings'.[10] The moral questions which faced the photographer, taking a picture during a moment of violent oppression, is an issue which appears within the fiction authored in the aftermath of 1976 by black writers. In Mongane Wally Serote's 1981 novel *To Every Birth Its Blood*, a disillusioned newspaper reporter called Tsi questioned his colleague about the purpose of his photography:

> 'I mean, I feel there is something about being there taking pictures while a fight, a clearly unbalanced fight goes on.'
>
> 'Unbalanced, what do you mean?'
>
> 'Morongwa could be locked up, purely because she is black, fighting a white person – and you know the price of that.'
>
> 'Well, I have a clear stand on that. I am a black photographer and that is how I fight.'
>
> 'What if she was killed?'
>
> 'I have recorded it.'
>
> 'What do the records help? Who believes them?'
>
> 'Records are not to be believed, but used, that is how I look at it.'
>
> 'Used? By whom? How can you use a thing if you do not value it?'[11]

Debates like this over the purpose and meaning of photography within the liberation struggle can help us understand the desires and anxieties that compelled the various archives of the struggle.[12] The making of these archives of struggle were painfully self-conscious and dangerous. The consequences of speech and silence in detention and on trial were fatal for many. There were also risks attached to speaking out through organisations like the Detainee Parent's Support Committee (DPSC). A 1986 report published by the American-based Lawyers Committee for Human Rights suggested that 'some who have spoken to the DPSC' had subsequently been visited by the army again.[13] In her testimony to the Johannesburg TRC youth hearing, one of the founders of the DPSC, Audrey Coleman, related the experience of a young man Sithole Edblumo, who appeared in a film made by the DPSC called *Children under Apartheid* and who was then interrogated by the Security Police and found dead four days after his release. Audrey Coleman suggested a direct link: 'I know because I was in the office myself when he came back from having been interrogated, that that was the reason for the questioning, the *Children under Apartheid*'.[14]

The photographer Gideon Mendel, a member of the Afripix collective who made some of the most widely circulated images of the struggle during the 1980s, told Patricia Hayes in a 2002 interview of his confusion over the purpose of photography during that time: 'I mean who was struggle photography for?'[15] Mendel describes a situation in which photographers might not have known why they were present at particular moments but they felt a need to be there. In light of this, Hayes draws our attention to the act of photographing itself as a 'component part of photography'.[16] She urges us to think 'beyond' the 'final product' of a photographic print that goes into circulation to consider the 'dynamic aspect of a growing presence of photographers with cameras' at moments of protest and in particular at political funerals during the 1980s.[17] Focusing on the photographer at political funerals, Hayes argues that they became a part of the rituals of such occasions – their presence with its invocation of an external audience could heighten emotions and tensions with the police – but also that the act of taking the photographs was itself important. Hayes argues that during the 1980s many reels of photographs were taken at funerals that were never developed. She points to these unseen photographs as 'images out of bounds. They constitute the boundaries of taste and judgement of what should be seen in their time'.[18] Considering these unseen photographs prompts her to ask, 'is it necessary for things to be visible in order to shape our political and historical consciousness?'[19] The way in which Hayes thinks about photographs and photography is instructive for thinking about acts of speech and the recording of voices. The seen, like the sayable, was constructed and contested. Do we need to start to think about the presence of academic researchers, seeking interviews during this period (and later ones) in the same way that Hayes thinks about the photographer – as part of the picture?

Telling stories differently

Visibility and audibility have a complex relationship in the archive. They are often simultaneous but also occasionally they become separated. In these instances, the presence of one can make the absence of the other all the more acute. This is the case with the main protagonist in this book: Masabata Loate. She emerges from the archive in glimpses and through interpreters. We cannot see and hear her through the same means. In the visual record of South African life that is contained within the society pages of South Africa's township edition newspapers Loate is a smiling, Afro-ed beauty queen. In the records of the apartheid court system, she is a state witness and later as a defendant herself, she is an ambiguous activist. In the written records of the anti-apartheid movement, she is a political prisoner and a martyr. In post-apartheid struggle memoirs, she appears as an emblematic loss to meaningless violence. These are all outlines of a young woman – a shadow that can be glimpsed moving through the records.

Where does the impossibility of Loate's story leave us if we are interested in young women's participation in the anti-apartheid movement and particularly its youth formations? I hope it can make us think again about the way we hear and reconstruct stories of activism. Head's description of Kuzwayo as writing a shadow history is typical of the ways in which women's stories are often framed as running alongside, behind or beneath a master narrative. As Emily Bridger has noted in her groundbreaking work on young women's activism within COSAS – it is not enough that we simply add young black women into the story of South Africa's youth. She argues that her own research provides four challenges to existing historical understandings of the struggle.[20] Firstly, female COSAS activists demonstrate that women could be mobilised and participate politically outside discourses of politicised motherhood and wifehood. Secondly, the lives and stories of these young women activists blur the boundaries between public and private, personal and political – narratives that struggle histories often uphold or unquestioningly reproduce. Thirdly, the difficulties and challenges of being and becoming activists that young women faced complicate any straightforward heroic picture of participation in the struggle. Fourthly, she argues that young women's narratives of their activism disrupt the temporal conception of 'the end of apartheid'. In these ways Bridger frames the young women of COSAS as 'talk[ing] back' to histories of the liberation struggle.[21] There is clearly much to be gained from eliciting stories of struggle from those ready and willing to share their experiences. Loate's story confirms all of these challenges and adds another: that we acknowledge the deep entanglement of what we know, with how we know it. Gendered narratives of the liberation struggle were integral to the waging of that struggle, and how it has been remembered. This we can hear and see in the dynamics of struggle speech.

Part of my aim in writing this book has been to try to work out if there is another way to position ourselves as historians and hear women's stories. Or to put it even more broadly than that, to open possibilities for *telling stories of the struggle differently*. I am borrowing the precise phraseology 'telling stories differently' from the work of Clare Hemmings. In *Why Stories Matter* Hemmings unearths and then dissects the common narratives of the development over time of feminist politics and philosophy that are found embedded within the work of feminists.[22] She reveals the shared assumptions, blind spots and omissions that underpin feminists' own understandings of the history of feminism as well as the emotional relationships and responses that are constituted through those narratives. She shows the ways in which different versions of the same story of feminism's history are implicated in various projects of (re)making its future. However, rather than simply telling a different story of feminism that tries to correct these assumptions, blind spots and omissions, Hemmings urges us to try to experiment with telling stories differently.

Hemmings's work is part of a recognition from feminists that the assumption of a 'linear move from silence to voice' as an 'unproblematic liberatory potential of research' is flawed.[23] A critique of voice has long been central to the theoretical contributions of postcolonial feminists and feminists of colour who have argued for the 'unspeakability' of certain deeply traumatic pasts like slavery.[24] In questioning whether the subaltern could speak, Gayatri Spivak argued that 'if in the context of colonial production, the subaltern has no history and cannot speak, the subaltern as female is even more deeply in shadow'.[25] Drawing on Spivak, Hemmings argues that 'Western feminist theorists need to interrupt their presumptive status as subjects to alter the grammar of the subject' and that the key to this is a 'consideration of *how one might figure in another's history*' (emphasis added).[26] For the historian of apartheid South Africa, the beginnings of a different way of telling stories of the past might lie in considering how the historian figured within the lives of the young men and women who mobilised politically against the State. Hemmings also suggests the importance of resisting making others 'fully readable' and thereby refusing to resolve the limits of self-knowledge, or knowledge of the other.[27] In the South African context, Jon Soske has suggested something similar, I think, in his insistence on aiming for 'an unusable image of the past'.[28] This insistence emerges from an acknowledgement of the politics of access (to interviewees, archives and so on) that are underpinned by the 'potential assimilation of the research process into political battles fought for ends that differ considerably from the researcher's own intellectual goals'.[29] This is perhaps particularly acute in a context like post-apartheid South Africa in which politics is shaped by 'public struggles for historical visibility'.[30] However, as we discussed earlier in relation to Hayes's focus on the photographer and the act of photography *within* the liberation struggle, this focus on the place of the historian or researcher within a political field could and should also be applied to the recent apartheid past. I want to suggest that the value of the fragment *as a fragment* is the attention it draws to the process by which we come to know, since we must continually acknowledge what we do not (yet) know. It is for this reason that I have not yet added to the archives about Loate, by interviewing surviving family and friends. That is another project.[31] My aim here has not been to render as full a portrait of her as might be possible, but rather to focus on the structures of knowledge that her shadowy presence is found within. So, what do the lines of fracture that splinter Masabata Loate's story tell us? Where do we see and hear her and why is that important?

The fragment

Loate is visible in the historical record as a beauty queen, a reminder of the particular space afforded to young black women within South Africa's urban modernity – one in which their bodies and appearance were up for scrutiny and read as carriers of cultural meaning. These glimpses of Loate should remind us of the lenses through which young women were viewed. In the 1978–9 trial of the Soweto Eleven we first heard Loate as a student activist turned state witness whose body the presiding judge felt free to pass comment on. She was heard as one of the young feminine speakers that rendered the youth anti-apartheid protests of the Soweto Uprisings as masculine. At the same moment Sibongile Mthembu (as she was then) was glimpsed as a rare exception in this male world and one whose own appearance, demeanour and religious belief were asserted as a sign of the respectability of the Soweto students in the face of the prosecution's attack on them as seditious revolutionaries. In the late 1970s young women student activists spoke but they were not accorded a voice – we heard how doors were closed on them, how they turned away from politics, but not how it was that they were there in the first place, or how they negotiated the emotionally fraught and dangerous crossing of (gendered) boundaries that their political participation entailed.

Chapter 2 argued for a nuanced understanding of the relationship between speaking about the struggle and political participation more broadly. I suggested that thinking about who speaks and when within the historical record can help us understand the dynamics of political practice. At the interface of political activism and the apartheid criminal justice system, young women were not silenced but spoke under multiple pressures. I showed the ways in which young women's presence and speech were central to both state and anti-apartheid depictions of youth politics as masculine within the courtroom during the trial of the Soweto Eleven. By considering what was sayable for young women we refocused our attention on the production of gendered narratives of struggle. Acknowledging the production of gendered narratives of struggle can dissolve the apparent contradiction between the portrayals of political participation that emerge from speaking about the struggle and other evidence like photographs or arrest statistics. We also saw the ways in which speech about the struggle was a part of the continual negotiation of gendered relationships that shaped political participation. The 'intimacies' of anti-apartheid politics shaped both, the daily practices that constituted that politics, and what it was that was (and is) said about those practices.

Young women experienced a struggle to speak because speech was so central a site of the struggle. In Chapter 3 I showed that struggles over speech intensified during the 1980s and that the life and death of Masabata Loate can help us to see the ways in which the sanctions for women who 'talked' or who spoke up, or out, became more violent during the 1980s. Recognising the importance of control over women's speech, as well as their bodies, is vital for unpicking the gendered dynamics of township struggle and the nature of the historical record and legacies it left. The States of Emergency created conditions under which decisions to speak were those of life and death. We heard Masabata Loate again in this context, as a defendant on trial as the alleged secretary of SAYRCO. The possibilities for Loate's ambiguous anti-apartheid activism to exist narrowed over time. Loate's ambiguity is central to her importance for struggle histories. Loate's story was not one that was sayable within struggle speech. Her version of her place within the anti-apartheid activist world that was told during her trial in 1982 was dismissed by the presiding magistrate as simply not credible. We might agree, in which case, the decision of her defence team to mount a line of argument that reiterated her earlier appearance as a state witness seems oddly ignorant of the risks of such a strategy. George Bizos judged her as a 'confused young woman' but we might instead suggest she was and is, confusing: she crossed boundaries of political affiliation and between the worlds of politics and urban social life that struggle speech tried to fix and uphold. She had the space to speak as a political defendant on trial but little of what she said in 1982 conformed to expectations of this position.

The story of Loate's death is a story of silencing and the erasure over time of the specificity of her murder; why she was killed remains obscured in the various versions of her death that have surfaced in newspaper reports, activist commentaries, the TRC and post-apartheid autobiographies. The stories of her silencing suggest the multiple logics of her murder and, by extension, the violence of the Emergency years in Soweto. In Chapter 4, and the book as a whole, I have argued for the potency of silence for unpicking the gendered dynamics of political participation and the historical record it leaves us. Reading the story of Loate's silencing alongside the strange clarity of imprisonment as a site for the articulation of a black, female, anti-apartheid activist self, shows us the contours of women's struggles to speak. Chapter 4 explored women's speech in the struggle during the 1980s and 1990s, as it was accorded a new set of potential meanings: that of breaking silences that had upheld or symbolised gendered oppressions. The circulation of black women's stories through domestic and international feminist spaces has had the effect of rendering ongoing silences as a barrier to knowledge of women's gendered experiences. However, reading silences within women's autobiographical projects can tell us a lot about the ongoing production of gendered narratives of struggle.[32]

Each chapter was centred on an archival appearance – a different glimpse of Loate. These fragments are separate from one another but also entangled. Narrating any one of these moments in Loate's life necessitates drawing on the others. Most obviously, Loate's second appearance in court, was all about her first. Holding the fragments against one another enables us to see each more clearly, since light and shade fall differently within the fragments, but they cannot be joined. Her story is splintered by the way it was recorded. The threats to Loate's physical safety after her testimony as a state witness are mentioned in her second trial but how this was connected, if it was, to her death and the way she was 'hunted' by her youth congress comrades in 1986, we do not know.[33] The threads are broken – by the time of her death, her appearance as a state witness is no longer remembered publicly. However, the two fragments do tell us she was subjected to a recurring risk of violence and her acts of speech, be that talking in court or speaking up within organisations, were what placed her at risk.

Shadows are present everywhere that there is light. Seeing shadows is dependent, not on their existence as such but on the orientation of the observer. There is always a danger that in trying to examine a shadow, an observer might step too close, and in the end see only the shade that they themselves are casting. In writing this book I was driven by an impulse to reckon with the refusals to speak that I, and others, had encountered. The shadow that I have drawn of Masabata Loate is indeed overlaid by my own and those of other historians and researchers; we are a part of this history. Yet I hope I have demonstrated that a persistent and recurring set of silences like those of young black women who were engaged with anti-apartheid politics are made, re-made and broken at different historical moments and by many different people, organisations and processes. It is not as simple as a failure to ask or a refusal to speak. Silences are made by many voices.

The shadows are a space with potentially negative connotations – a space of the unknown, the frightening. When we speak of people becoming a shadow of themselves, we usually mean they are diminished in some way, no longer what they were. I borrow something of this meaning when I speak of my biography of Masabata Loate as a shadow portrait – for I am indeed suggesting the limits to my knowledge. However, I am also drawing on an idea of darkness as a refuge and space of creativity. Reflecting on a real darkness, that of load-shedding hours during the #RhodesMustFall occupation of Azania House, at the University of Cape Town, Thuli Gamedze has reworked the idea of darkness as a space of potential for finding a full sense of self:[34]

> . . . this darkness has provided a new kind of safety for a diverse group of some of the best people I have ever met. Intersectionality gives us a key into finding each other in this darkness, and feeling each other out without having to carry with us the burden of inhumanity, which comes with the 'perspective' offered by colonial lighting. When we discover ourselves in this dark, invisible, mysterious space, I cannot begin to imagine the inventive languages and visualities we will use in our struggle towards re-defining black humanity in the larger South African space.[35]

With this in mind, I do not want to imply that Loate languishes in the shadows. She lives there. She is alive, with a fullness that we cannot grasp. She is beyond our ability to see her clearly, but neither is she fully lost to us. She was there – her shadow is what she has left behind.

Notes

1. Ellen Kuzwayo, *Call Me Woman* (London: Women's Press, 1985), xiii.
2. Gillian Whitlock, *The Intimate Empire* (London: A&C Black, 2000), 147–8.
3. Mtutuzeli Matshoba, *Call Me Not a Man / Mtutuzeli Matshoba* (Johannesburg: Ravan Press, 1979).
4. See for example: Jeremy Seekings, 'Whose Voices? Politics and Methodology in the Study of Political Organisation and Protest in the Final Phase of the "Struggle" in South Africa', *South African Historical Journal* 62, no. 1 (2010): 7–28, http://dx.doi.org/10.1080/02582471003778300; Hilary Sapire, 'Township Histories, Insurrection and Liberation in Late Apartheid South Africa', *South African Historical Journal* 65, no. 2 (1 June 2013): 167–98, http://dx.doi.org/10.1080/02582473.2013.777089; Arianna Lissoni et al., *One Hundred Years of the ANC: Debating Liberation Histories Today* (Johannesburg: Wits University Press, 2012).
5. For the former see, Seekings, 'Whose Voices?' and for the latter, Jacob Dlamini, *Askari: A Story of Collaboration and Betrayal in the Anti-Apartheid Struggle* (Johannesburg: Jacana Media, 2014).

6. In this I have been inspired by the call from Woodward et al. for approaches that examine the 'processes through which gendered subjects locate and relocate themselves in the world: how they move between being vocal and mute, between centre-stage limelight and the shadowy wings': Wendy Woodward, Patricia Hayes and Gary Minkley, *Deep Histories: Gender and Colonialism in Southern Africa* (Amsterdam: Rodopi, 2002), xxv.

7. This phraseology is borrowed from the insightful discussion of biography in Nancy J. Jacobs and Andrew Bank, 'Biography in Post-Apartheid South Africa A Call for Awkwardness', *African Studies* 78, no. 2 (3 April 2019): 165–82, https://doi.org/10.1080/00020184.2019.1569428.

8. David William Cohen, *The Combing of History* (Chicago: University of Chicago Press, 1994), 118.

9. They ask the evocative question, 'where does history reside and power hide in this image?' See: Gary Minkley and Ciraj Rassool, 'Photography with a Difference: Leon Levson's Camera Studies and Photographic Exhibitions of Native Life in South Africa, 1947–1950', *Kronos*, no. 31 (2005): 192.

10. Santu Mofokeng, 'Trajectory of a Street Photographer', *Nka Journal of Contemporary African Art* 2000, no. 11–12 (1 May 2000): 45, https://doi.org/10.1215/10757163-11-12-1-41.

11. Mongane Serote, *To Every Birth Its Blood* (Johannesburg: Picador Africa, 2004), 106.

12. Ann Laura Stoler, *Along the Archival Grain Epistemic Anxieties and Colonial Common Sense* (Princeton, NJ: Princeton University Press, 2009).

13. Helena Cook and Diane Orentlicher, *The War against Children: South Africa's Youngest Victims* (New York: Lawyers Committee for Human Rights, 1986), 52.

14. Audrey Coleman, Truth and Reconciliation Commission, Special Hearings, Children's Hearing, Johannesburg, Day 1, 12 June 1997, accessed June 2024, www.justice.gov.za/trc/special/children/acoleman.htm.

15. Patricia Hayes, 'Political Funerals in South Africa: Photography, History and the Refusal of Light (1960s–80s)', in *Love and Revolution in the Twentieth-Century Colonial and Postcolonial World: Perspectives from South Asia and Southern Africa*, ed. G. Arunima, Patricia Hayes and Premesh Lalu, Palgrave Studies in the History of Social Movements (Cham: Springer International Publishing, 2021), 304.

16. Hayes, 'Political Funerals in South Africa', 305.

17. Hayes, 'Political Funerals in South Africa', 302.

18. Hayes, 'Political Funerals in South Africa', 303.

19. Hayes, 'Political Funerals in South Africa', 302.

20. Emily Bridger, *Young Women against Apartheid: Gender, Youth and South Africa's Liberation Struggle* (Woodbridge, Suffolk; Rochester, NY: James Currey, 2021), 221–3.

21. Bridger, *Young Women against Apartheid*, 222.

22. Clare Hemmings, *Why Stories Matter: The Political Grammar of Feminist Theory* (Durham, NC: Duke University Press Books, 2011).

23. Róisín Ryan-Flood and Rosalind Gill, eds., *Secrecy and Silence in the Research Process: Feminist Reflections, Secrecy and Silence in the Research Process: Feminist Reflections*, Transformations: Thinking through Feminism (Abingdon, Oxon: Routledge, 2010), 2.

24. Bibi Bakare-Yusuf, 'The Economy of Violence: Black Bodies and the Unspeakable Terror', in *Gender and Catastrophe* (London: Zed Books, 1997), 171–84; see the insightful discussion on trauma and silence in Nthabiseng Motsemme, 'The

Mute Always Speak: On Women's Silences at the Truth and Reconciliation Commission', *Current Sociology* 52, no. 5 (2004): 914–17, https://doi.org/10.1177/0011392104045377.

25. Gayatri Chakravorty Spivak, 'Can the Subaltern Speak?', in *Marxism and the Interpretation of Culture*, ed. Lawrence Grossberg and Carry Nelson (Urbana, IL: University of Illinois Press; Basingstoke: Macmillan, 1988), 288.

26. Hemmings, *Why Stories Matter*, 214.

27. Hemmings, *Why Stories Matter*, 223.

28. Jon Soske, 'Open Secrets, Off the Record: Audience, Intimate Knowledge, and the Crisis of the Post-Apartheid State', *Historical Reflections / Réflexions Historiques* 38, no. 2 (2012): 68, http://www.jstor.org/stable/23267796.

29. Soske, 'Open Secrets, Off the Record', 67.

30. Soske, 'Open Secrets, Off the Record', 67.

31. There are very few leads to follow. The most recent and promising was a 2020 public recollection of Loate by one of the surviving Soweto Eleven, Thabo Ndabeni, who was jailed for refusing to testify at Loate's 1982 trial, at a June 16 commemoration: 'Masabata shouldn't have died the way she did. For someone who sacrificed as much as she did and to die in an undignified way. Necklacing! That was the worst that could befall a soldier for the revolution such as her.' The author of the blog post, Veli Mbele, who reported this comment, also expresses a wish to 'hold a proper and dignified memorial for Masabata'. Veli Mbele, 'June 16 Uprising and the Untold Story of Masabata Loate', Culture Review, accessed June 2024, https://web.archive.org/web/20201030135628/https://culture-review.co.za/june-16-uprising-and-the-untold-story-of-masabata-loate.

32. Motsemme, 'The Mute Always Speak: On Women's Silences at the Truth and Reconciliation Commission'.

33. This chilling description comes from the report that 'her comrades allegedly came out of a street committee meeting to hunt her' in 'Anti-necklace ex-beauty queen murdered', *Cape Times*, 20 October 1986.

34. 'Load-shedding hours' refers to periods of electricity black-outs when demand for electricity outstrips supply available to the government-owned national power provider, ESKOM. Since 2007 in South Africa this has become a frequent problem, so that power is rationed by shutting down sections of the supply grid on a pre-set schedule. For the history of electricity supply in South Africa see: Faeeza Ballim, *Apartheid's Leviathan: Electricity and the Power of Technological Ambivalence*, New African Histories (Athens, OH: Ohio University Press, 2023).

35. Thuli Gamedze, 'Azania House Intersectionality as a Catalyst for Black Imagination', *The Johannesburg Salon (The Joannesburg Workshop in Theory and Criticism)* 9 (2015): 123.

Bibliography

Archival collections

Historical Papers (WHP), University of the Witwatersrand:

AD1450: Trials:
Supreme Court of South Africa (Transvaal Provincial Division), *State vs. W.W.C. Twala and Ten Others*, case K/P 282/78.
AD2021: SAIRR Security Trials 1958–82:
State vs. Mary Masabate Loatse and others, case: 41/4115/81 Magistrates Court, District of Johannesburg.
State vs. Stanley Radebe, Ephraim Mthuthuzele Madalane, Ernest Lebana Mohakala and Innocentia Nonkululeka Mazibuko, Case: SH 635/82, Regional Court for the Regional Division of the Southern Transvaal (Kempton Park).
AG 2523: Detainee Parents Support Committee.

South African Historical Archive (SAHA), University of the Witwatersrand:

AL2607: Congress of South African Students (COSAS).

London School of Economics (LSE), The Women's Library (TWL):

6TWP: The Women's Press.

Digital archives

'Archive', *"I Saw a Nightmare": Doing Violence to Memory, The Soweto Uprising, June 16, 1976*, Gutenberg-e.org. http://www.gutenberg-e.org/pohlandt-mccormick/archive/.
Digital Innovation South Africa. https://disa.ukzn.ac.za/.
Struggles for Freedom: Southern Africa (ALUKA). https://www.jstor.org/site/struggles-for-freedom/southern-africa/.

Government and official publications

Goldblatt, Beth, and Shiela Meintjes. 'Gender and the Truth and Reconciliation Commission', May 1996. http://www.doj.gov.za/trc/submit/gender.htm.

South Africa, *Report of the Commission of Inquiry into the Riots at Soweto and Elsewhere from the 16th of June 1976 to the 28th of February 1977.* Pretoria: Govt. Printer, 1980.

South African Institute of Race Relations. 'Survey of Race Relations in South Africa 1982'. Pietermaritzburg, 1982.

'Statement of the National Executive Committee of the African National Congress on the Emancipation of Women in South Africa'. *Agenda* 6, no. 8 (1 January 1990): 19–23. https://doi.org/10.2307/4065629.

Truth and Reconciliation Commission of South Africa, *Truth and Reconciliation Commission of South Africa Report*, vols 1–5, Cape Town: Truth and Reconciliation Commission, 1998.

Interviews, hearing transcripts, speeches

Bizos, George. 'Memoirs as related to Thomas Karis and Gail Gerhart' (New York, 1989), accessed 14 March 2023. https://www.jstor.org/stable/al.sff.document.gerhart0018.

Coleman, Max, and Audrey Coleman. Interview 10 April 2007, in *Between Life and Death: Stories from John Vorster Square.* Johannesburg: Doxa Natural Knowledge, 2007.

Mandela, Nelson. Address to rally in Cape Town on his release from prison, 11 February 1990. Verbatim transcript, accessed June 2024. https://atom.nelsonmandela.org/index.php/za-com-mr-s-16.

Musi, Rebecca. Interview with Rachel Johnson, Johannesburg, September 2008.

Truth and Reconciliation Commission, Public Hearings of Human Rights Violation Committees. Full hearing transcripts, accessed 26 June 2024. https://www.justice.gov.za/trc/.

Newspapers, magazines

Associated Press (AP) News
Cape Times
City Press

Financial Mail
Frontline
Mail & Guardian
Rand Daily Mail
Sowetan
Time Magazine
United Press International (UPI)
Weekly Mail and Guardian

Websites and online journalism

'List of BCM Heroes and Heroines', AZAPO, last updated 5 January 2003; accessed June 2024. https://web.archive.org/web/20190511202049/http://azapo.org.za/azapohistory/azanian-peoples-organisation/.

Mbele, Veli. 'June 16 Uprising and the Untold Story of Masabata Loate', Culture Review, posted 17 June 2020; accessed June 2024. https://web.archive.org/web/20201030135628/https://culture-review.co.za/june-16-uprising-and-the-untold-story-of-masabata-loate.

Mngxitama, Andile. 'June 16, 1976 in Perspective: Tsietsi and Khotso, Brothers in Arms', Black Opinion, first posted 21 January 2004; reposted 15 June 2016; accessed June 2024. https://web.archive.org/web/20160618051602/http://blackopinion.co.za/2016/06/15/june-16-1976-perspective-tsietsi-khotso-brothers-arms/.

Msimang, Sisonke. 'Winnie Mandela (1936–2018)', posted 4 June 2016. https://jacobinmag.com/2018/04/winnie-mandela-south-africa-obituary-anc.

Paul Brunton Philosophic Foundation. 'Illustrated Biography', posted 19 November 2023. https://www.paulbrunton.org/about-paul-brunton/illustrated-biography/.

'To cap? Or not cap "Black"?', Who We Are, posted 8 August 2021, https://www.who-are-we.online/article2.html.

Political journals

APUDSA Views
Horizon
Sash: The Black Sash Magazine
Sechaba: Official Organ of the African National Congress South Africa
The Voice of Women

Scholarship

Alegi, Peter. 'Rewriting Patriarchal Scripts: Women, Labor, and Popular Culture in South African Clothing Industry Beauty Contests, 1970s–2005'. *Journal of Social History* 42, no. 1 (2008): 31–56. https://doi.org/10.1353/jsh.0.0070.

Alegi, Peter, and Chris Bolsmann. 'From Apartheid to Unity: White Capital and Black Power in the Racial Integration of South African Football, 1976–1992'. *African Historical Review* 42, no. 1 (1 June 2010): 1–18. https://doi.org/10.1080/17532523.2010.483783.

Allman, Jean. 'The Disappearing of Hannah Kudjoe: Nationalism, Feminism, and the Tyrannies of History'. *Journal of Women's History* 21, no. 3 (11 September 2009): 13–35. https://doi.org/10.1353/jowh.0.0096.

Allo, Awol. *The Courtroom as a Space of Resistance: Reflections on the Legacy of the Rivonia Trial.* London: Routledge, 2016. https://doi.org/10.4324/9781315615073.

Amin, Shahid. 'Approver's Testimony, Judicial Discourse: The Case of Chauri Chaura'. In *Subaltern Studies V*, edited by Ranajit Guha, 166–202. Oxford: Oxford University Press, 1987.

Asheeke, Toivo Tukongeni Paul Wilson. *Arming Black Consciousness: The Azanian Black Nationalist Tradition and South Africa's Armed Struggle.* African Studies Series. Cambridge: Cambridge University Press, 2023.

Bakare-Yusuf, Bibi. 'The Economy of Violence: Black Bodies and the Unspeakable Terror'. In *Gender and Catastrophe*, edited by Ronit Lentin, 171–84. London: Zed Books, 1997.

Ballim, Faeeza. *Apartheid's Leviathan: Electricity and the Power of Technological Ambivalence.* New African Histories. Athens, OH: Ohio University Press, 2023.

Beall, Jo, M. Friedman, Shireen Hassim, R. Posel, L. Stiebel and Alison Todes. 'African Women in the Durban Struggle, 1985–6: Towards a Transformation of Roles', *South African Review* 4 (1987): 93–103.

Bethlehem, Louise. 'Stenographic Fictions: Mary Benson's At the Still Point and the South African Political Trial'. *Safundi* 20, no. 2 (3 April 2019): 193–212. https://doi.org/10.1080/17533171.2019.1576963.

Bizos, George. *Odyssey to Freedom.* Johannesburg: Penguin Random House South Africa, 2011.

Boehmer, Elleke. *Stories of Women: Gender and Narrative in the Postcolonial Nation.* Knowledge Unlatched. Manchester: Manchester University Press, 2009. https://doi.org/10.2307/j.ctt155j4ws.

Bonner, Philip. 'Fragmentation and Cohesion in the ANC: The First 70 Years'. In *One Hundred Years of the ANC: Debating Liberation Histories Today*, edited by Arianna Lissoni, Jon Soske, Natasha Erlank, Noor Nieftagodien and Omar Badsha, 1–12. Johannesburg: Wits University Press, 2012.

Bozzoli, Belinda. *Theatres of Struggle and the End of Apartheid*. Edinburgh: Edinburgh University Press, 2004.

Bridger, Emily. 'Apartheid's "Rape Crisis": Understanding and Addressing Sexual Violence in South Africa, 1970s–1990s'. *Women's History Review* 33, no. 2 (23 February 2024): 265–84. https://doi.org/10.1080/09612025.2023.2219535.

Bridger, Emily. 'From "Mother of the Nation" to "Lady Macbeth": Winnie Mandela and Perceptions of Female Violence in South Africa, 1985–91'. *Gender & History*, 1 August 2015. https://doi.org/10.1111/1468-0424.12133.

Bridger, Emily. 'Functions and Failures of Transnational Activism: Discourses of Children's Resistance and Repression in Global Anti-Apartheid Networks'. *Journal of World History* 26, no. 4 (2015): 865–87.

Bridger, Emily. 'Soweto's Female Comrades: Gender, Youth and Violence in South Africa's Township Uprisings, 1984–1990'. *Journal of Southern African Studies* 44, no. 4 (4 July 2018): 559–74. https://doi.org/10.1080/03057070.2018.1462591.

Bridger, Emily. *Young Women against Apartheid: Gender, Youth and South Africa's Liberation Struggle*. Woodbridge, Suffolk; Rochester, NY: James Currey, 2021.

Bridger, Emily, and Erin Hazan. 'Surfeit and Silence: Sexual Violence in the Apartheid Archive'. *African Studies* 81, no. 3–4 (2 October 2022): 286–305. https://doi.org/10.1080/00020184.2023.2212606.

Brooks, Alan, and Jeremy Brickhill. *Whirlwind Before the Storm: The Origins and Development of the Uprising in Soweto and the Rest of South Africa from June to December 1976*. London: International Defence and Aid Fund for Southern Africa, 1980.

Brown, Julian. 'An Experiment in Confrontation: The Pro-Frelimo Rallies of 1974'. *Journal of Southern African Studies* 38, no. 1 (1 March 2012): 55–71. https://doi.org/10.1080/03057070.2012.644978.

Brown, Julian. *The Road to Soweto: Resistance and the Uprising of 16 June 1976*. Woodbridge, Suffolk: James Currey, 2016.

Brunton, Paul. *The Hidden Teaching beyond Yoga*. Tenth Impression. London: Rider & Company, 1941.

Bundy, Colin. 'Street Sociology and Pavement Politics: Aspects of Youth and Student Resistance in Cape Town, 1985'. *Journal of Southern African Studies* 13, no. 3 (April 1987): 303–30. https://doi.org/10.1080/03057078708708148.

Butler, Judith. *Excitable Speech: A Politics of the Performative*. New York: Routledge, 1997.

Cameron, Marsaili. 'What the Hell Is Feminist Editing?' In *In Other Words: Writing as a Feminist*, edited by Gail Chester and Sigrid Nielsen, 119–25. London: Hutchinson, 1987.

Campbell, Catherine. 'Learning to Kill? Masculinity, the Family and Violence in Natal'. *Journal of Southern African Studies* 18, no. 3 (September 1992): 614–28. https://www.jstor.org/stable/2637301.

Carolin, Andy. 'Locating Sexual Rights in the Anti-Apartheid Movement: Simon Nkoli and the Making of Post-Apartheid Protest Theatre'. *Critical Arts* 32, no. 5–6 (2 November 2018): 35–50. https://doi.org/10.1080/02560046.2018.1560342.

Chabani Manganyi, N., and Andre Du Toit, eds. *Political Violence and the Struggle in South Africa*. London: Palgrave Macmillan, 1990. http://link.springer.com/book/10.1007/978-1-349-21074-9.

Cherry, Janet. '"We Were Not Afraid": The Role of Women in the 1980s Township Uprising in the Eastern Cape'. In *Women in South African History: They Remove Boulders and Cross Rivers*, edited by Nomboniso Gasa, 281–314. Cape Town: HSRC Press, 2007.

Chubb, Karin. *Between Anger and Hope: South Africa's Youth and the Truth and Reconciliation Commission*. Johannesburg: Witwatersrand University Press, 2001.

Clayton, Cherry. 'Radical Transformations: Emergent Women's Voices in South Africa'. *English in Africa* 17, no. 2 (1990): 25–36. https://hdl.handle.net/10520/AJA03768902_330.

Coetzee, Carli. *Written under the Skin: Blood and Intergenerational Memory in South Africa*. Woodbridge, Suffolk; Johannesburg, South Africa: James Currey; 2019.

Cohen, David William. *The Combing of History*. Chicago: University of Chicago Press, 1994.

Cole, Catherine. 'Justice in Transition: South African Political Trials, 1956–1964'. In *The Courtroom As a Space of Resistance: Reflections on the Legacy of the Rivonia Trial*, edited by Awol Allo, Emilios Christodoulidis and Sharon Cowan, 81–122. London: Taylor & Francis Group, 2015. http://ebookcentral.proquest.com/lib/durham/detail.action?docID=4442706.

Coleman, Max. *A Crime Against Humanity*. Cape Town: David Philip, 1998.

Cook, Helena, and Diane Orentlicher. *The War against Children: South Africa's Youngest Victims*. New York: Lawyers Committee for Human Rights, 1986.

Coombes, Annie E., 'The Gender of Memory in Postapartheid South Africa: The Women's Jail as Heritage Site'. In *Museum Transformations*,

The International Handbooks of Museum Studies Volume 4, edited by Annie E. Coombes and Ruth B. Phillips, 207–226. Chichester: John Wiley and Sons, 2015.

Cronin, Jeremy. '"The Law That Says/Constricts the Breath-Line (. . .)" South African English Language Poetry Written by Africans in the 1970s'. *English Academy Review* 3, no. 1 (January 1985): 25–49. https://doi.org/10.1080/10131758585310031.

Curnow, Robyn, and Thandi Modise. 'Thandi Modise, a Woman in War'. *Agenda* 43 (2000): 36–40.

Das, Veena. *Life and Words: Violence and the Descent into the Ordinary.* Berkeley: University of California Press, 2006.

Delius, Peter, and Clive Glaser. 'Sexual Socialisation in South Africa: A Historical Perspective'. *African Studies* 61, no. 1 (2002): 27–54. https://doi.org/10.1080/00020180220140064.

Dlamini, Jacob. *Askari: A Story of Collaboration and Betrayal in the Anti-Apartheid Struggle.* Johannesburg: Jacana Media, 2014.

Drew, Allison. *Discordant Comrades: Identities and Loyalties on the South African Left.* London: Routledge, 2019.

Driver, Dorothy. 'Imagined Selves, (Un)Imagined Marginalities'. *Journal of Southern African Studies* 17, no. 2 (1991): 337–54. https://doi.org/10.1080/03057079108708281.

Dubow, Saul. *Apartheid, 1948–1994.* Oxford: Oxford University Press, 2014.

Erlank, Natasha. 'Christianity and African Nationalism in South Africa in the First Half of the Twentieth Century'. In *One Hundred Years of the ANC: Debating Liberation Histories Today,* edited by Arianna Lissoni, Jon Soske, Natasha Erlank, Noor Nieftagodien and Omar Badsha, 77–96. Johannesburg: Wits University Press, 2012.

Erlank, Natasha. 'Gender and Masculinity in South African Nationalist Discourse, 1912–1950'. *Feminist Studies* 29, no. 3 (2003): 653–72. https://www.jstor.org/stable/3178733.

Everatt, David, and Elinor Sisulu, eds. *Black Youth in Crisis: Facing the Future.* Braamfontein: Ravan Press, 1992.

Federation of Transvaal Women, *A Woman's Place Is in the Struggle, Not Behind Bars.* Reprinted by The Africa Fund, New York, 1988.

Field, Sean. 'Turning up the Volume: Dialogues about Memory Create Oral Histories'. *South African Historical Journal* 60, no. 2 (1 June 2008): 175–94. https://doi.org/10.1080/02582470802416393.

Fish, Patrick. 'Malan, the Movie: The BBC Version of Rian Malan's "My Traitor's Heart"'. *South African Theatre Journal* 5, no. 1 (January 1991): 98–108. https://doi.org/10.1080/10137548.1991.9688031.

Fourie, Enid. 'The UN Convention on the Rights of the Child and the Crisis for Children in South Africa: Apartheid and Detention

Symposium: UN Convention on Children's Rights'. *Human Rights Quarterly* 12, no. 1 (1990): 106–14.
Friedman, Steven. 'The Sounds of Silence: Structural Change and Collective Action in the Fight against Apartheid'. *South African Historical Journal* 69, no. 2 (3 April 2017): 236–50. https://doi.org/10.1080/02582473.2017.1293719.
Gaitskell, Deborah. '"Wailing for Purity": Prayer Unions, African Mothers and Adolescent Daughters 1912–1940'. In *Industrialisation and Social Change in South Africa: African Class Formation, Culture, and Consciousness, 1870–1930*, edited by Shula Marks and R. J. A. R Rathbone, 383–57. Harlow: Longman, 1982.
Gamedze, Thuli. 'Azania House Intersectionality as a Catalyst for Black Imagination'. *The Johannesburg Salon (The Johannesburg Workshop in Theory and Criticism)* 9 (2015): 122–3.
Glaser, Clive. *Bo Tsotsi: The Youth Gangs of Soweto, 1935–1976*. Oxford: James Currey, 2000.
Glaser, Clive. 'Soweto's Islands of Learning: Morris Isaacson and Orlando High Schools Under Bantu Education, 1958–1975'. *Journal of Southern African Studies* 41, no. 1 (2 January 2015): 159–71. https://doi.org/10.1080/03057070.2015.991573.
Gqola, Pumla Dineo. *Rape: A South African Nightmare*. Auckland Park, South Africa: MF Books Joburg, 2015.
Gready, Paul. 'The Sophiatown Writers of the Fifties: The Unreal Reality of Their World'. *Journal of Southern African Studies* 16, no. 1 (1990): 139–64. http://www.jstor.org/stable/2636643.
Gready, Paul. 'The Witness: Rian Malan's "My Traitor's Heart" and Elsa Joubert's "Poppie"'. *Current Writing* 7, no. 1 (January 1995): 88–104. https://doi.org/10.1080/1013929X.1995.9677949.
Gready, Paul. *Writing as Resistance: Life Stories of Imprisonment, Exile, and Homecoming from Apartheid South Africa*. Lanham, MD: Lexington Books, 2003.
Gunner, Liz. 'The Politics of Language and Chief Albert Luthuli's Funeral, 30 July 1967'. In *One Hundred Years of the ANC: Debating Liberation Histories Today*, edited by Arianna Lissoni, Jon Soske, Natasha Erlank, Noor Nieftagodien and Omar Badsha, 182–210. Johannesburg: Wits University Press, 2012. https://www.cambridge.org/core/books/one-hundred-years-of-the-anc/politics-of-language-and-chief-albert-luthulis-funeral-30-july-1967/E613C1E81B5CD1EFE8F8052C8EA2AC04.
Hadfield, Leslie Anne. 'Challenging the Status Quo: Young Women and Men in Black Consciousness Community Work, 1970s South Africa'.

Journal of African History 54 (2013): 247–67. https://doi.org/doi:10.1017/S0021853713000261.

Hadfield, Leslie Anne. *Liberation and Development: Black Consciousness Community Programs in South Africa*. East Lansing, MI: Michigan State University Press, 2016.

Hanisch, Carol. 'The Personal Is Political'. In *Radical Feminism: A Documentary Reader*, edited by Barbara A. Crow, 113–16. New York: New York University Press, 2000.

Hartman, Saidiya. 'Venus in Two Acts'. *Small Axe* 12, no. 2 (2008): 1–14. https://doi.org/10.1215/-12-2-1.

Hassim, Shireen. 'Democracy's Shadows: Sexual Rights and Gender Politics in the Rape Trial of Jacob Zuma'. *African Studies* 68, no. 1 (1 April 2009): 57–77. https://doi.org/10.1080/00020180902827431.

Hassim, Shireen. 'Not Just Nelson's Wife: Winnie Madikizela-Mandela, Violence and Radicalism in South Africa'. *Journal of Southern African Studies* 44, no. 5 (3 September 2018): 895–912. https://doi.org/10.1080/03057070.2018.1514566.

Hassim, Shireen. 'The Impossible Contract: The Political and Private Marriage of Nelson and Winnie Mandela'. *Journal of Southern African Studies* 45, no. 6 (2 November 2019): 1151–71. https://doi.org/10.1080/03057070.2019.1697137.

Hassim, Shireen. *Women's Organizations and Democracy in South Africa: Contesting Authority*. Madison: University of Wisconsin Press, 2006.

Hayes, Patricia. 'Political Funerals in South Africa: Photography, History and the Refusal of Light (1960s–80s)'. In *Love and Revolution in the Twentieth-Century Colonial and Postcolonial World: Perspectives from South Asia and Southern Africa*, edited by G. Arunima, Patricia Hayes and Premesh Lalu, 291–366. Palgrave Studies in the History of Social Movements. Cham: Springer International Publishing, 2021.

Healy-Clancy, Meghan. 'The Family Politics of the Federation of South African Women: A History of Public Motherhood in Women's Antiracist Activism'. *Signs* 42, no. 4 (2017): 843–66. https://doi.org/10.1086/690916.

Heffernan, Anne. 'Blurred Lines and Ideological Divisions in South African Youth Politics'. *African Affairs* 115, no. 461 (1 October 2016): 664–87. https://doi.org/10.1093/afraf/adw052.

Heffernan, Anne. *Limpopo's Legacy: Student Politics and Democracy in South Africa*. Woodbridge, Suffolk: Boydell & Brewer, 2019. https://doi.org/10.2307/j.ctvc16j21.

Heffernan, Anne, Noor Nieftagodien, Sifiso Mxolisi Ndlovu, Bhekizizwe Peterson, Ian Macqueen and Arianna Lissoni. *Students Must Rise: Youth Struggle in South Africa before and beyond Soweto '76*. Johannesburg: Wits University Press, 2006.

Hemmings, Clare. *Why Stories Matter: The Political Grammar of Feminist Theory*. Durham, NC: Duke University Press, 2011.

Hirson, Baruch. *Year of Fire, Year of Ash: The Soweto Revolt: Roots of a Revolution?* London: Zed Press, 1979.

Hlongwane, Khangela Ali. 'Bricks-and-Mortar Testimonies: The Interactive and Dialogical Features of the Memorials and Monuments of the June 16 1976 Soweto Uprisings'. In *The Road to Democracy in South Africa: Volume 7: Soweto Uprisings: New Perspective, Commemorations and Memorialisation*, 195–226. Cape Town: Unisa Press, 2017.

Hlongwane, Khangela Ali, Sifiso Mxolisi Ndlovu and Mothobi Mutloatse, eds. *Soweto '76*. Houghton: Mutloatse Arts Heritage Trust, 2006.

Holmes, Rachel. 'Queer Comrades: Winnie Mandela and the Moffies'. *Social Text*, no. 52/53 (1997): 161–80. https://doi.org/10.2307/466738.

Hunt, Lynn. *Family Romance of the French Revolution*. London: Routledge, 1992. https://doi.org/10.4324/9781315003306.

Hyslop, Jonathan. *The Classroom Struggle; Policy and Resistance in South Africa, 1940–1990*. Pietermaritzburg: University of Natal Press, 1999.

Jacobs, Nancy J., and Andrew Bank. 'Biography in Post-Apartheid South Africa: A Call for Awkwardness'. *African Studies* 78, no. 2 (3 April 2019): 165–82. https://doi.org/10.1080/00020184.2019.1569428.

Johnson, Rachel. '"The Girl About Town": Discussions of Modernity and Female Youth in Drum Magazine, 1951–1970'. *Social Dynamics* 35, no. 1 (1 March 2009): 36–50. https://doi.org/10.1080/02533950802666899.

Johnson, Shaun, ed. *South Africa: No Turning Back*. Basingstoke: Macmillan, 1988.

Kane-Berman, John Stuart. *Soweto: Black Revolt, White Reaction*. Johannesburg: Ravan Press, 1978.

Karimakwenda, Nyasha. 'Safe to Violate: The Role of Gender in the Necklacing of Women During the South African People's War (1985–1990)'. *Journal of Southern African Studies* 45, no. 3 (4 May 2019): 559–74. https://doi.org/10.1080/03057070.2019.1642646.

Kessel, Ineke Van. *Beyond Our Wildest Dreams: The United Democratic Front and the Transformation of South Africa*. Charlottesville: University Press of Virginia, 2000.

Kuzwayo, Ellen. *Call Me Woman*. London: Women's Press, 1985.

Lee, Hermione. *Virginia Woolf's Nose: Essays on Biography*. Princeton, NJ: Princeton University Press, 2018. https://doi.org/10.1515/9780691188607.

Lee, Rebekah. 'Death "On the Move": Funerals, Entrepreneurs and the Rural-Urban Nexus in South Africa'. *Africa: Journal of the International African Institute* 81, no. 2 (2011): 226–47. https://www.jstor.org/stable/41485275.

Le Roux, Elizabeth. 'Miriam Tlali and Ravan Press: Politics and Power in Literary Publishing during the Apartheid Period'. *Journal of Southern African Studies* 44, no. 3 (4 May 2018): 431–46. https://doi.org/10.1080/03057070.2018.1450007.

Limb, Peter. *The ANC's Early Years: Nation, Class and Place in South Africa before 1940*. Pretoria: University of South Africa, 2010. https://doi.org/10.25159/882-5.

Lissoni, Arianna, Jon Soske, Natasha Erlank, Noor Nieftagodien and Omar Badsha, eds. *One Hundred Years of the ANC: Debating Liberation Histories Today*. Johannesburg: Wits University Press, 2012.

Lobban, Michael. *White Man's Justice: South African Political Trials in the Black Consciousness Era*. Oxford: Clarendon Press, 1996.

Lodge, Tom. *Red Road to Freedom: A History of the South African Communist Party 1921–2021*. Woodbridge, Suffolk; Rochester, NY: James Currey, 2022.

Lodge, Tom. 'The Destruction of Sophiatown'. *The Journal of Modern African Studies* 19, no. 1 (1981): 107–32.

Lowe, Lisa. 'The Intimacies of Four Continents'. In *Haunted by Empire: Geographies of Intimacy in North American History*, edited by Ann Laura Stoler, 191–212. American Encounters/Global Interactions. Durham, NC: Duke University Press, 2006.

Macqueen, Ian M. *Black Consciousness and Progressive Movements under Apartheid*. Scottsville, South Africa: University of KwaZulu-Natal Press, 2018.

Magaziner, Daniel R. 'Two Stories about Art, Education, and Beauty in Twentieth-Century South Africa'. *The American Historical Review* 118, no. 5 (1 December 2013): 1403–29. https://doi.org/10.1093/ahr/118.5.1403.

Magaziner, Daniel R. 'Pieces of a (Wo)Man: Feminism, Gender and Adulthood in Black Consciousness, 1968–1977'. *Journal of Southern African Studies* 37, no. 1 (1 March 2011): 45–61.

Magaziner, Daniel R. *The Law and the Prophets: Black Consciousness in South Africa, 1968–1977*. Athens, OH: Ohio University Press, 2010.

Magubane, Bernard. *The Making of a Racist State: British Imperialism and the Union of South Africa, 1875–1910*. Trenton, NJ: Africa World Press, 1996.

Magubane, Zine. 'Attitudes towards Feminism among Women in the ANC, 1950–1990: A Theoretical Re-Interpretation'. In *The Road to Democracy in South Africa: Volume 4, Part 2.*, 975–1033. Cape Town: Unisa Press, 2010.

Malan, Rian. *My Traitor's Heart.* London: Vintage, 1991.

Maphunye, Kealeboga J. 'Legacy Underplayed or Ignored? Tsietsi Mashinini: The Forgotten Warrior of South Africa's Liberation Struggle'. *African Historical Review* 49, no. 2 (3 July 2017): 22–47. https://doi.org/10.1080/17532523.2017.1414675.

Marks, Monique. *Young Warriors: Youth Politics, Identity and Violence in South Africa.* Johannesburg: Witwatersrand University Press, 2001.

Marschall, Sabine. *Landscape of Memory: Commemorative Monuments, Memorials and Public Statuary in Post-Apartheid South-Africa.* Leiden: Brill, 2010.

Martin, Yasmina. '"Now I Am Not Afraid": Simon Nkoli, Queer Utopias and Transnational Solidarity'. *Journal of Southern African Studies* 46, no. 4 (3 July 2020): 673–87. https://doi.org/10.1080/03057070.2020.1780022.

Mashinini, Emma. *Strikes Have Followed Me All My Life: A South African Autobiography.* London: Women's Press, 1989.

Matandela, Mbalenhle. 'Redefining Black Consciousness and Resistance: The Intersection of Black Consciousness and Black Feminist Thought'. *Agenda* 31, no. 3–4 (2 October 2017): 10–28. https://doi.org/10.1080/10130950.2017.1402410.

Mathiane, Nomavenda. *Beyond the Headlines: Truths of Soweto Life.* Johannesburg: Southern Book Publishers, 1990.

Matshoba, Mtutuzeli. *Call Me Not a Man / Mtutuzeli Matshoba.* Johannesburg: Ravan Press, 1979.

Matteau-Matsha, Rachel. '"I Read What I Like": Politics of Reading and Reading Politics in Apartheid South Africa'. *Transformation: Critical Perspectives on Southern Africa* 83, no. 1 (27 December 2013): 56–85.

Mattera, Don. 'Six Poems'. *Index on Censorship* 3, no. 4 (1974): 19–24. https://doi.org/10.1080/03064227408532368.

Miller, Kim. 'Moms with Guns: Women's Political Agency in Anti-Apartheid Visual Culture'. *African Arts* 42, no. 2 (2009): 68–75. http://www.jstor.org/stable/20626992.

Milton, J. R. L. 'Criminal Law in South Africa—1976–1986'. *Acta Juridica* 1987 (1987): 34–54.

Minkley, Gary, and Ciraj Rassool. 'Photography with a Difference: Leon Levson's Camera Studies and Photographic Exhibitions of Native Life in South Africa, 1947–1950'. *Kronos*, no. 31 (2005): 184–213.

Mkhabela, Sibongile. *Open Earth and Black Roses: Remembering 16 June 1976*. Braamfontein, South Africa: Skotaville Press, 2001.
Moffett, Helen. 'Sexual Violence, Civil Society and the New Constitution'. In *Women's Activism in South Africa: Working Across Divides*, edited by Hannah Britton, Jennifer Fish and Sheila Meintjes, 155–84. Scottsville, South Africa: University of KwaZulu-Natal Press, 2009.
Moffett, Helen. '"These Women, They Force Us to Rape Them": Rape as Narrative of Social Control in Post-Apartheid South Africa'. *Journal of Southern African Studies* 32, no. 1 (1 March 2006): 129–44. https://doi.org/10.1080/03057070500493845.
Mofokeng, Santu. 'Trajectory of a Street Photographer'. *Nka Journal of Contemporary African Art* 2000, no. 11–12 (1 May 2000): 41–46. https://doi.org/10.1215/10757163-11-12-1-41.
Moloi, Tshepo. '"Oral Testimonies by Former Members of the Azanian National Youth Unity (AZANYU): The Sayable and Unsayable in an Oral History Interview"'. In *Oral History: Representing the Hidden, the Untold and the Veiled'. Proceedings of the Fifth and Sixth Annual National Oral History Conference*. Pretoria: Research Institute for Theology and Religion, University of South Africa, 2013. https://www.sahistory.org.za/sites/default/files/archive-files/ohasa_2008-2008-22-05-2013_oral_history_conference_papers.pdf.
Molteno, Frank. 'The Uprising of 16th June: A Review of the Literature on Events in South Africa 1976'. *Social Dynamics* 5, no. 1 (June 1979): 54–89. https://doi.org/10.1080/02533957908458236.
Moosage, Riedwaan. 'A Prose of Ambivalence: Liberation Struggle Discourse on Necklacing'. *Kronos* 36, no. 1 (2010): 136–56.
Motsei, Mmatshilo. *The Kanga and the Kangaroo Court: Reflections on the Rape Trial of Jacob Zuma*. Sunnyside: Jacana, 2007.
Motsemme, Nthabiseng. 'The Mute Always Speak: On Women's Silences at the Truth and Reconciliation Commission'. *Current Sociology* 52, no. 5 (2004): 909–32.
Mukonde, Kasonde T. '"If You Belong to My Generation and You Never Read James Hadley Chase, Then You Are Not Educated": Everyday Reading of High School Students in Soweto, 1968–1976'. *Journal of Southern African Studies* 49, no. 2 (4 March 2023): 205–24. https://doi.org/10.1080/03057070.2023.2204782.
Murray, Simone. *Mixed Media: Feminist Presses and Publishing Politics*. London: Pluto, 2004.
Ndebele, Njabulo. 'Memory, Metaphor and the Triumph of Narrative'. In *Negotiating the Past: The Making of Memory in South Africa*, edited by

Sarah Nuttall and Carli Coetzee, 19–28. Oxford: Oxford University Press, 1998.
Ndlovu, Hlengiwe. 'Womxn's Bodies Reclaiming the Picket Line: The "Nude" Protest during #FeesMustFall'. *Agenda* 31, no. 3–4 (2 October 2017): 68–77. https://doi.org/10.1080/10130950.2017.1391613.
Ndlovu, Sifiso Mxolisi. 'The Anatomy of the Crowd'. In *The Road to Democracy in South Africa: Volume 7: Soweto Uprisings: New Perspective, Commemorations and Memorialisation*, 41–78. Cape Town: Unisa Press, 2017.
Nieftagodien, Noor, and Sally Gaule. *Orlando West, Soweto: An Illustrated History*. Johannesburg: Wits University Press, 2012. https://www.cambridge.org/core/books/orlando-west-soweto/3C379146F2C62F49B9EC6EF41C0DCE4C.
Niehaus, Isak. 'Towards a Dubious Liberation: Masculinity, Sexuality and Power in South African Lowveld Schools, 1953–1999'. *Journal of Southern African Studies* 26, no. 3 (September 2000): 387–407. https://doi.org/10.1080/713683581.
Nkomo, Suzi. 'Organising Women in SANSCO: Reflections on the Experience of Women in Organisation'. *Agenda* 10 (1991): 10–15. https://doi.org/10.2307/4065449.
Nkwanyane, Thami, 'No lavish funeral for Seatlholo, icon of '76', City Press, 21 February 2004. https://www.news24.com/citypress/southafrica/news/no-lavish-funeral-for-seathlolo-icon-of-76-20100614.
Nnaemeka, Obioma. 'Imag(in)Ing Knowledge, Power and Subversion in the Margins'. In *The Politics of (M)Othering: Womanhood, Identity and Resistance in African Literature*, edited by Obioma Nnaemeka, 1–25. London: Routledge, 2005.
O'Connell, Siona. 'The Spring Queen Pageant and the Postapartheid Archive'. *Safundi* 18, no. 2 (3 April 2017): 168–76. https://doi.org/10.1080/17533171.2016.1272239.
Odendaal, André. *The Founders: The Origins of the ANC and the Struggle for Democracy in South Africa*. Johannesburg: Jacana Media, 2012.
O'Meara, Dan. 'The Afrikaner Broederbond 1927–1948: Class Vanguard of Afrikaner Nationalism'. *Journal of Southern African Studies* 3, no. 2 (1 April 1977): 156–86. https://doi.org/10.1080/03057077708707970.
Osinubi, T. A. 'Abusive Narratives: Antjie Krog, Rian Malan, and the Transmission of Violence'. *Comparative Studies of South Asia, Africa and the Middle East* 28, no. 1 (1 January 2008): 109–23. https://doi.org/10.1215/1089201x-2007-059.
Passerini, Luisa. *Fascism in Popular Memory: The Cultural Experience of the Turin Working Class*. Studies in Modern Capitalism. Cambridge: Cambridge University Press, 2010.

Pohlandt-McCormick, Helena. 'Controlling Woman: Winnie Mandela and the 1976 Soweto Uprising'. *The International Journal of African Historical Studies* 33, no. 3 (2000): 585–614. https://doi.org/10.2307/3097436.

Pohlandt-McCormick, Helena. *'I Saw a Nightmare . . .' : Doing Violence to Memory, The Soweto Uprising, June 16, 1976*. New York: Columbia University Press, 2008. http://www.gutenberg-e.org/pohlandt-mccormick/index.html.

Portelli, Alessandro. *The Death of Luigi Trastulli, and Other Stories: Form and Meaning in Oral History*. Albany, NY: State University of New York Press, 1991.

Portelli, Alessandro. 'Oral Testimony, the Law and the Making of History: The "April 7" Murder Trial'. *History Workshop*, no. 20 (1985): 5–35. https://www.jstor.org/stable/4288647.

Portelli, Alessandro. *The Voice and the Text: Writing, Speaking, Democracy, and American Literature*. New York: Columbia University Press, 1994.

Rassool, Ciraj. 'Rethinking Documentary History and South African Political Biography'. *South African Review of Sociology* 41, no. 1 (April 2010): 28–55. https://doi.org/10.1080/21528581003676028.

Reddy, Vasu, and Cheryl Potgieter. '"Real Men Stand up for the Truth": Discursive Meanings in the Jacob Zuma Rape Trial'. *Southern African Linguistics and Applied Language Studies* 24, no. 4 (2006): 511–21. https://doi.org/10.2989/16073610609486438.

Reddy, William M. *The Navigation of Feeling: A Framework for the History of Emotions*. Cambridge: University Press, 2001. https://doi.org/10.1017/CBO9780511512001.

Ribane, Nakedi. *Beauty: A Black Perspective*. Scottsville, South Africa: University of KwaZulu-Natal Press, 2006.

The Road to Democracy in South Africa: Volume 7: Soweto Uprisings: New Perspective, Commemorations and Memorialisation. Cape Town: Unisa Press, 2017.

Robinson, Jenny. '(Dis)Locating Historical Narrative: Writing, Space and Gender in South African Social History'. *South African Historical Journal* 30 (May 1994): 144–57. https://doi.org/10.1080/02582479408671788.

Ross, Fiona. *Bearing Witness: Women and the Truth and Reconciliation Commission in South Africa*. London: Pluto, 2002.

Ross, Fiona. 'Linguistic Bearings and Testimonial Practices'. In *Discourse and Human Rights Violations*, edited by Christine Anthonissen and Jan Blommaert, 101–13. Amsterdam: John Benjamins, 2007.

Ross, Fiona. 'On Having Voice and Being Heard: Some After Effects of Testifying before the South African Truth and Reconciliation

Commission'. *Anthropological Theory* 3 (2003): 325–41. https://doi.org/10.1177/14634996030033005.

Roux, Daniel. 'Jonny Steinberg's the Number and Prison Life Writing in Post-Apartheid South Africa', 2009. http://hdl.handle.net/10019.1/12473.

Royston, Robert, ed. *Black Poets in South Africa*. African Writers Series. London: Heinemann, 1974.

Rueedi, Franziska. 'Narratives on Trial: Ideology, Violence and the Struggle over Political Legitimacy in the Case of the Delmas Treason Trial, 1985–1989'. *South African Historical Journal* 67, no. 3 (3 July 2015): 335–55. https://doi.org/10.1080/02582473.2015.1092573.

Rueedi, Franziska. '"Siyayinyova!": Patterns of Violence in the African Townships of the Vaal Triangle, South Africa.1980–86', *Africa* 85, no. 3 (August 2015): 395–416. https://doi.org/doi:10.1017/S0001972015000261.

Rueedi, Franziska. *The Vaal Uprising of 1984 and the Struggle for Freedom in South Africa*. Woodbridge, Suffolk: James Currey, 2021.

Russell, Diana E. H. *Lives of Courage: Women for a New South Africa*. New York: Basic Books, 1989.

Ryan-Flood, Róisín, and Rosalind Gill, eds. *Secrecy and Silence in the Research Process: Feminist Reflections*. Transformations: Thinking through Feminism. Abingdon, Oxon: Routledge, 2010. https://doi.org/10.4324/9780203927045-8.

Samuelson, Meg. *Remembering the Nation, Dismembering Women? Stories of the South African Transition*. Scottsville, South Africa: University of KwaZulu-Natal Press, 2007.

Sandwell, Rachel. 'Fantasy States: Nationalism, Intimacy, and Transgression in South African Women's Political Memoirs'. *Signs: Journal of Women in Culture and Society* 47, no. 3 (March 2022): 765–87. https://doi.org/10.1086/717734.

Sandwell, Rachel. '"Love I Cannot Begin to Explain": The Politics of Reproduction in the ANC in Exile, 1976–1990'. *Journal of Southern African Studies* 41, no. 1 (2 January 2015): 63–81. https://doi.org/10.1080/03057070.2015.991988.

Sapire, Hilary. 'Township Histories, Insurrection and Liberation in Late Apartheid South Africa'. *South African Historical Journal* 65, no. 2 (1 June 2013): 167–98. http://dx.doi.org/10.1080/02582473.2013.777089.

Scarry, Elaine. *The Body in Pain: The Making and Unmaking of the World*. New York: Oxford University Press, 1985.

Schuster, Lynda. *A Burning Hunger: One Family's Struggle Against Apartheid*. Athens, OH: Ohio University Press, 2006.

Seekings, Jeremy. 'Gender Ideology and Township Politics in the 1980s'. *Agenda* 10 (1991): 77–85. https://doi.org/10.2307/4065458.

Seekings, Jeremy. *Heroes or Villains? Youth Politics in the 1980s*. Johannesburg: Ravan Press, 1993.
Seekings, Jeremy. *The UDF: A History of the United Democratic Front in South Africa, 1983–1991*. Oxford: James Currey, 2000.
Seekings, Jeremy. 'Whose Voices? Politics and Methodology in the Study of Political Organisation and Protest in the Final Phase of the "Struggle" in South Africa'. *South African Historical Journal* 62, no. 1 (2010): 7–28. http://dx.doi.org/10.1080/02582471003778300.
Serote, Mongane. *To Every Birth Its Blood*. Johannesburg: Picador Africa, 2004.
Sider, Gerald, and Gavin Smith. 'Introduction'. In *Between History and Histories: The Making of Silences and Commemorations*, edited by Gerald Sider and Gavin Smith, 3–28. Toronto: University of Toronto Press, 1997.
Simbao, Ruth Kerkham. 'The Thirtieth Anniversary of the Soweto Uprisings: Reading the Shadow in Sam Nzima's Iconic Photograph of Hector Pieterson'. *African Arts* 40, no. 2 (1 July 2007): 52–69.
Simpson, Thula. *History of South Africa: 1902 to the Present*. London: C Hurst & Co Publishers Ltd, 2022.
Slovo, Gillian. *Every Secret Thing / Gillian Slovo*. London: Little, Brown, 1997.
Soske, Jon. 'The Family Romance of the South African Revolution'. In *Love and Revolution in the Twentieth-Century Colonial and Postcolonial World: Perspectives from South Asia and Southern Africa*, edited by G. Arunima, Patricia Hayes and Premesh Lalu, 175–201. Palgrave Studies in the History of Social Movements. Cham: Springer International Publishing, 2021. https://doi.org/10.1007/978-3-030-79580-1_7.
Soske, Jon. 'Open Secrets, Off the Record: Audience, Intimate Knowledge, and the Crisis of the Post-Apartheid State'. *Historical Reflections / Réflexions Historiques* 38, no. 2 (2012): 55–70. https://doi.org/10.3167/hrrh.2012.380205.
Spivak, Gayatri Chakravorty. 'Can the Subaltern Speak?' In *Marxism and the Interpretation of Culture*, edited by Lawrence Grossberg and Carry Nelson, 271–313. Urbana, IL: University of Illinois Press; Basingstoke: Macmillan, 1988.
Spivak, Gayatri Chakravorty. 'The Rani of Sirmur: An Essay in Reading the Archives'. *History and Theory* 24, no. 3 (1985): 247–72. https://doi.org/10.2307/2505169.
Steinberg, Jonny. *Winnie and Nelson: Portrait of a Marriage*. Johannesburg: Jonathan Ball, 2023.
Stoler, Ann Laura. *Along the Archival Grain Epistemic Anxieties and Colonial Common Sense*. Princeton, NJ: Princeton University Press, 2009.

Suttner, Raymond. 'Women in the ANC-Led Underground'. In *Women in South African History: They Remove Boulders and Cross Rivers*, edited by Nomboniso Gasa, 233–55. Cape Town: HSRC Press, 2007.
Switzer, Les, and Mohamed Adhikari. *South Africa's Resistance Press: Alternative Voices in the Last Generation Under Apartheid*. Athens, OH: Ohio University Press, 2000.
Thomas, Lynn M. *Beneath the Surface: A Transnational History of Skin Lighteners*. New York: Duke University Press, 2020.
Thomas, Lynn M. 'The Modern Girl and Racial Respectability in 1930s South Africa'. *The Journal of African History* 47, no. 3 (2006): 461–90. https://doi.org/10.1017/S0021853706002131.
Tomaselli, Keyan G., and P. Eric Louw, eds. *The Alternative Press in South Africa*. London: James Currey, 1992.
Trouillot, Michel-Rolph. *Silencing the Past: Power and the Production of History, 20th Anniversary Edition*. 2nd Revised edition. Boston, MA: Beacon Press, 2015.
Unterhalter, Elaine. 'The Work of the Nation: Heroic Masculinity in South African Autobiographical Writing of the Anti-Apartheid Struggle'. *European Journal of Development Research* 12, no. 2 (December 2000): 157. https://doi.org/10.1080/09578810008426770.
Walker, Cherryl. 'Conceptualising Motherhood in Twentieth Century South Africa'. *Journal of Southern African Studies* 21, no. 3 (September 1995): 417–37. https://doi.org/10.1080/03057079508708455.
White, Luise, Stephan Miescher and David William Cohen. *African Words, African Voices: Critical Practices in Oral History*. African Systems of Thought. Bloomington: Indiana University Press, 2001.
Whitlock, Gillian. *The Intimate Empire*. London: A&C Black, 2000.
Woodward, Wendy, Patricia Hayes and Gary Minkley, eds. *Deep Histories: Gender and Colonialism in Southern Africa*. Amsterdam: Rodopi, 2002.
Xaba, Thokozani. 'Masculinity and Its Malcontents: The Confrontation Between "Struggle Masculinity" and "Post-Struggle Masculinity" (1990–1997)'. In *Changing Men in Southern Africa*, edited by Robert Morrell, 105–24. London: Zed Books, 2001.

Unpublished dissertations and theses

Cooper-Hockey, Emily. 'Whose Agenda? The Negotiation of Gender, Race and "Difference" in a Feminist Journal in South Africa, 1987–1993'. BA Honours Dissertation, University of Durham, 2017.

Dennie, Garrey Michael. 'The Cultural Politics of Burial in South Africa, 1884–1990'. PhD, The Johns Hopkins University. https://www.proquest.com/docview/304348729/abstract/16FF58AFF3F34936PQ/1.

Fester, Gertrude M.N. 'Women and Citizenship Struggles: A Case of the Western Cape, South Africa 1980–2004'. PhD, Gender Institute L.S.E., 2007.

Gobodo-Madikizela, Pumla Phillipa. 'Legacies of Violence: An In-Depth Analysis of Two Case Studies Based on Interviews with Perpetrators of a "Necklace" Murder and with Eugene de Kock'. PhD, University of Cape Town (South Africa). https://www.proquest.com/docview/304663465/abstract/2F0BA56C5C8F463APQ/1.

Hurley, Kameron. 'The Voice of Women? The ANC and the Rhetoric of Women 's Resistance, 1976–1989'. MA thesis, University of Natal, 2003.

Johnson, Rachel E. 'Making History, Gendering Youth: young Women and South Africa's Liberation Struggles after 1976'. PhD, University of Sheffield, 2010.

Moloi, Tshepo. 'Youth Politics: The Political Role of AZANYU in the Struggle for Liberation: The Case of AZANYU Tembisa Branch, 1980s to 1996'. Research Report, University of the Witwatersrand, 2005. https://core.ac.uk/download/pdf/39664456.pdf.

Rassool, Ciraj. 'The Individual, Auto/Biography and History in South Africa'. University of the Western Cape, 2004.

Valela, Ntombizikhona. '"I Am 22 Million": Reading Winnie Madikizela as the Intellectual Face of Anti-Apartheid Popular Struggle'. MA thesis, Rhodes University, 2017.

Index

www.ingramcontent.com/pod-product-compliance
Lightning Source LLC
LaVergne TN
LVHW052016300826
846742LV00019B/71
9781915249456